THE
GUN DIGEST BOOK
OF
RIFLESMITHING

By
Jack Mitchell

DBI BOOKS, INC., NORTHFIELD, ILLINOIS

About Our Cover

The subject of Riflesmithing in America would be less than a reality without the products made and distributed by Bob and Frank Brownell — it's that simple.

Brownell's has been literally "writing the book" on gunsmithing tools for almost a half century. With those thoughts in mind, we surrounded the FN (in-the-white) Mauser action with a selection of currently-available Brownell's gunsmithing tools. It's a fitting tribute to both Brownell's gunsmithing tools and the riflesmiths who use them.

PUBLISHER
Sheldon Factor

EDITORIAL DIRECTOR
Jack Lewis

ART DIRECTOR
Sonya Kaiser

ASSISTANT ARTISTS
Dana Silzle
John Vitale

PHOTO SERVICES
Kristen Tonti

PRODUCTION
Betty Burris

COPY EDITOR
Dorine Imbach

CONTRIBUTING EDITOR
Dean Grennell

Produced by

Charger Productions

ISBN 0-910676-47-X   Library of Congress Catalog Card Number 82-072293

CONTENTS

ACKNOWLEDGEMENTS

I never realized until now that the Acknowledgement is the most gratifying part of a book. Since it is written last, it indicates that the project is completed. I'm not saying that I didn't enjoy doing this book, but there were occasions when I was tempted to take one of the rifles on which I was working and place a few well-aimed shots through the vitals of my typewriter. Fortunately, reason prevailed.

If this book is lacking in certain areas, I accept responsibility. If it proves worthwhile, the credit rightfully goes to the outstanding publishing staff, the professional riflesmiths who shared their knowledge and time, and the many manufacturers within the firearms industry that supplied information and products for testing and evaluation.

I especially want to thank my sweetheart of a wife, Elaine, who has been a tower of patience and understanding during my self-exile chained to the typewriter these past several months. I want to thank my boys, Brian and Brad, for not getting too upset that I haven't spent more time with them.

I owe a debt to my dad for teaching me to shoot and understand the responsibility of firearms safety. I especially want to thank my mom for allowing her 11-year-old to fire several thousand rounds of .22 ammo through his rifle in the family cellar, using the bullet trap that Dad built during the cold winter months in Saugus, Massachusetts. And thanks to "Annie" for all her help and support during my college years.

Without the splendid cooperation of riflesmith Sterling Davenport and gunsmith Joe Reid, both of Tucson, Arizona, who performed many of the tasks illustrated throughout this book, this project never would have been completed.

Industry folks like Frank Brownell, Dick Dietz of Remington, Chub Eastman of Leupold, Steve Yorba of Pachmayr, Bob Ray of Buehler, Bob Sconce of Miniature Machine Corporation, and Bill Rogers of Springfield Sporters never batted an eye in offering their full help and support during my panic calls for assistance, products or photographs.

Pete Grisel, Ken Jantz and Ted Blackburn supplied both expertise and products for demonstration purposes. The photos of the late Lenard Brownell's custom rifles were sent by his lovely wife to illustrate the immense talent of this gifted riflesmith.

Duane Johnson of Calico Hardwoods and George Peterson of Western Gunstock deserve special recognition. Their companies supplied Davenport and me with some of the most exquisite stock blanks for this project that I have ever layed my eyes on.

Just thank you is insufficient to express my feelings for the magnificent job performed by my fellow workers at Charger Productions. Jack Lewis translated my dangling participles, split infinitives and incomplete sentences back into the English language. Bob Arsenault, showed the patience of Job as I stole time to work on this book while correspondence continued to pile up on my desk. Dean Grennell drew the thankless task of making all the photo captions fit. Kristy Tonti spent untold hours developing, printing and reprinting my pictures until they turned out right. And last, but certainly not least, I want to thank Sonya Kaiser, our overworked art director, for doing such a magnificent job of putting this book together.

Jack Mitchell

INTRODUCTION

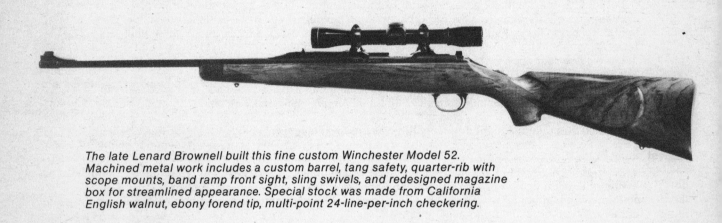

The late Lenard Brownell built this fine custom Winchester Model 52. Machined metal work includes a custom barrel, tang safety, quarter-rib with scope mounts, band ramp front sight, sling swivels, and redesigned magazine box for streamlined appearance. Special stock was made from California English walnut, ebony forend tip, multi-point 24-line-per-inch checkering.

THE MOST difficult part of writing a book on the subject of riflesmithing is getting started. The hundreds of different types of rifles, the myriad individual tasks necessary to build one almost from scratch and the seemingly endless techniques used to accomplish each task are of staggering proportions. It's like sitting down at the dinner table with knife and fork and attempting to eat an elephant. Neither a 256-page book nor a stomach can house it all. And even if there were a way to assemble all the information into one text, a problem arises in that I don't know it all. But, I doubt anyone really does.

Rather than write a condensed version of the general trade, I have attempted to concentrate on what I feel are the most important facets of the riflesmithing profession. Although such fields as welding, polishing, bluing and engraving are part of the business, they are best learned by first-hand instruction. It's like learning how to kiss: you can read all about it, but until you've actually tried it, you're languishing in the dark.

This book is an attempt to share with the reader individual tasks performed by the practicing riflesmith. These individuals are members of a unique fraternity quite apart from the general gunsmith performing everyday repair work. They are specialists carrying on the tradition of excellence begun hundreds of years before them.

A custom rifle is the end result of countless labors. The stock must be shaped and fitted to the customer, inletted, bedded, finished and checkered. The metal parts are machined, ground, filed, welded, drilled, aligned, checkered, polished and blued. The efforts required to marry wood and metal into one strong, reliable, accurate and harmonious piece termed the custom rifle are many and painstaking. It requires experience, talent and a dedication to perfection. Fortunately, there are those individuals in this business who continue to strive for that goal. We — the shooters, hunters, collectors, and writers — who appreciate this talented group of artisans are the recipients of the fruits of their labors.

A customer commissions the custom riflesmith to create a special, one-of-a-kind rifle with the same expectations of one who has commissioned an artist to create a unique work of art on canvas. Almost without exception, the custom riflesmith or artist is motivated first by the challenge of the work, professional pride in his craft, talents, and the experience of learning each and every time he sets foot into his shop. The satisfaction of learning, growing, and creating are the true rewards of the custom riflesmith. Financial remuneration, if the truth be known, serves only as fuel to purchase more supplies and begin new projects. This premise may sound idealistic, but I have never met a rich riflesmith. On the other hand, I have been extremely fortunate in meeting and knowing some exceptionally talented people who continue to strive for that elusive goal known as perfection.

Dale Goens produced this exquisite example of the riflesmith's art, beginning with a pre-'64 Winchester Model 70. Custom barrel is chambered for 7mm Remington magnum cartridge. Ted Blackburn built the trigger guard and floorplate. Figured stock constructed of imported exhibition-grade Circassian walnut finely checkered to match the wood pattern.

The wonderful part about this business is all the things there are to learn...and no one ever really absorbs them all. At least, I've never met anyone that has. An instructor at gunsmithing school told me he had been a gunsmith for over forty-three years and hardly a week went by that a student didn't bring in some strange firearm he'd never seen or heard of before and didn't have the vaguest idea how, or in some cases, why it worked. It is the journey, not the destination, that really matters to this unique fraternity of craftsmen.

It is damn near impossible to perfect all the physical, mechanical and artistic aspects that encompass the term riflesmithing in only one lifetime. Because a rifle — or certain labors performed to it — is looked upon as an art form, certain criteria are used in judging its merits and those of the artist.

Unfortunately, this industry, like so many others, is quick to attach labels and titles. The terms "master gunsmith" or "master riflesmith" are thrown around by firearms writers with increasing regularity. In the field of art a master, as defined by Webster, is "an artist regarded as great." Granted, there are many individuals in the field of riflesmithing who specialize in certain areas and should

rightfully be termed masters. I believe few would disagree that Dale Goens, the late Lenard Brownell, or Jerry Fisher are master stockmakers. Monty Kennedy, Al Lind and John Hearn are deservedly acknowledged to be master checkers. Winston Churchill, Lynton McKenzie and Leonard Francolini are truly master engravers. But the truth is, there are probably less than a handful of master gunsmiths or riflesmiths.

The field of riflesmithing is made up of specialists. To perfect such skills as metalwork, stockmaking, checkering or engraving requires a great deal of time, experience, talent and desire. I know many outstanding stockmakers who dread metalwork and vice versa. Working on any aspect of the trade that takes time away from one's chosen specialty becomes a chore instead of a labor of love. Many riflesmiths farm out work they do not have the time or desire to perform to other top riflesmiths. This leaves them time to do the best job possible within their own specialty; this is in their own best interests and certainly those of the customer. The end result is a truly custom rifle that will be delivered to the customer. The work being shared by those most competent to complete each phase is to the benefit of all.

Custom-stocked Remington Model 700 chambered for .270 Win., built by Sterling Davenport. Stock wood is French walnut and features Fleur-de-lis with ribbon pattern, 26-line-per-inch checkering.

Chapter 1

TOOLS OF THE TRADE

Listing And Discussing Some — Not Necessarily All! — Of The Tools And Products Needed In Day-To-Day Riflesmithing

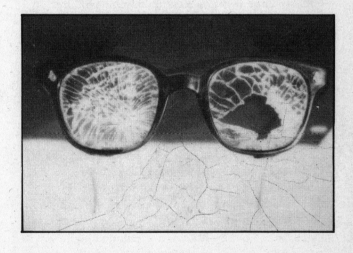

Safety glasses should be worn when working on any firearm. The pair at right undoubtedly saved author a serious eye problem, might even have saved his life.

WHETHER YOU are a weekend and evening gun tinkerer or a professional riflesmith there's one thing you can count on: You'll never have enough tools. Most of the gunsmithing books I've read over the years almost always begin their chapters on tools stating rather boldly that much of the gunsmithing work can be accomplished with a minimum of tools. That may be so if you have the patience of Job, an innate mechanical aptitude, and are not afflicted with man's almost universal desire for more and better tools. Man's fascination with mechanical contrivances began right after he got tired of swinging from vines and seems to run rampant in folks hooked on gunsmithing. After all, a firearm is nothing more than a tool. Granted, some firearms are sufficiently ornate to be considered works of art and are displayed throughout the museums of the world. Many have design features that border on pure genius. With the myriad of differently

designed firearms it is no wonder that they require specialized tools, both to improve their mechanical capabilities and bring them to a highly artistic level. Many of the tools required to work on firearms are ingenious unto themselves. To complete certain tasks without the proper tools when working on rifles is certainly more difficult, if not impossible.

To adequately outfit a riflesmith's shop requires an incredible number of individual tools that amount to several thousand dollars. The reason for requiring so many different types of tools is due to the many different aspects of riflesmithing, or general gunsmithing for that matter. Although there are two general categories of riflesmithing, namely metalworking and woodworking, each has several different aspects within its own area.

The metalworking side of riflesmithing can be broken down into the following: die-making, welding, heat-treating, tool-making, drilling, reaming, rifling, barrel turning,

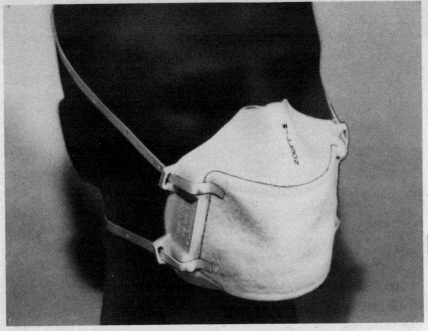

When working with any type grinder, dust mask should be worn to prevent harmful wood, ivory or polishing dust from reaching the lung area.

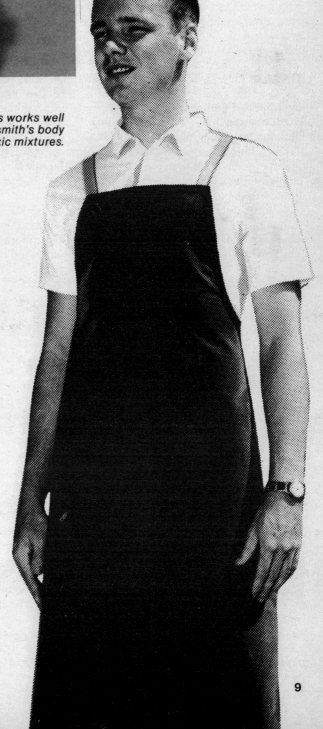

A shop apron of heavy-duty neoprene always works well to protect the clothing and even the riflesmith's body when he is working on rifles or using toxic mixtures.

chambering, headspacing, grinding, lapping, polishing, bluing, browning, relining barrels, manufacturing sights, spring-making, engraving, metal checkering, forging, filing, milling, sandblasting and burnishing. I've probably forgotten a task or two, but you get the general idea.

The woodworking side of riflesmithing includes a large number of different aspects, also. They include: sanding, sawing, chiseling, carving, checkering, inlaying, bedding, inletting, designing, finishing, feathering and shaping. If you've only just been bitten by the gunsmithing bug you may be getting the idea that there's quite a bit to this centuries-old field of endeavor. Don't be disheartened. Even the old pros started from square one.

The obvious question is how does one obtain all the necessary tools to complete the many different types of work necessary for riflesmithing? The answer is, one doesn't. Probably the only fellow I've ever met that has just about one of every conceivable tool and accessory is Frank Brownell of Montezuma, Iowa. But don't be jealous of old Frank. He sells them to folks like you and me whenever we need them. His catalog is probably the best single first purchase you could make if you're interested in pursuing this hobby or career. His reputation for selling quality merchandise is world renowned and he's a heck of a nice guy to boot.

Unless you have a bankroll large enough to choke a horse the best way to go is to purchase a few of the basic riflesmithing tools and purchase others as the need arises. Whichever tools you choose remember one important axiom: Always buy good-quality merchandise. There's no such thing as a good "cheap" tool in this business. A seventy-five-cent screwdriver found in the local grocery store will last slightly less time than it takes to complete

It's virtually impossible to be a gunsmith without an array of files for special purposes. One of the basic tools is the Nicholson mill file for metalworking use.

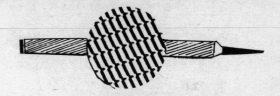

The Nicholson Magicut file is favored by any number of riflesmiths for woodworking on the various facets of a rifle stock. Inset illustrates arrangement of teeth.

your first disassembly of a rifle. Buy quality tools, take care of them and they'll probably be around longer than you will.

The very first purchase you should make in your tool inventory is a pair of safety glasses. Buy them and WEAR THEM EVERY TIME YOU STEP INTO THE SHOP, REGARDLESS OF THE TASK PERFORMED. I've seen experienced gunsmiths fail to wear them on more than one occasion only to be severely injured. There are damned few blind gunsmiths.

Probably the most basic tools useful for a great variety of work are the hacksaw, file, hammer, drill, screwdriver and vise. Let's begin with which type is best suited to a riflesmith's needs.

A hacksaw is invaluable around the shop. They come with either pistol grip or straight handle, solid or adjustable frame. One with sliding studs allows four different position settings. The blade tension may be adjusted by turning the handle or wingnut. Buy quality blades made in high-speed steel or tungsten alloy as they have hardened teeth for long life yet are flexible. When the blades do become worn out cut them into strips to serve as scrapers for wood inletting or as flat springs. The blades vary in length from eight to twelve inches and with fourteen to thirty-two teeth per inch. A fourteen-tooth blade works well on large pieces and mild steels. A blade with eighteen teeth per inch works well on tool, high-speed, and carbon steel. A twenty-four-tooth blade is better suited to copper, brass, iron pipe, angle iron, and electrical conduit. A thirty-two-tooth blade is used for thin tubing and sheet metal.

An important aspect in selecting the type of blade for

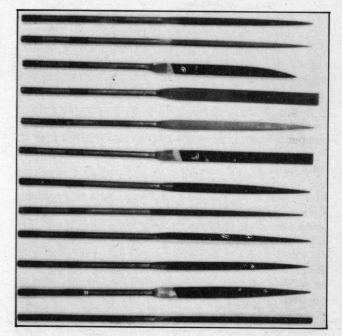

Although needle files may be purchased as needed, this professional-quality set for gunsmithing has each item shaped for a special use for medium- to fine-range cuts.

hacksaws involves its set of teeth. A "standard" set has one tooth right and one tooth left in progression. A "wave" set blade has teeth cut in pairs. Since the set of the blade determines the amount of blade clearance as it cuts through the metal it is an important consideration.

Although hacksaw blades are only approximately .025-inch thick and either 7/16 or ½ inch in width, they will last considerably longer if used properly. Blade life is directly proportional to both cutting speed and amount of pres-

This particular style for working on stock wood is called the Swiss cabinet file, it's used for shaping.

This is termed a no-clog file, as it can be used without the space between its teeth filling up with wood dust.

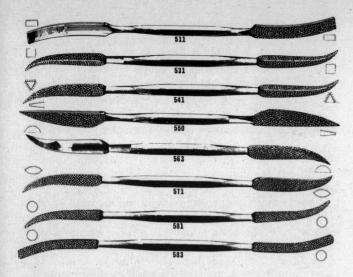

This assortment of double-end rasps allows fast cutting on stocks. The differing shapes make it a much simpler matter to get into the difficult areas and curvatures.

Before we go further on the subject of tools, perhaps we should briefly discuss the subject of cleanliness. In gunsmithing, it's virtually impossible. Woodworking results in dust, wood chips, and lots of inletting black on hands and clothes while bedding an action to a stock. Metalwork causes metal chips and filings that cling to everything. One of the handiest accessories for the shop and protection for clothing is the Neoprene shop apron. They won't keep your hands and face clean, but they'll go a long way in keeping clothes clean. They're inexpensive (under $6) and available through Brownell's.

Another basic, and definitely the most used tool in the shop is the file. Although available in a multitude of sizes and shapes, there are three divisions of files, single cut, double cut, and rasp cut. A single-cut file is used for draw filing, saw filing, and finishing surfaces. They work equally well on steel, brass, or bronze. A double-cut file is used for roughing out metal and fast removal, but leaves a rough finish. Rasps are utilized for removing wood, bone, or other soft materials. There are also specialty files such as: checkering, vixen, lead float, Swiss and American Swiss, blunt, safe edge, tapered, and increment cut with teeth of different heights.

The best quality files are manufactured by Simmonds, Nicholson, Hayes, Disston, American Swiss, and Grobbet. Two of the finest individual gunsmithing files are Nicholson's Mill File for metalwork and Nicholson's Magicut File on wood. These companies also make sets of small needle files that are indispensable for precision work.

The file's cutting edges or teeth determine whether it may be classified as a bastard, second cut, smooth, or

sure applied. Approximately forty strokes per minute during cutting is best. Sawing faster will actually draw the temper from the steel and dull the teeth. Applying too much pressure will result in a broken blade although too little pressure will cause the teeth to slip over the work causing a glazing effect. Sawing at forty strokes per minute allows the riflesmith to work at a pace that is not tiring. If you can afford only one blade to begin with, an eighteen-tooth will be the most versatile.

Metal-checkering files range from 20 to 50 lines per inch. They are necessary for checkering of bolt knobs, sight ramps and bolt stops, the author contends. All files should be outfitted with screw handles (top) for hand protection.

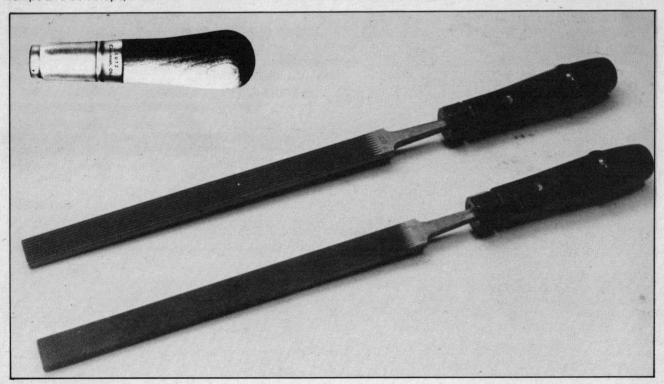

FILES

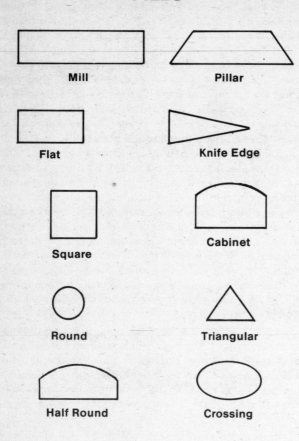

Mill

Pillar

Flat

Knife Edge

Square

Cabinet

Round

Triangular

Half Round

Crossing

dead smooth. There are a total of ten different cutting edges ranging from 00, 0 and one through eight. Remember, the shorter the file the finer the cut.

Files will cut better and have less tendency to "load up," (metal filings clog in the teeth of the file) if they are first rubbed with ordinary blackboard chalk. A file brush should always be handy to also remove filings and prevent them from causing scratches after each pass with the file on the work. File handles are one of the best investments against injury you can make. If a file is used without a handle it can slip and the tang can cause serious injury.

There is a lot more to filing than just picking one up and removing metal until you get the desired results. Experience is the best teacher. However, there are certain procedures to follow when filing: Check the height of the work to the height of the vise. Remove any burrs or fins to prevent injury. Hold the file with two hands, one on the handle and the other at the end of the file. Always check the hardness of the metal before attempting to file it. Approximately forty strokes per minute will produce the best results with a minimum of fatigue. File flat on the work and lift it completely off the work on the return stroke. This is

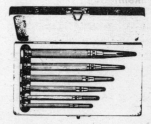

Precision screwdrivers are a must to remove tiny internal screws such as those found on rifle scope bases.

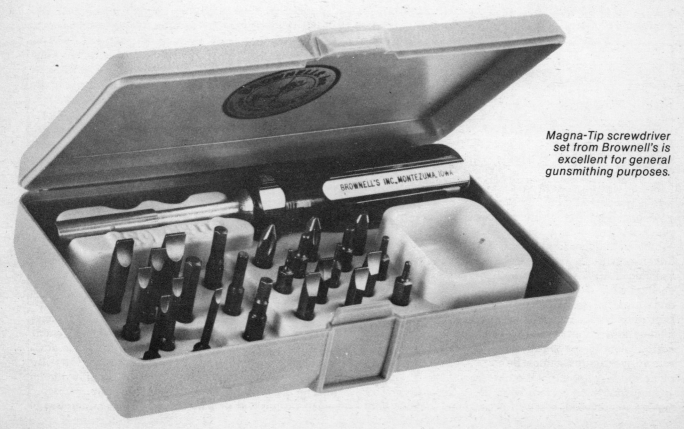

Magna-Tip screwdriver set from Brownell's is excellent for general gunsmithing purposes.

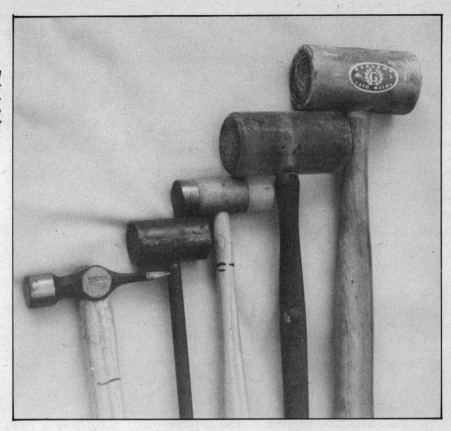

Hammers are essential tools around any gunsmithing shop. From left: ball peen, brass-, nylon-, plastic- and rawhide-head hammers all are used on a daily basis during any custom rifle building operation.

Soft jaws placed in a vise reduce the likelihood of scratching, marring the stock wood or any metal parts.

known as "draw filing" and is the best method of keeping the work square.

Wrapping abrasive paper around a file is an excellent way to polish metal rapidly.

Keep files from hitting each other during storage to prevent breaking off the cutting teeth.

Riflesmithing requires using the proper size screwdrivers or burred screwheads will invariably result. Don't use screwdrivers that have rounded edges as they will easily slip out of the screwhead when pressure is applied and scratch the surrounding metal or wood. Purchase the best quality tool steel screwdrivers and they'll last a lifetime with proper care. Certain screws have extremely narrow slots in the screwhead requiring grinding the screwdriver blade to match. Be careful to not overheat the blade during grinding or the blade will lose its temper.

Small precision screwdrivers are a necessity for removing tiny internal screws from triggers, actions, and

scope bases. They range in width from .04 through .14 inch and are available in sets of six.

Large screwdrivers with long shanks will be needed to remove stock bolts from certain rifles. Some rifles require specialty-type screwdrivers, such as the diminutive Browning .22 caliber automatic.

An excellent screwdriver set made especially for the gunsmithing industry is the twenty-four-piece Brownell Magna-Tip Set. The magnetized chuck is extremely helpful in holding small screws to the bit while positioning them in hard-to-get-at recesses in rifles. The bits are hollow-ground to give excellent metal-to-metal contact and there are enough bits to fit most popular rifles. Since they are also fully guaranteed, they are a wise investment.

A variety of hammers is essential to the riflesmith. A medium-weight ball peen hammer is a must for drifting out small pins. Different size brass hammers are necessary to install and remove rifle sights. Plastic-head hammers and better yet, rawhide-head hammers will not mar metal surfaces. Large, round wooden mallets are excellent to use on chisels for shaping stocks.

A good vise is an absolute essential to just about all aspects of riflesmithing work. A four-inch vise that bolts to the edge of the workbench with a locking screw that allows it to be turned or securely locked in place will suffice. Sears runs sales on their heavy-duty four-inch vise from time to time at prices that won't take too big a chunk out of the wallet. To prevent pressure from the vise damaging work, a good set of soft jaws are needed. They also act to prevent the work from moving as they provide an excellent gripping surface. Bronze vise jaws are also a welcome addition as they not only prevent marring of

Above: Many rifle stocks require that a stock bolt hole be drilled to mate stock to the receiver. This specialized tool can be made or bought. (Right) Carbide center drills are excellent for removing frozen screws.

Drilling holes in both wood and metal are musts in custom rifle work. A selection of quality bits in letter, fractional and number sizes is required for precision gun work.

metal, but act as a heat-sink while holding pieces that are being heated with a torch.

A drill is one of the most frequently used tools in riflesmithing. A hand drill will get the job done, a portable power drill is better, but a drill press should be used for precision work. A large selection of drill bits are needed to accommodate the hundreds of different size holes used by the many rifle manufacturers. Ideally, one should have two complete sets of "number" drills (one high-carbon and one high-speed steel), one set of "letter" drills, and a set of "fractional" drills. High-speed drills have an advantage over high-carbon drills in that they can be used continuously without drawing the temper. Since drills will become dull when making holes in hardened steel or, worse, may break, a riflesmith should learn how to resharpen them. The easiest way is to purchase a special jig that is used to hold the drill when resharpening on a bench grinder. It cuts a perfect fifty-nine-degree angle to the axis of the drill and the necessary twelve-degree clearance angle on the cutting edge.

Three additional drills will be necessary for rifle work. To drill butt stocks for stock screws a one-half-inch-diameter by eighteen-inch-shank drill must be made or purchased. Also a one-quarter-inch by fourteen-inch-shank drill is needed for the same purpose. The last drill, usually a one-quarter-inch by twenty-inch-shank drill is necessary to remove stuck cases.

Even though we have only covered the most basic tools needed by the riflesmith, one can realize that due to the many different types or styles of hammers, drills and so on, and their high cost, the beginner must be prudent in his decision as to which tool to purchase and their priorities in importance before plunking down his money.

To accomplish most gunsmithing chores there are many other small hand tools and accessories quite necessary to turn out quality work. Rifles are precision tools. It follows then that other precision tools are a must, to complete most jobs. Let's continue with a brief discussion of some of the more important ones.

PRECISION MEASURING TOOLS

Before getting into the various tools in this category one thing anyone that works on metal will need is a can of Dykem Steel Blue. It is a blue layout liquid that is spread over the metal prior to taking any measurements. Any scribe marks made in it will stand out in sharp relief giv-

ing excellent definition to the layout. It sells for under $3 per four-ounce can and lasts for years.

A four-inch square with a straight blade is necessary for keeping all work squared. A six-inch stainless steel rule graduated in tenths and hundredths on one side and thirty-seconds and sixty-fourths on the other makes layouts simple. Both tools being quite inexpensive, they should be at the top of the buying list.

A firing pin protrusion gauge is essential to check the

Dykem layout fluid is applied to metal to allow exact layout with a scribe. Even with daily use, the author has discovered one eight-ounce can will last for years.

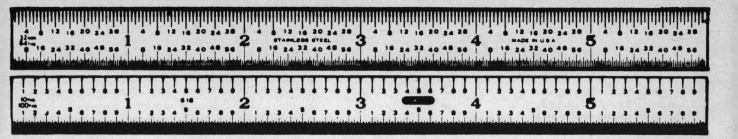

Most gunsmiths carry a six-inch stainless steel ruler in the shop apron, using it hundreds of times a week.

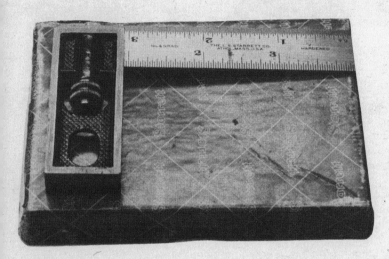

A four-inch square is one of the most useful tools found in a shop. Used to check ninety-degree angles for both wood and metal parts, it aids in many riflesmithing jobs.

Firing pin protrusion gauge is a precision instrument for checking critical firing pin protrusion on any type of firearm. Simple to use, it is accurate to .0001 inch.

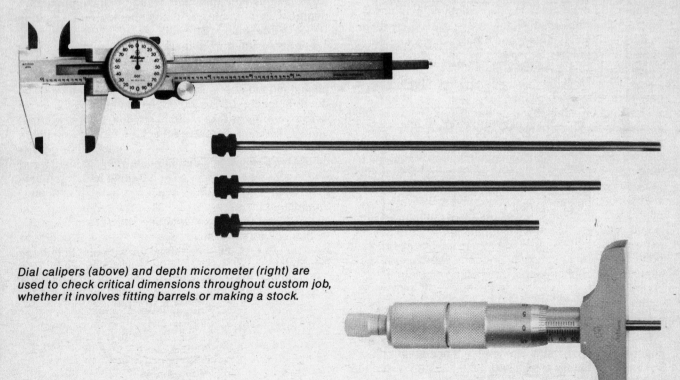

Dial calipers (above) and depth micrometer (right) are used to check critical dimensions throughout custom job, whether it involves fitting barrels or making a stock.

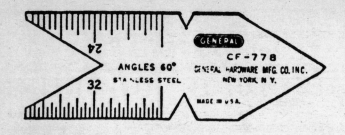

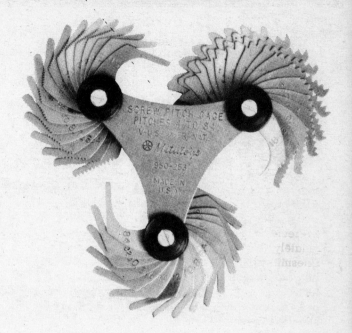

Left: A 60-degree center gauge is a must for lathe work. It is especially useful to gauge lathe bits or in setup for thread cutting. (Below) A thread pitch gauge is used to identify number of threads per inch on various screws.

firing pin protrusion on any firearm. They are extremely accurate up to .0001 inch. Firing pins that are either under or over proper length will cause faulty ignition or puncturing of the primer. Since exact protrusion is critical to the performance and reliability of the rifle, this gauge is at the top of the buying list.

Dial calipers give fast, accurate outside, inside, depth and step measurements. They are easier to use than a vernier caliper and probably the most used measuring tool in riflesmithing. Although the dial caliber will perform the functions of a depth micrometer, the depth micrometer is usually also purchased because of its high degree of finite accuracy. It is a better tool for measuring critical barrel and action work.

For doing lathe work a sixty-degree center gauge is needed to gauge lathe bits or doing set-up for thread cutting. Another good tool used around the lathe is a thread pitch gauge to check threads per inch (tpi) settings. The gauge measures all American National, V and U.S. Standard sixty-degree threads from size four to eighty-four. It makes checking threads per inch on any screw simple and quick. Speaking of screws, a handy little gadget called the Screw Chek'r makes checking the thread and size of all screws, machine, wood, sheet metal, self-tapping, drive and standard rivets a breeze. It tells size, threads per inch, length, diameter, tap series, body drill size, and tap drill. It comes with a special screw-cutting tool for cutting unhardened screws to length, straightens bent screws and battered threads. It's available through Brownell's.

A six-inch precision level is a good investment for checking work in milling machines, Universal grinders,

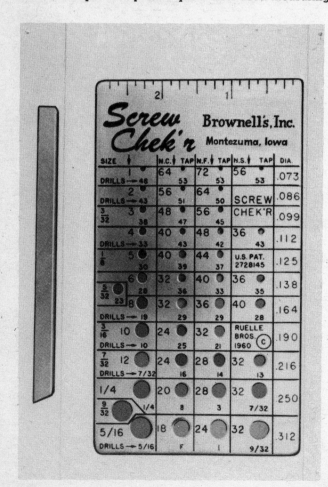

Screw Check'r is an ingenious tool to identify thread size of various gun screws. It also tells which size of tap to use to match screw, aids in cutting to length.

A 6-inch precision machinist level is necessary to true up work in a milling machine. (Right) Adjustable pull for hunting or target rifles is exacting task. Trigger pull weights are accurate way of measuring this factor.

and lathes as well as drill presses during drilling and tapping.

Nothing works as well for measuring the trigger pull on rifles as a set of Trigger Pull Weights. Accurate readings are especially important for adjusting the trigger pull on target rifles.

Precision measuring tools are quite expensive. Unfortunately, they are also quite essential to most phases of riflesmithing. There is little room for error in building rifles and these tools should be among the first initial purchases for serious gun enthusiasts or professionals. The good news is they should last a lifetime if used correctly and stored properly.

SPECIALIZED RIFLESMITHING TOOLS

One of the handiest tools found on most gunsmithing benches is the Bench Block. Usually made of heavy-duty precision steel they're excellent for driving out pins in either flat or round work. They have a number of different size holes which allow the pins to drop through while being driven out of the work. Recently I began using a

nylon bench block manufactured by Vanco Company, P.O. Box 1658, Natchez, MS 39120. So far it has stood up well to abusive pounding, and being made of nylon, it does not scratch the work's metal surface.

Tap and die kits are a must for anyone that works on guns. I prefer using carbon-steel taps. They are easier to remove if broken than high-speed steel; and everyone breaks taps. The carbon tap will shatter in the hole if beaten with a steel punch whereas the high speed just

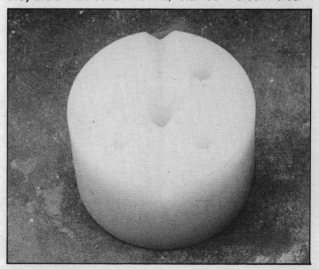

A good bench block is a necessity to remove pins when disassembling any rifle. This accessory is available in either steel or nylon. They prevent the loss of pins, as they are drifted out of the rifle, retained in block holes.

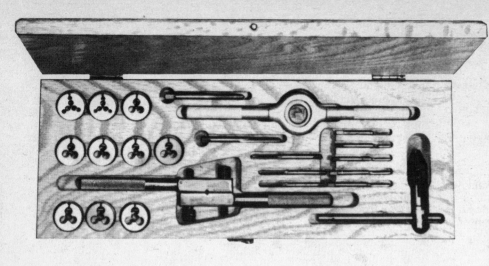

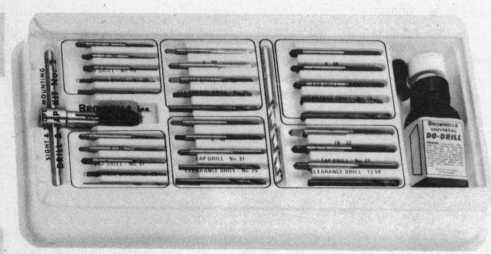

A die and tap kit such as those at left is a must for tapping screw holes in rifles and to thread screws. The kits shown offer a selection of the most commonly used drills and taps.

peens deeper into the threads. When buying tap sets make sure to get extras in popular sizes like the 6x48. Tapping should never be attempted without first applying a good cutting oil to the work. Brownell's Do-Drill or Tap Magic are excellent.

POLISHING AND SHARPENING STONES

As I discussed in my *The Gun Digest Book of Pistolsmithing* a good variety of stones is essential for polishing parts and sharpening cutting tools. Two invaluable oilstones are

Cutting oil is essential for metal cutting. Do-Drill and Tap Magic are excellent for cutting, tapping and drilling jobs encountered.

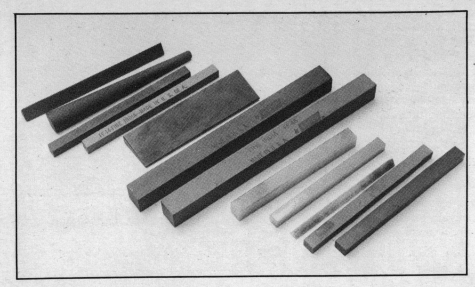

A variety of course, medium, fine India, hard Arkansas, ruby stones in different shapes are needed to polish, hone critical bearing surfaces such as sears, hammers.

called India and Arkansas. Another faster-cutting stone than the Arkansas is the Washita. The last ranges in grades from perfect crystallized and porous whetstone grit to vitreous flint and hard sandstone. The amount of crystallization in these stones determines their sharpness of grit. Good whetstones are quite porous, but uniform in texture and are made of silica crystals. Solid or smooth-looking Washita stones should be avoided as they gen-erally have hard spots which prevent the work from cut-ting uniformly. They range in colors from white to yellow or are red-streaked.

Arkansas stones are harder and denser than Washita stones. They are excellent for cutting purposes as well as for polishing hard metals such as reamers. Available in a number of sizes and shapes, they are best for finish-polishing.

Using plastic stock templates, Sterling Davenport prepares to lay out a Mauser stock on a piece of French walnut. Such templates may be made to match the layout of any stock style, thus eliminating the laborious hand layout method.

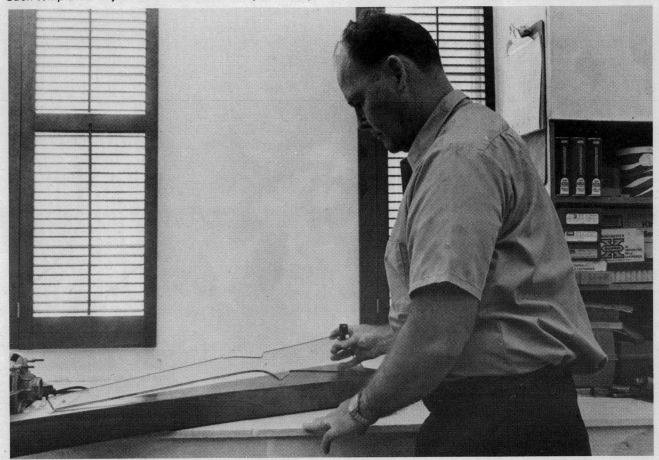

India stone is a man-made product. Available in coarse, medium, and fine, all should be part of the riflesmith's tool inventory. Since stones have a tendency to dry out if left exposed to air, it is best to keep them soaking in a jar of oil. Stones should also be cleaned regularly by washing in gasoline, wiping dry, and storing in oil.

Stones are excellent for removing small burrs or fins, removing machine marks, and polishing bearing surfaces on rifles such as the rails and trigger sears.

STOCKMAKING TOOLS

Transforming a blank of solid hardwood into a finished stock requires a variety of specialized woodworking tools. Although many riflesmiths prefer buying semi-inletted

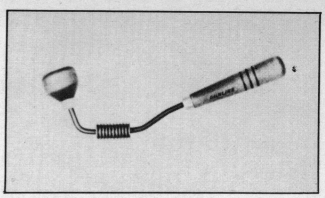

Barrel bedding tools in differing sizes are essential for perfect bedding of barrel to stock for accuracy.

Tool known as the Spoke Shave long has been relied upon by stockmakers for fast removal of wood in stockmaking.

stock blanks, or have their own duplicating machines, many prefer to work strictly from a raw blank.

Rather than going through the tedious procedure of laying out the stock with different measuring devices such as dividers, a much faster and I believe, more efficient approach is by using a plastic template. They are easily made after tracing the desired shape from a blank already laid out. The tracing is then transferred to the plastic or plexiglass plate and cut to shape on a bandsaw.

If working from a blank, initial shaping is accomplished with chisels and hammer. Chisels should be kept razor sharp to best control the tools. After rough shaping,

further shaping is accomplished with a spoke shave, rasps and woodworking files. Sterling Davenport, a fine custom riflesmith recently showed me a rather innovative way to alter rasps better suited to working a stock blank. He heats and bends them slightly. The heat does not destroy the rasp's or file's cutting ability. The slight bend makes the tool more adaptable to stock work. This is especially true when inletting barrel channels. However, it is still a good idea to have a variety of barrel bedding and inletting tools for initial bedding requiring removal of large amounts of wood.

Serious stockmakers should also consider making their own wood chisels. Davenport makes them by taking steel and heating it to a cherry red, then pounding it with a hammer on an anvil to desired shape. It is then shaped on a grinder, filed and polished smooth on buffing wheels. The tools are then heat treated.

Scrapers, necessary for removing hair-thin amounts of wood during the final inletting of barreled action to stock may also be made in any desired shape. The metal used to make scrapers should be quality spring steel. Davenport makes them by first honing them flat on a hard Arkan-

A number of different styles and shapes of wood rasps are a necessity to handle chores involved in stock work.

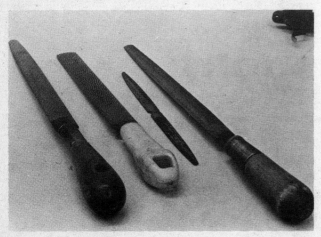

Davenport heats and bends rattail files for easier use. Heating them doesn't destroy the cutting quality of tool.

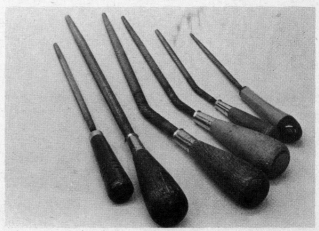

A number of sizes and shapes of wood chisels are required to shape custom rifle stocks. Sterling Davenport makes his own by heating, shaping, tempering to achieve the desired configuration.

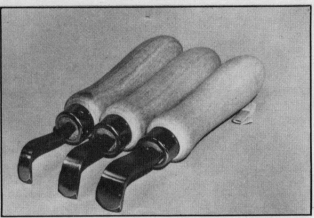

Curl scrapers are used to handle wood removal in final inletting work. Handle gives control of cutting edge.

This set of scrapers was made from spring stock, as is suggested by the odd shapes. They also may be bought.

sas stone. The surfaces are then polished on a felt wheel. After the edges are razor sharp, Sterling uses a burnisher to make a small curl on the edge allowing them to now cut very fine amounts of wood with each pass. These tools are absolutely necessary to get the professional light-tight fit between metal and wood insuring strength of stock and accurate shooting characteristics.

Stockmaker's hand screws are used for final accurate fitting of the stock to the action. Sets for popular rifles such as Mausers, Springfield, Enfield, Winchester Model 70, Sako, and Remington 700s should be included in the riflesmith's tool box.

ABRASIVES

One of the most time-consuming aspects of riflesmithing is involved with sanding and polishing. A good supply of garnet paper ranging in grits from 80 through 280 is necessary to remove all scratches from a stock before applying the finish coats. If any scratches do remain in the wood they will be highlighted when the finish is applied and are the mark of amateurism. The same holds true in

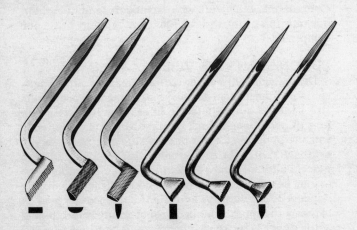

Small bottoming rasps can be an aid to a stockmaker in making cuts in difficult-to-reach recesses in a stock.

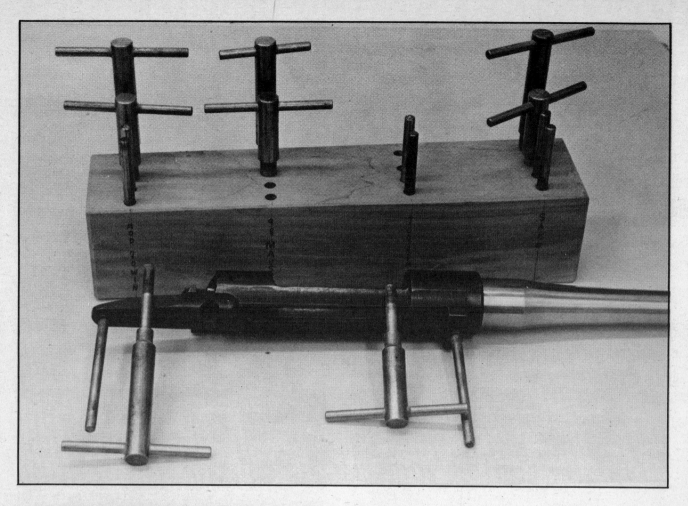

Stockmaker's hand screws are used for fitting stock to action. Sets for each action style are required. (Left) Garnet paper and wet-or-dry paper in various grades are needed. Mitchell's abrasive cord, tape is excellent for sanding, polishing difficult recesses.

For accurate metal-to-metal fit, such as the locking lugs to the lug recesses in the receiver, lapping compound is required. A supply of various grit silicon carbide and aluminum oxide works extremely well. The latter also works well when fitting steel to aluminum. It also does an excellent job of lapping chambers. The silicon carbide is an extremely hard abrasive and should be thoroughly cleaned out of the work with either kerosene ot trichloroethane after the desired fitting or lapping has been completed.

PUNCHES AND PIN VISES

Drift punches are used to drive pins holding triggers, sears, and the like out of their holes. A number of different size punches are required to fit the many different size pins. A good bench block should be used in conjunction with the punches. Center punches are also necessary to establish spots to be drilled or for staking small parts into place. Full-time smiths generally prefer adjustable power punches. A hammer is not needed and the tool may be adjusted to deliver anywhere from fourteen to fifty pounds of pressure to clearly mark any spot on hardened steel. If a drift punch is broken it can be squared up and returned

polishing metal. Wet-or-dry paper from 80 grit through 600 is essential to remove any machine marks or scratches prior to bluing. The wet-or-dry type works better and the paper lasts longer if cut with kerosene.

I recently began using abrasive cords and tapes from the E.C. Mitchell Company of Middleton, Massachusetts. Trying to polish out small recesses such as trigger guards is difficult and time consuming. Using these flat tapes or abrasive cords in various diameter greatly speeds up the polishing of these difficult-to-reach regions.

Silicone carbide (above, left) and aluminum oxide (right) lapping compounds are needed to lap action, jewel bolts.

Drift punches (right) are among the most-used tools in any gunshop. They are used to remove, replace pins in assembly, disassembly of a rifle. (Below) Center punches are used to make starter holes for drilling, for staking parts and screws in place.

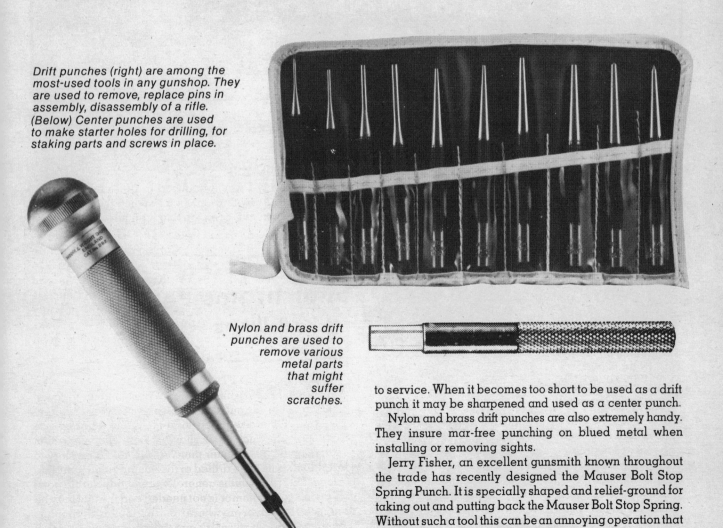

Nylon and brass drift punches are used to remove various metal parts that might suffer scratches.

to service. When it becomes too short to be used as a drift punch it may be sharpened and used as a center punch.

Nylon and brass drift punches are also extremely handy. They insure mar-free punching on blued metal when installing or removing sights.

Jerry Fisher, an excellent gunsmith known throughout the trade has recently designed the Mauser Bolt Stop Spring Punch. It is specially shaped and relief-ground for taking out and putting back the Mauser Bolt Stop Spring. Without such a tool this can be an annoying operation that often results in marring the metal.

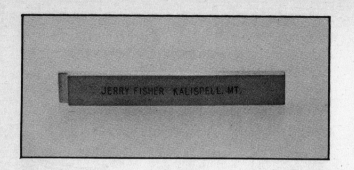

Left: A new tool designed by Jerry Fischer is a Mauser bolt stop spring punch. Easy to use, it makes assembling and disassembling bolt stop springs simple. (Below) Pin vises in varying sizes work well in grinding, polishing small parts. Vise keeps them in place on buffing wheel.

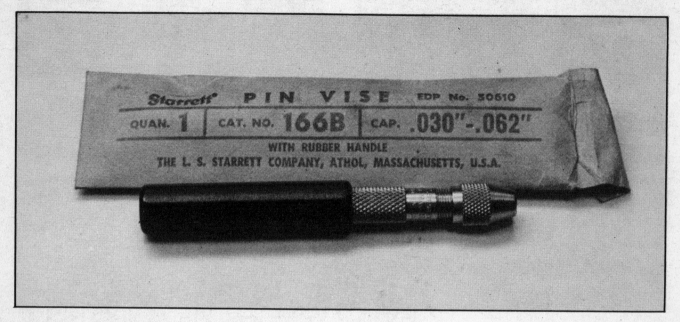

Pin vises come in very handy for holding small pins or screws, especially when grinding or polishing them. Trying to hold on to a small pin when polishing it on a buffing wheel ofttimes leads to the pin flying out of the fingers to parts unknown. The pin or screw also heats up quickly making the task of holding on to it even trickier. Pin vises come in a variety of sizes and like most of the other tools mentioned to this point, are available through Brownell's.

POLISHING AIDS

From the day I was introduced to brass belt buckles and the U.S. Army Airborne's insistence that it be kept mirror-polished I've been looking for a faster and easier

Simichrome polish and Flitz, a new import from Germany, are the best polishing agents author has discovered.

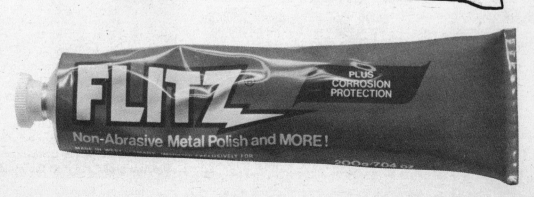

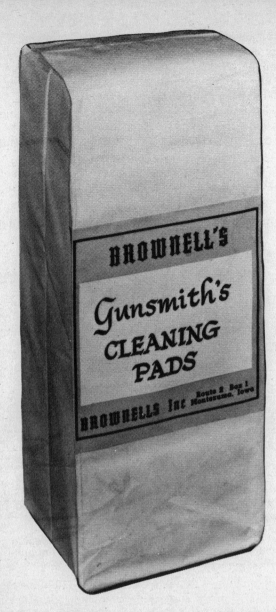

Brownell's cleaning pads are designed specifically for polishing or wiping down firearms with oil. The 100% non-woven cotton doesn't leave any telltale scratches.

material than Brasso. After building several firearms that had brass furniture I've had much time for experimentation. Once a piece of brass has been shaped and polished to a mirror brilliance it can easily be scratched if the wrong kind of cloth is used during future polishings. Brownell's sells special cleaning pads of one-hundred-percent non-woven cotton that are excellent for polishing brass or blued metal. They are also lint free which is a nice feature when wiping down a rifle for display purposes.

For the last several years the finest single polish I have found for polishing brass furniture on rifles is a metal polish called Simichrome. It also works well on other metals such as aluminum, silver, gold and plastic. It works faster and better than any other conventional polishing liquid I've tried. Now, another new non-abrasive metal polish from West Germany called Flitz has hit the U.S. Market. It, like Simichrome is outstanding for polish-

ing, but also imparts a thin film to help prevent rust. Either product is excellent.

BONDING AGENTS

Many times customers will bring in rifles with worn, or extra-loose screws or pins. A dab of a product called Lock N' Seal quickly remedies the situation. It sets up to 3400 pounds per square inch (psi) which will definitely hold up under most conditions. It works quite well on sight

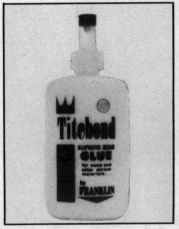

Locktite Lock N' Seal has long been a favorite for holding screws in place on firearms. Good for attaching forend tips, pistol grip caps is Franklin's Titebond.

screws even in the big magnum caliber rifles. If you don't have Lock N' Seal handy a drop of medicinal iodine works well.

A product called Acra-Weld is an excellent epoxy compound that works equally well on metal or wood. It is also not susceptible to oils, vibration, or solvents and can be colored to match the surrounding surfaces.

For installing forend tips, Titebond aliphatic resin glue works great. It should be applied to both mating surfaces

Acra-Weld is a two-part bonding agent, featuring resin in one tube, a hardening agent in the other. The two are mixed together per instructions prior to their use.

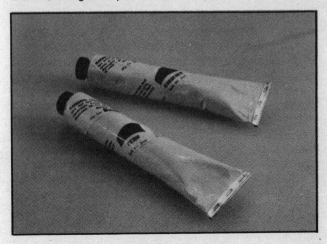

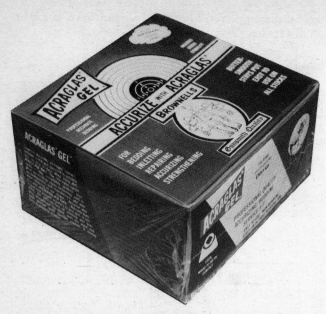

Brownell's Acraglas long has been a mainstay for barrel bedding work. It's now available in a newer gel form.

and held together under pressure using either C-clamps or strong rubber bands fashioned from old car or bicycle inner tubes until it has set up.

Possibly the most famous bonding material and the stuff I cut my teeth on learning gunsmithing is Brownell's Acraglas. It does an incredible job of repairing broken or cracked stocks. I understand it is now also available as a

Stock repair pins are used in conjunction with Acraglas to repair cracked or broken stocks. The combination will provide added strength in the area that's been damaged.

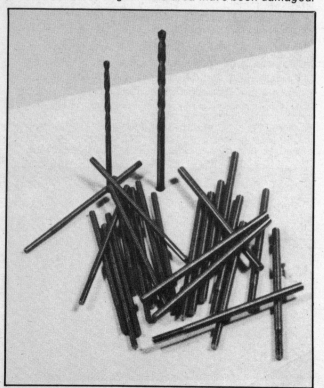

gel which cuts down on the possibility of runovers. Acraglas, or the new Acragel, will give professional results when repairing, bedding or inlaying stocks, and they are not affected by most chemicals or natural elements.

When repairing broken or cracked stocks on high-powered rifles I also will use stock repair pins in conjunction with Acraglas just to be on the safe side. With both a pin and the Acraglas I know if the stock ever does break again it won't be in the same spot.

JIGS AND FIXTURES

Certain jigs and fixtures are absolutely essential to completing many riflesmithing tasks and turning out pre-

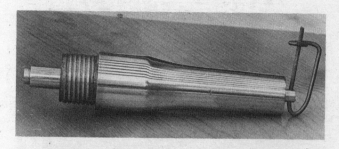

The author made this bolt-lapping jig. It is invaluable as an aid in obtaining the 80 percent contact of bolt locking lugs to the lug recesses located in receiver.

Author also made this bolt-handle welding jig for use in bolt handle jigs. It is available commercially, too.

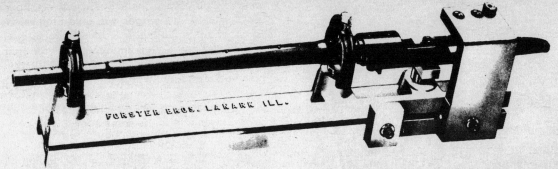

Forster universal sight-mounting fixture has gained popularity over the years with riflesmiths. It is used to drill and tap scope base holes precisely, accurately.

locking recesses of the receiver. The contact amount is checked by painting the lugs with Dykem. It is a tool that should be included in any serious riflesmith's inventory.

Another handy jig is the bolt-handle welding jig. It can be made of angle iron, or purchased through Brownell's. It does make welding the new or altered bolt handle at precisely the right angle a simpler task than just laying the bolt in a vise and jockeying it to the right angle. It is one tool that pays for itself during its first use.

The Forster Universal Sight Mounting Fixture is invaluable for drilling and tapping holes for the mounting of scope mounts and receiver sights. It adapts to any bolt-action, lever or pump rifle. This precision instrument will greatly reduce any possibility of ruining a barrel or receiver due to drilling off-center.

A handy little tool called a Ramp Soldering Jig eliminates any possibility of the front sight slipping while being soldered in place. It is designed to allow easy access to the soldering area for perfect jobs and will work on just about any type of front sight now manufactured.

Ramp-soldering jigs make installation of front sights an easier job. They hold the sight in exact position; open design offers easy access for heating with a torch.

The B-Square recoil pad jig is a favorite tool of the author. It allows precise fitting of the pad and also eliminates possible damage to stock, finish during job.

cise, quality work. Some must be purchased while a few can be made. Although often quite expensive, they will usually pay for themselves within the first few times they are used.

One important jig used in fitting barrels to actions is the bolt-lapping jig. I made the one pictured at gunsmithing school. It was made from a piece of scrap metal, but one similar could be fashioned from a used barrel. It is a device threaded to the particular receiver to be fitted to a new barrel. It has a spring-loaded push bar that engages the bolt face when screwed to the receiver. After applying lapping compound to the locking lugs the bolt is opened and closed with the push bar applying enough pressure to lap the bolt to the desired eighty percent contact in the

The B-Square bolt jeweling jig holds the rifle bolt in position for symmetrically jeweled patterns. Set up in a drill press, jeweling is created with lapping compound.

Tung oil is one of the most simple oil finishes to apply, giving the stock the finest possible professional finish.

The easiest and fastest method of fitting recoil pads to butt stocks is done with the B-Square Recoil Pad Jig. I have done this task by hand and eyeballing, but this ingenious little tool allows error-free fitting with no chance of damaging the stock so as to necessitate refinishing.

Many customers will request that the bolt on their favorite rifle be jeweled. It is a nice cosmetic touch and does result in a smooth bearing surface. The only way to accomplish this operation is with the B-Square Bolt Jeweling Jig. When set up on a drill press creating the jeweled effect with 120-grit silicone carbide and small wire brush turning in the drill press it is a simple task.

STOCK FINISHING SUPPLIES

Putting a perfect finish on a stock can be one of the most difficult parts of riflesmithing. Amateurs are lulled into a false sense of security with the many claims of various manufacturers of both oil and plastic type finishes. Applying that "perfect" finish takes a great deal of experience and a lot of patience. Probably the best single method of stock finishing is explained by Sterling Davenport in my chapter on finishing.

After the last coat of finish has been applied, rubbed out, the almost legendary Lin-Speed oil or Stock Sheen & Conditioner from Birchwood Casey can be utilized to provide the wood of stock with rich professional sheen.

Shellac sticks are available in different colors to aid in hiding scratches, holes, cracks in damaged stocks. It is necessary to melt a drop of the shellac over the problem area, then sand it flush with the wood when dry.

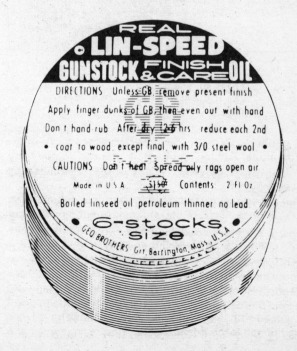

Birchwood Casey long has been a supplier of products of use to the professional gunsmith. Water-base stain is excellent, as is the maker's Stock Sheen & Conditioner. The former can be wiped on the wood prior to finishing.

Whether the riflesmith prefers a plastic or oil finish is a matter of personal taste. I have used both in many different commercial brands with varying degrees of success. However, there are a few individual products the amateurs and professionals should have on hand. When repairing stocks prior to finishing, an assortment of shellac sticks to match the color and grain of the wood is helpful. Acraglas mixed with sanding dust from the same stock will also work. The stick is simply heated and the drops fill the crack or hole. It is then allowed to dry and sanded smooth.

One of the three most popular types of finish used by the majority of riflesmiths today because of its ease of working, excellent results, and good water-resistant quality is tung oil. Although not as durable, perhaps, as some of the newer plastic finishes, it does fill the wood pores and makes for a beautiful finish to any stock. It also is a simple task to sand out and repair any scratches with this type of finish.

There will be many times when a customer will desire to have his rifle refinished. Many times these stocks will need to be stained or restained. Birchwood Casey's water-base stain has long been the favorite in the industry. It may be applied directly to the wood and then finished or mixed with the finish beforehand.

Regardless of the finish applied to a stock, nothing will bring out the lustre and beauty of the wood as the two products that have been around for years. One is Birchwood Casey's Stock Sheen & Conditioner. The other is Lin-Speed.

Both products produce outstanding results if proper directions are followed.

POWER TOOLS

While a number of power tools are cost-prohibitive to the amateur, many are needed by the professional. From a business point of view, they are a sound business in-

One of the most-used tools in many gunsmithing phases is the Dremel Moto-Tool. The variable-speed Model 380 can save hours of handwork for professional results.

Few gunsmiths could get along without a bench grinder. The Baldor 6-inch one-third horsepower model can be used for numerous tasks, providing many years of service.

Disc sanders can be used to cut recoil pads, shape wood, grind metal, sharpen tools and more. Author built this floor stand from scrap with machinist Mike Sprague.

vestment since they may be a legitimate business write-off, will greatly speed up the amount of work a person can produce, and will bring good resale dollars if sold or traded at a later time.

An outstanding investment at a moderate price is a variable-speed Dremel Moto-Tool and its line of accessories. The Dremel Model 380 is probably the most popular in the general gunsmithing trade. It will save a lot of man-hours around the shop grinding, cutting, sanding, drilling, and polishing. It is a tough, well-made tool that lends itself to practically every phase of gunsmithing or hobby work.

A sturdy bench grinder gets a great deal of use around the gunshop. The professional should purchase one with

A lathe is essential in fitting and chambering a barrel to an action. It is an expensive tool and, unless one does barrel work in volume, it will not pay for itself. It can be used for many projects needing precision results.

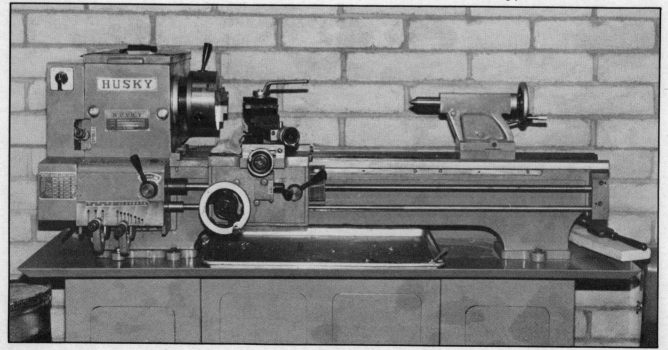

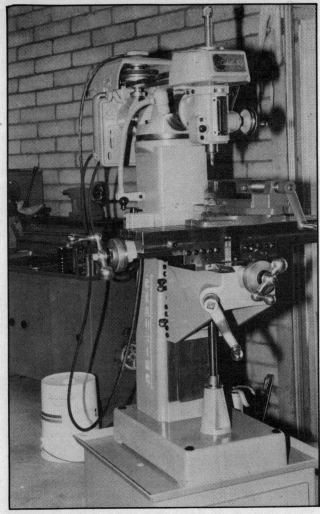

The milling machine, like the lathe, is an expensive investment. Finding a good used machine like Clausing model shown is desirable for doing precision work.

One can use a hand drill for many projects but a bench or floor model is more versatile. Corbin Manufacturing of Phoenix, Oregon, carries a wide line at good prices.

a minimum of a one-third-horsepower motor, double ended and sealed. Get a model that will handle ten-inch wheels. It is better to buy one with roller or ball bearings since the less expensive brass-bushing models will not produce the same quality results over an extended period of time. Coarse, medium, and fine wheels are a must for the variety of different types of grinding necessary in riflesmithing. Be sure to get a dressing stone to keep the grinding wheels running true.

A disc grinder may not be the most essential tool in the shop and is quite expensive, but nothing comes in handier for installing recoil pads, butt plates, squaring blanks, surface grinding, or sharpening tools. I made one and saved a good deal of money, but it is not an easy project if a large disc and powerful motor are to be used.

Unless a riflesmith intends to have his actions barreled up by one of the gunsmithing services advertised in various firearms publications, a lathe is an expensive but necessary investment. If possible, buy a used lathe and check it to make certain it is in good condition and runs within the necessary acceptable tolerances for gun work.

For riflesmithing purposes, buy one with a minimum of a five-foot bed, three feet between centers, and with a 1⅜-inch spindle. The accessories, such as a steady rest, et cetera, are also quite expensive, but many times they are available with used models. One of the best places to purchase a new lathe is through Corbin Mfg., Phoenix, Oregon. As unpatriotic as it might sound, foreign imports, especially Japanese or Taiwanese power equipment is much less expensive and every bit as reliable as the U.S.-manufactured lathes.

To own a good-quality milling machine, like a Clausing, is like dying and going to gunsmith heaven. Absolutely dead perfect machining can be done with a mill. Although any riflesmith worth his salt can cut a dovetail in a rifle barrel using a couple of files and a hacksaw, a milling machine will accomplish this same task in a fraction of the time and do the job better. Although it is not an absolute must, it is a welcome addition insuring precise and quality work if operated properly.

Another power tool not on the "must have" list for riflesmithing, but ever so handy, is the power bandsaw. It cuts

The Rockwell commercial-duty Speed Bloc sander is best investment author ever made, he says. For final sanding and shaping stocks, it saves endless number of hours.

A belt sander is less expensive than a disc sander and will do any job of a disc sander. Many models currently are available from Brownell's and Corbin Manufacturing.

both metal and wood and is indispensable for cutting stock blanks to shape. They are available from prices of $175 to $16,000, but even the least expensive are a welcome and useful addition to the shop.

Either a sturdy bench-mounted or floor-model drill press should be the first purchase made if quantity gunsmithing work is expected. Used to drill holes for scope mounts, making tools, polishing metal parts, and too many other jobs to mention, a drill press is needed to accomplish precision drilling. Be sure to order a good compound vise for securing work for drilling. Corbin Mfg. carries a large variety of drill presses in several price ranges.

Looking back over the years at all the many tools I have

An air compressor is used with air grinder to polish metal parts or work wood. It also can be used to clean firearms during work.

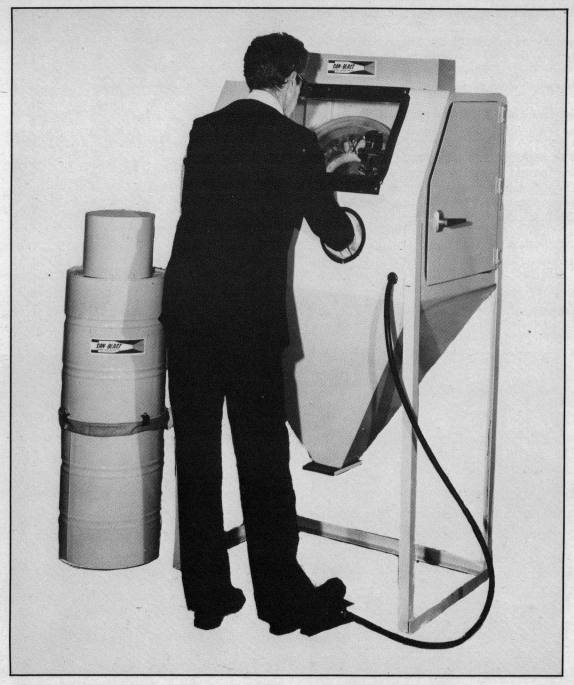

While it may do more than the average gunshop needs, a compressor with a blast cabinet is used to remove rust or corrosion from metal parts quickly or to prepare them for matte-finish bluing process.

purchased, none has given more valuable service than the Rockwell Commercial Duty, Speed-Bloc Sander. No other tool will work as well for sanding down stocks to that glass-smooth preparation for finish coating. Used with 80-grit garnet paper it will actually shape a stock. I've used mine continuously for over nine years without a single problem and it has seen more than an average amount of use.

The Rockwell belt sander is one of the most versatile tools used by the riflesmith. It is excellent for polishing metal, sanding, shaping stocks, or attaching recoil pads.

Although available in a great range of prices, a $150 model will serve well.

A good air compressor is invaluable for cleaning parts, sandblasting, or for use with air tools. Since air grinders are gaining more and more favor among the riflesmithing trade, a good compressor will pay for itself within a few months. Sandblasting rusted parts or giving a matte finish to gun parts by compressed air is much faster than attempting it by hand. A company called Trumans, Inc., 17 Kenmore Avenue, Youngstown, OH 44507 manufactures a line of blast cabinets and accessories that will greatly add to the amount of productivity from a one-man gun shop.

Air grinders are excellent for polishing both flat and round surfaces. They are especially handy on octagonal barrels. They will polish out scratches and pits in the metal, but do not round the edges which is of paramount importance in the restoration of older rifles. It then takes only a few minutes to sandblast the metal, giving it a rather flat, but attractive finish when blued.

WELDING, BRAZING, SOLDERING EQUIPMENT

Welding, brazing, and soldering are a daily way of life for the riflesmith. Running perfect welds in the gunsmithing trade is an absolute necessity. An improperly welded bolt handle could break, ruining a hunt. Tool steel must be brazed rather than welded. Recoil reducers and small parts must be silver soldered. The riflesmith must have the equipment on hand to complete the majority of rifle

Welding equipment is a must for any riflesmith, but half tanks of oxygen and acetylene gas such as those shown are less expensive, easier to handle than full sizes.

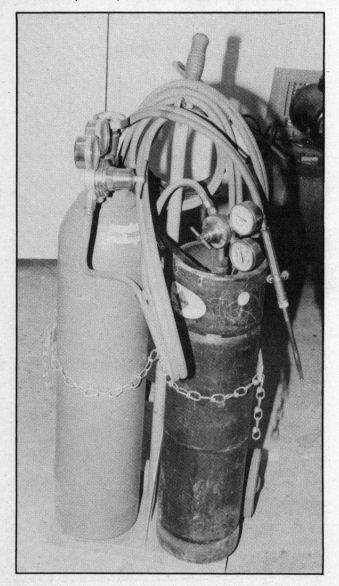

Brownell's Heat Stop helps prevent heat from running to the lug area during welding, destroying hardening. PBC non-scaling compound is used to prevent steel scaling.

work that comes through his shop door.

Since the majority of welding will be done on small parts, half tanks of oxygen and acetylene are all that are required. Depending upon location, it may be less expensive and more convenient to lease welding equipment rather than buying outright. It is wise to shop around for torches and regulators as there is a good deal of competition among the many manufacturers and it is possible to obtain these products at reasonable prices. The riflesmith should have welding tips in small, medium and large sizes on hand to tackle any job. Cutting heads are

threads on the acetylene connection are left-handed while the oxygen coupling is right-handed. Keep the welding tips cleaned by running small tip cleaners through them before beginning each task.

When welding on bolts, barrels or receivers it is a good

Kasenit is an industry standard for hardening plain-carbon or low-carbon alloy steels. (Below) Tempilaq is inexpensive liquid for determining certain melting temperatures. It is excellent to use when hardening steel parts.

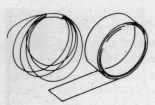

Brownell's Hi-Force 44 solder and Silvaloy silver solder in ribbon form are excellent for high-temperature soldering work such as for front sight ramps.

generally not needed, but are a nice luxury item.

The welding rig should be portable. Most riflesmiths opt for a twelve-foot length of hose. They can be purchased quite reasonably through surplus industrial outlets. Remember, this equipment may be depreciated each year and supplies of welding rod are a one-hundred-percent write-off.

Welding equipment can be dangerous if not handled and used properly. Oil and oxygen do not mix. That is the purpose for the brass fittings. The tanks should be kept upright at all times. If they should have to be moved be certain to attach the safety cap to the oxygen tank. If it should fall without the cap the entire tank can become a missile. Acetylene is highly flammable and poisonous. When oxygen pressure drops below twenty-five pounds, it is time to have the tanks refilled. Maximum pressure on the acetylene tank should not exceed fifteen pounds. When attaching the hoses to the tanks, remember that the

idea to use a product such as Brownell's Heat Stop to prevent the heat from running to other areas of the part. A product called PBC may also be used if welding on barrels, to prevent scaling.

Brazing is the utilization of brass or copper to bind two pieces of steel together, producing an extremely strong bond. The work is heated with an acetylene torch as in welding, and should only be done while wearing the proper welding goggles.

Silver soldering is nothing more than another form of brazing requiring heat, but using silver as the filler agent along with a flux. Brownell's Hi-Force 44 solder does an excellent job of bonding. However, there are times when I prefer Silvaloy which is available in a thin ribbon. It is a simple matter to place a small piece of ribbon between front sight and barrel and complete the bond. It is a good idea to use soldering talc around the surrounding area in case any solder leaks out. Cleaning up any runovers are

Soldering talc works well to prevent runovers of solder from adhering to surrounding metal, easing clean-up.

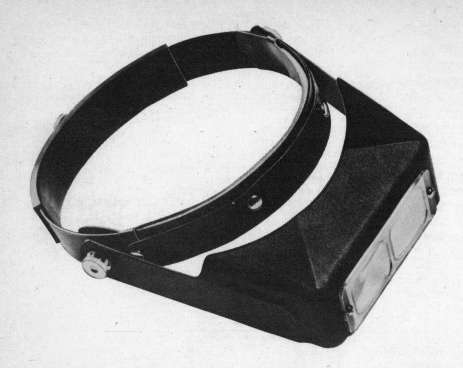

The OptiVisor is available in many different magnifications for doing metal work, checkering or for any other type of close-up viewing.

much easier as the solder won't adhere to the metal if the talc is first applied.

Two other products should be considered for the riflesmith's bench if welding and heat treating are to be performed. The first is an old standby, Kasenit. It is one of the easiest hardening compounds to use and gives excellent results. The other, Tempilaq, is a liquid that sets up hard and then melts at a given temperature during hardening or tempering. Just select the right temperature for the particular job and use a small smear of liquid from a corresponding temperature-controlled bottle and heat the metal until the Tempilaq melts.

Welding, brazing, soldering, heat treating, and tempering gun parts are everyday operations for the practicing gunsmith. These services are also excellent moneymakers. It is wise to thoroughly understand and perfect this aspect of riflesmithing early in your career.

The least expensive tool listed in this chapter is this gauge for making master lines prior to checkering. It also has grids to determine lines per inch on finished work. (Below) Checkering cradles make the job easier, as it allows proper positioning, stability for checkering work.

CHECKERING EQUIPMENT

In the world of riflesmithing most often there are two types of individuals that checker stocks. The first group is made up of those folks that pursue it as an art form, enhancing the appearance and functionality of the firearm. The other group, of which I am a charter member, are those that can technically perform the task, but would be far better off to have shipped the stock off to the first group for optimum results. I don't mean to cast a pall over any of

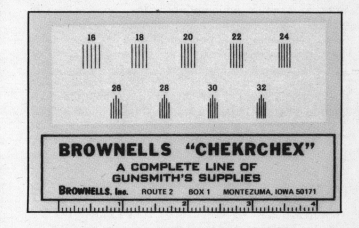

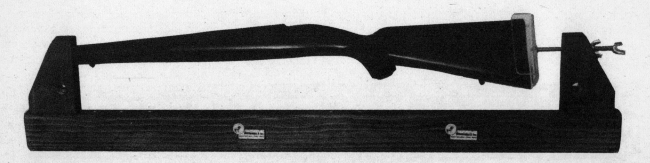

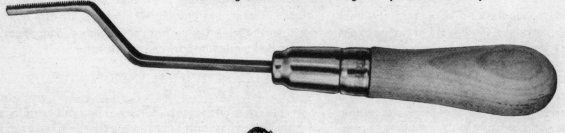

Dembart long has supplied quality wood-checkering tools. A starter set with different types of cutting heads is marketed. (Below) The jointer is utilized to straighten checkering lines. Tool was designed by Monte Kennedy.

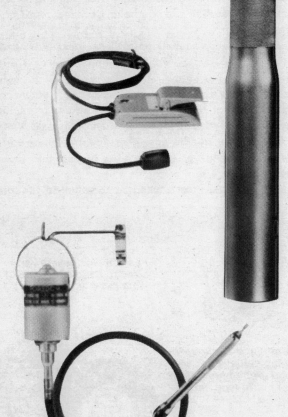

Many professional checkerers prefer to use an electric checkering unit. Popular is the MMC rotary checkering head with Foredom industrial-grade CC motor, flexible shaft, rheostat and handpiece. Only three or four checkering jobs will pay for unit.

you beginning would-be checkerers, but there is much more to this art other than merely scratching straight lines in a piece of wood.

Checkering is best left to that group that also have the ability to draw and are gifted with artistic conception. A custom firearm that belongs in the custom category can look dreadful if a mediocre checkering job is performed. Besides each individual diamond being perfect and each line between diamonds being straight, the overall pattern is as distinctive as the quality and figure of the wood.

I find nothing wrong in checkering as a hobby, or doing simple patterns on certain rifles intended to be meat-getters. However, I would not think of performing this service on custom rifles in my shop. Custom checkering requires completing extensive checkering patterns perfectly in a minimal amount of time if it is to be at all profitable. I have personally done a few extensive checkering jobs that were technically perfect — or close to it — but lacked the overall flair that should enhance the lines of the rifle and complement the individual characteristics of the wood. Of the four hundred or so gunsmiths I have known over the years, there are less than a handful that have truly mastered this phase of the riflesmith's art. I suggest anyone really interested in learning quality checkering to study the works of Al Lind, Dale Goens, Al Biesen, Monty Kennedy, Lenard Brownell, Jerry Fisher, and Steve Fischer.

Before I've scared everyone away from checkering let me emphasize that there is a big difference between checkering for a living and checkering for fun. I checker many of my own guns, but prefer to have any expensive custom rifles checkered by the experts. Of course, the only way anyone can find out if they have the aptitude for it is to get some tools and begin practicing. After a few practice projects most people are able to perform reasonably good checkering patterns.

Checkering requires specialized hand tools and, in some cases, electric tools. A steady hand is important, but good vision is a must. Many professional checkerers use a binocular magnifier glass known as the OptiVisor. It affords the checkerer magnified pinpoint clarity.

A checkering cradle is a tremendous aid. The work can be turned in the cradle, allowing the checkering hand to remain absolutely vertical. This is important to keep the lines running dead straight. The cradle also eliminates any wobble, allowing the cutting tool to make a precise cut. They sell for less than $20 and are available through Brownell's.

Another handy little tool is the Chekrchex. It is a small transparent rule that acts as a guide when cutting in pattern lines on curved or flat surfaces. It also has several different measurement lines to determine the lines per inch of checkering on completed rifles.

One of the most popular sets of checkering tools is made by Dem-Bart. The set consists of regular cutters, skipline cutters, and bordering tools, available in eighteen- through twenty-four-line-per-inch settings. Another excellent tool is the "Jointer" designed by Monty Kennedy. It has a long, straight cutting plane to help straighten any crooked lines. I've used it on more than one occasion to bring the lines back to proper angle without anyone knowing I'd cut less than a perfect pass.

Many custom checkerers use an electric checkering outfit. The MMC Rotary Checkering Head, attached to a Foredom industrial-grade CC Motor, flexible shaft, CFL-15 Rheostat and handpiece will cut much faster than attempting to do it by hand. The entire set sells for just over $575. Still, it does not guarantee perfect results. It takes a steady hand and an artist's touch to turn out professional work.

I would suggest that everyone interested in working with wood and interested in stockmaking give checkering a try. Just go slow and even slower the closer you get to finishing a project for best results. And practice, practice, practice!

BUFFING AND POLISHING EQUIPMENT

A good double-ended buffing and polishing wheel setup is essential for the riflesmith. They can be made or purchased. A minimum of a one-horsepower motor is recommended. The motor should be sealed as buffing and polishing is one of the dirtiest jobs encountered in this business. Use a motor that will turn a minimum of 1750 revolutions per minute (rpm) and use the largest wheels possible. Muslin-stitched wheels are excellent and hold a head of polishing compound better than felt wheels. Felt wheels are also much more expensive. Two sets of wheels are needed as brass will have to be polished and buffed from time to time. Brass filings will catch in the wheel and scratch steel. A 240-, 400-, 500-, and 600-grit wheel are all necessary to bring the metal to a mirror finish. A matte and carding set of wheels are also handy to remove rust and grime from metal parts and for imparting a soft matte finish on certain firearms.

MISCELLANEOUS RIFLESMITHING AIDS

No riflesmith could get through a day in the shop without a supply of spring stock and replacement striker springs. Springs are constantly being lost by customers when disassembling guns or from wearing out. Brownell's carries replacement striker springs for most of the popular rifles, but it is still up to the riflesmith to make many unusual-size springs as replacements.

Many times riflesmiths are asked to reline rifle barrels. This is especially true with many of the older, but still popular, .22 caliber rifles. Special barrel liner drills and liners are available through Brownell's. Relining barrels is not a difficult operation and can be an excellent moneymaker for the shop.

There are many functions in riflesmithing that one would swear has to be done with three hands. A set of vise-grips can be that third hand. They also are terrific for holding small pieces during welding or tempering. Another handy set of pliers is one made for removing bolt extractors. It greatly simplifies an otherwise frustrating task. A variety of long-jawed needle-nose pliers are a welcome addition when trying to get small screws or pins into inaccessible spots.

Probably the most abused part on rifles are the screws.

Felt wheels come in various sizes to handle the type of work to be accomplished.

Matte and carding wheels remove rust, corrosion and prepare gun parts for matte-type finish.

For polishing, buffing, stitched- and loose-muslin wheels work well, are less expensive than soft, hard felt type. They are needed for preparing metal parts for bluing.

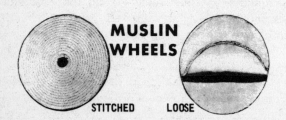

MUSLIN WHEELS

STITCHED   LOOSE

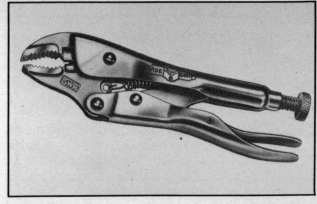

As springs have a tendency to wear out or break, it is a good idea to have a supply of striker springs (above) on hand, as well as a supply of music wire (below) for spring stock. Latter is used in making unusual springs.

Vise grips are almost like having an extra pair of hands and are usual for holding small parts when working on them with a torch. (Below) Bolt-extractor pliers make assembly, disassembly of extractor easier and safer.

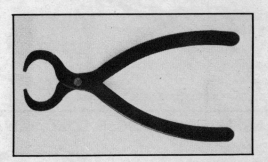

Moneymaker for the gun shop is ability to reline rifle barrels in .22 caliber. It is not difficult and is less expensive for the customer. Special drills and barrel liners are necessary; they are available from Brownell's.

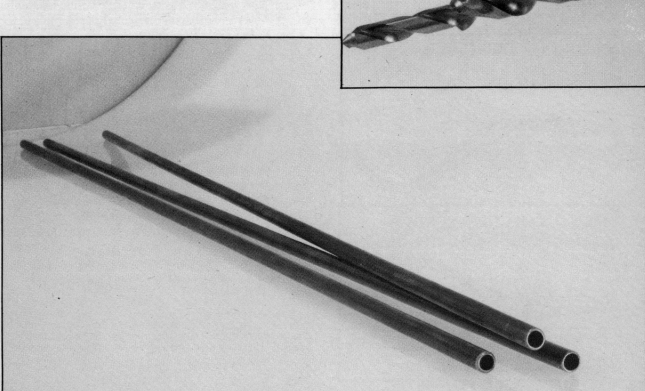

No. 134 FLAT NOSE

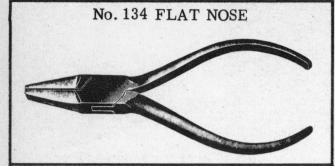

No. 137 ROUND NOSE

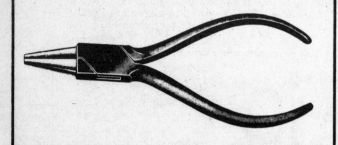

No. 143 ROUND NOSE LONG JAW

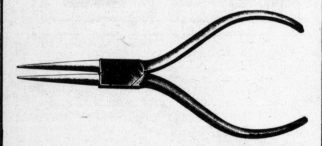

No. 152 DUCK BILL

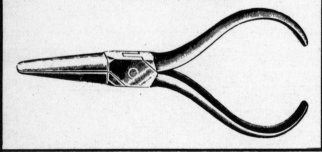

No. 153 STRAIGHT NEEDLE
No. 154 CURVED-NOSE NEEDLE

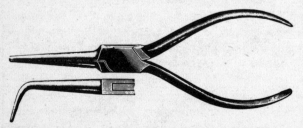

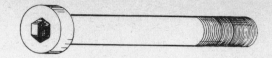

Screw heads take great abuse and replacement often is a faster process than repair. An assortment of trigger-guard screws, sight-base screws and fillister-head type is a necessity if one is building or repairing rifles.

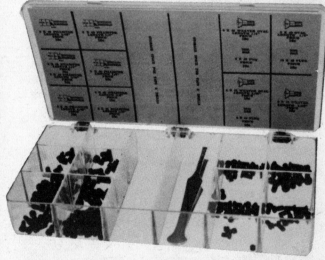

Amateur gun tinkers seem to delight in marring or burring the screwheads with mismatching screwdrivers. They are also one of the first pieces lost, bent, mutilated or cross-threaded by the uneducated. A good replacement selection of trigger-guard screws, as well as fillister-head, and sight-base screws in various sizes is a good investment. The cost is rather small when you consider the alternative is making a new screw which takes time.

Every working gunsmith should have an assortment of pliers within reach. There are special shapes for those special purposes one finds on various firearms models.

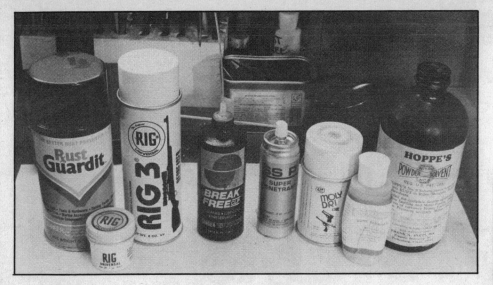

Both amateurs and professionals in the riflesmithing ranks need good solvents to clean and maintain the firearms, lubricants to aid in functioning and preservatives to keep them from rusting during an extended period of storage or in less than ideal climatic conditions.

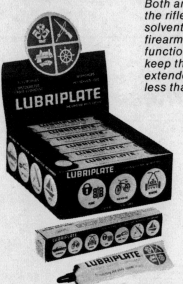

Two recent products to remove rust without damage to bluing are Rust Free and Hoppe's MDL. They are favored over the old oil and steel wool treatment.

SOLVENTS AND LUBRICANTS

There is no shortage of manufacturers of lubricants and solvents in the gunsmithing trade. Some are better than others. Most work well for their intended purpose. Unfortunately, many folks don't understand that there is a difference between a solvent, decreaser, lubricant, or preservative. A good solvent should aid in removing corrosion, unburned powder, and lead from chamber and bore. Three outstanding products I have used for years in this area are Hoppe's, Corbin, and Wipe-Away.

One of the best degreasers on the market is called RIG #3. Degreasers are used to clean firearms preparatory to cold bluing and removing oils and grease.

To lubricate bearing surfaces Break Free, Lubriplate, and RIG do an excellent job. I prefer using Moly-Dri to lubricate the surfaces between barrel and receivers on shotguns which have a tendency to gall.

When storing a firearm over extended periods of time I like RIG, G-96's Gun Treatment, and Break Free.

New on the market to remove rust without damaging

bluing are Rust Free and Rust Guardit. Both seem to work with the limited amount of testing I've managed to complete thus far.

There you have it, a rather ponderous shopping list guaranteed to sap all but the most affluent of men. And, I've probably forgotten one or twenty or so can't-do-without items. The best way to assemble the many necessary tools is to buy on an as-needed basis. Start by buying the most basic items. As you progress through the many phases of riflesmithing and gain experience, the priority of tools will become more clear. But please start your shopping list with a pair of safety glasses. And only buy quality tools. Good luck!

Chapter 2

LOCKING SYSTEMS

There Are Good And Bad Systems ——Custom Riflesmiths Have Their Favorites

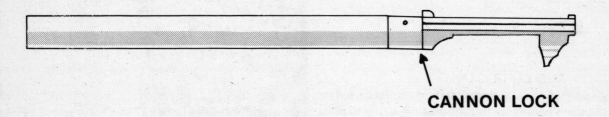

CANNON LOCK

SINCE THE invention of gun powder in the mid-Thirteenth Century and the subsequent development of firearms to the present time, man has tried continually to improve upon the firearm's breech-locking system. A rifle is no stronger than the relationship between the bolt face, cartridge and chamber. Before the invention of repeating arms several locking systems were attempted in single-shot rifles with varying degrees of success. Several volumes could be written — and have been — on one type of locking system or another, but it is important to note that there are differences.

The first locking system devised was the *cannon lock.* The smallarms version was commonly cylindrical in form and about nine inches in length. There was not an actual lock. The gunpowder was ignited through a touchhole on top of the barrel. Oftentimes the muzzle had an outer ring to strengthen it. This type of firearm was a single unit from muzzle to breech. Simple in design, this system is one of the strongest ever designed.

The *screwed breech* was the next locking system of note, being developed in the mid-1600s. This system, used on flintlocks and the later percussion rifles, had the barrel threaded at the chamber end allowing a breech

Breech plug   **Barrel**

SCREWED BREECH

plug to be screwed securely into position. This system also is quite strong and reliable.

One of the earliest known breech-loading rifles was the *Ferguson breech,* named after a Scottish soldier in the employ of the British during the 1770s. It contained a breech plug with a quick thread which was turned one-half revolution to open the breech for loading. The plug in the breech section was smooth to prevent fouling which could jam the action. He also added metal to the bottom of the breech to accept the screw thread. This was so the plug could be lowered below chamber level to facilitate cleaning of the bore. This rifle was brought to the colonies and used against Revolutionary troops.

This locking system was the first breech-loading system to be used in military action.

There were other breech-loading systems of merit such as the Hall breech-loading carbine, but the next important locking system was the *falling-* or *sliding-block locking system* using paper cartridges in early percussion Sharps rifles. When metallic cartridges evolved, the case was extracted and ejected, further advancing the design. This action proved extremely rugged because of the solid breech-block that traveled up and down in the rear of the chamber. When the block is in a locked position, the chambered cartridge is locked in place by a solid block of steel.

The *rolling-block* locking system started with Remington and its rolling-block rifles. This system is actually an improvement on an earlier Geiger split-breech rolling-block design developed by Remington in 1867 and is ingenious in its simplicity of design. The two main parts of the action are the hammer and breech block. They are held in place in the receiver by two large pins with extremely close fits to eliminate any give during recoil.

To operate, the hammer is pulled back to the full-cock position with the thumb. The thumb then is moved to the thumb-piece on the breech block and pulled back and down or rolled back. With the chamber exposed the cartridge is loaded. The block is closed and the rifle may be fired. Although possibly not as strong as the Peabody-Martini *hinge-block* system, the rolling block proved strong and reliable.

The hinge-block system was erected in more than one design, ranging from rather poor to exceedingly strong. One type, the *trap door,* gained attention with the Trap Door Springfield rifles. This single-shot was opened by pivoting the breech block up and forward. This rifle was actually a conversion of the 1865 Springfield muzzleloading rifle. The conversion was accomplished by milling out a portion of the top rear of the breech end of the barrel and replacing it with a swinging breech block. The block was attached to a hinge butt that had been fastened to the barrel either by brazing or with screws. The breech block contained the firing pin with an extractor that pivoted on the hinge pin. The original lock was used with the hammer nose changed to strike the firing pin rather than the nip-

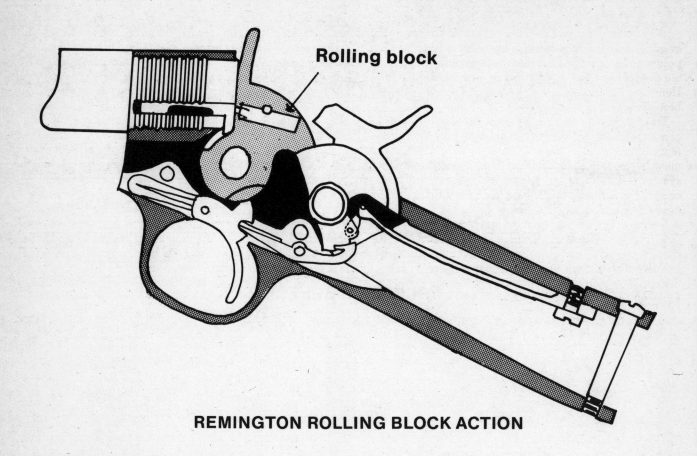

Rolling block

REMINGTON ROLLING BLOCK ACTION

ple. This system was not considered to be a strong action.

Another variation of the hinge-block locking system was the *Snider Converter*. Jacob Snider, an American inventor, was hired by the British government in 1866 to convert their muzzleloading Enfields to breech loading. Snider used a system pretty much copied after Henry VIII's breech-loading Harquebus firearm invented in 1537. To load the Snider Converter Enfield the breech piece was hinged up from the left, exposing the chamber. It was largely successful due to the recent invention of the brass case which would expand on firing providing a breech seal against escaping gas. The system proved adequate for that period, but is not as strong as the *Peabody-Martini* system.

The Peabody-Martini locking system and further variants led to the *Martini-Henry* system, by far the strongest hinge-block system in this class. The system first evolved in 1862 when Boston inventor Henry Peabody submitted his rifle to the army for testing. The breech block hinged at the rear and above the axis of the bore. Unlocking was accomplished by moving the trigger guard down and forward, which dropped the front of the block below the chamber line to permit loading. The rifle had an external hammer and automatic extractor. Although an excellent new design, the Civil War had ended and the government no longer was interested.

The Peabody action was improved upon by a Swiss master mechanic, Frederich von Martini. He first modified Peabody's design by changing the leverage arrangement to cock the hammer as the action opened. However, his second modification entailed removing the exposed hammer, replacing it with an internal lock within the breech block. This greatly streamlined the entire design.

Although Peabody originally invented his unique breech block system, the names Peabody-Martini and Martini-Henry are heard much more often. The Martini-Henry came into being after Martini submitted his modified Peabody action to England for tests. Alexander Henry began fitting rifled barrels to the new Martini action. The polygonal bore with lands and grooves greatly added to the accuracy of the rifle. However, both the Martini and Henry modifications were performed on Peabody's breech block design.

The last locking system design in the single-shot rifles of note is the *break-open* or *top-break* action. This action is used today, but almost exclusively in shotguns. The most successful commercial venture using this locking system belonged to J. Stevens & Company of Massachusetts. He called his rifle the Tip-Up, which first began appearing in volume after 1870.

The barrel is hinged from the front part of the frame. Stevens' design included a siding extractor under the breech end of the barrel and connected to the frame by a link. When the action was opened with the breech end of the barrel tipping up, the extractor was activated. A locking device running through the frame locked the barrel in a closed position. The firing pin was fitted in the standing breech. Although not considered to be a strong action the Stevens Tip-Up rifles were a great financial success.

The break-open action ranges from miserable to excellent. Due to the incredible pressures brought to bear on the locking system with smokeless powder, the strength of the bolt and the methods employed to lock the action are critical. Crossbolt locks such as those used in Greener actions have proved quite reliable, but this system overall is not as strong as some of the others already listed.

There are many single-shot rifles not included here, but those listed are unique in that they were original. Certain innovative improvements and new designs made many extremely strong, such as the historic Farquharson and today's Ruger Number One.

LOCKING SYSTEMS FOR REPEATING ARMS

The first successful repeating rifle was the 1860 Spen-

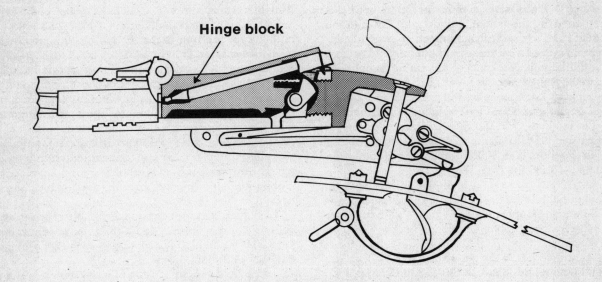

Hinge block

HINGE BLOCK LOCKING SYSTEM
MODEL 1873 "TRAPDOOR" SPRINGFIELD

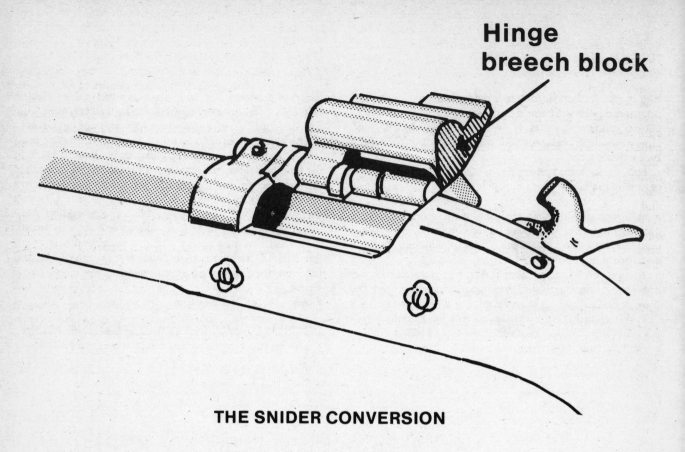

Hinge breech block

THE SNIDER CONVERSION

cer lever action. It employed what is known today as a *rotary-block* locking system. A semi-circular breech block was activated by the trigger guard lever, causing the block to fall and rotate. With the breech opened, a magazine spring moved a cartridge out where it could be held against the breech block face by a spring finger until chambered by the thrust of the lever. The hammer required thumb cocking. Later models used a magazine cut-off to keep additional cartridges locked in the magazine tube located in the buttstock. The Spencer was a seven-shot repeater using a .56/52 rimfire cartridge. A little over 12,-000 rifles and more than 94,000 carbines were sold to the government during the Civil War.

Another highly successful lever-action rifle with its beginnings in the 1860s used a *toggle-block* locking system. This was the Henry rifle. The same system also was used in the Winchester Model 1866, and improved upon in the Winchester Models 1873 and 1876 by strengthening the action to handle the .44-40 center-fire cartridge. German Luger pistols also use this locking system.

Henry rifles had the magazine situated below the barrel. This model was loaded by pulling the coil magazine spring up into the muzzle end of the tube. The muzzle section then was pivoted to permit cartridges to be inserted head first down the tube. When pivoted back in place a coil spring compressed and pushed the cartridges back toward the breech.

The Henry's breech block is a true toggle lock. By pull-

ing the trigger guard lever downward, the toggle is disjointed and thus unlocked. Continued motion of the toggle arm draws the breech bolt back in a direct line to the axis of the bore. The rear of the breech block rides down to cock the hammer. The carrier block holding the next cartridge from the magazine tube is now drawn into alignment with the breech block. By drawing the lever back the cartridge now is driven into the chamber and the carrier descends to receive the next cartridge from the magazine tube. During the last bit of lever motion in coming to the closed position, the toggle joint is straightened to lock and support the breech bolt against the cartridge case rim. The trigger is now in position to be pulled, actuating the sear and allowing the hammer to fall on the firing pin housed in the breech bolt.

Although this system enjoyed incredible success, especially in the Winchester Model 1873, it is not considered to be a strong locking system and is not suitable for modern heavy-caliber cartridges.

The *vertical-sliding* locking block system is one of the finest, simplest and strongest locking systems ever devised for lever-action rifles. It should come as no surprise to gun buffs that it was the brainchild of John Browning. This system is still used in Winchester Model 94 and Marlin Model 36 rifles.

Since Browning used hand tools and a minimum of machinery, most parts were not kept to close tolerances, except where necessary. The results were a smoother and better operating action less susceptible to jamming due to foreign matter such as dust and dirt. The lock featured twin locking bolts riding up in mortises in the receiver walls and cuts in the sides or rear of the breech block. They are visible on the top of the gun when the action is closed. The bolts are raised and lowered by rearward or forward movement of the lever.

In later versions, like the Winchester Model 94, the lock rises behind the breech block head to accommodate long cartridge models. As the lever is opened the firing pin is pulled back into the bolt and locked until the bolt is again closed and ready to be fired. A hook on the finger lever pulls the cartridges out of the magazine into the carrier block. This allows for a lighter magazine spring which makes loading cartridges into the magazine tube easier. As the lever is closed the cartridge is pulled off the carrier and into the chamber by the forward movement of the breech bolt. This locking system permitted chambering the rifle for the .50/110, the largest and highest-powered cartridge then available. It is no surprise that Winchester and Marlin continue to use this system in their currently manufactured lever-action rifles.

The *tipping-bolt* locking system, also called the hump lock system, probably would mean little to gun enthusi-asts until two legendary firearms are mentioned that use this extremely strong locking system. The first is the shotgun known as the "perfect repeater," Winchester's Model 12. The other is a rifle of equal fame heralded by many as the strongest lever-action rifle ever built: the Savage Model 1899. This rifle is still in manufacture eighty-three years later, a tribute to the design genius of Arthur Savage.

Savage designed his tipping-bolt system with two excellent features, the magazine and the breech lock. The magazine is a revolving box-type housed below the bolt. This type of magazine had been in use in Europe for quite some time, but it was the first time for an American lever-action rifle. The cartridges are separated at all times, so there is little possibility or cartridge deformation. However, it was the hammerless, enclosed-breech firing mechanism and exceptionally strong lock that set it apart from other locking systems of that period. It is the only other system that rivals the turning-bolt locking system in strength. The breech block is machined from a solid steel block to close tolerances with the receiver walls.

The system operates by lowering the lever which lowers the breech block out of the locking mortises in each receiver wall. After clearing the locking seat it then is

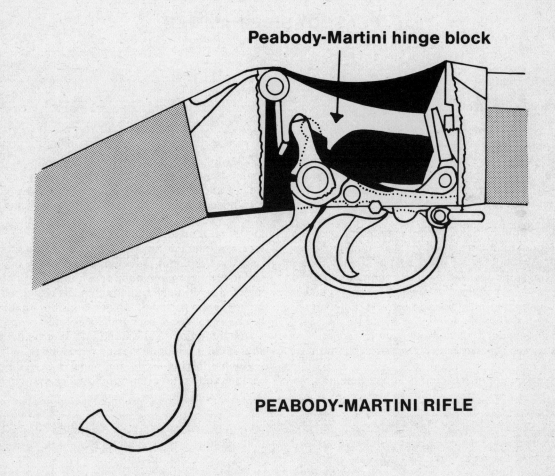

Peabody-Martini hinge block

PEABODY-MARTINI RIFLE

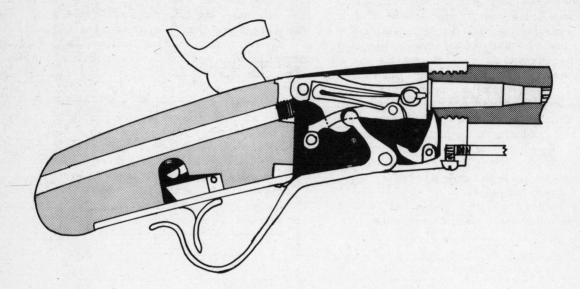

PEABODY SIDE-HAMMER

drawn rearward, extracting and ejecting the fired cartridge. As the lever is returned to the closed position the breech block pushes a cartridge ahead to the chamber and is elevated into the locked position in the receiver recess with its face against the cartridge case head and its rear securely positioned against the solid steel receiver.

In 1902 certain National Guard units purchased the Savage Model 1899 chambered in the .30-30 Winchester cartridge. Although never used by the United States Army or Navy, it does hold the distinction of being the only rifle used by a military service in this country in that caliber. The tipping-bolt locking system is quite strong, having been tested successfully using .50 caliber machine-gun cartridges under sustained automatic fire conditions. Few locking systems can match it for strength and reliability.

A little-encountered reasonably strong action is the *locking-flaps* locking system. It is found predominantly in Colt-Sauer rifles. Colt introduced this line of rifles in 1972 with the J.P. Sauer & Sohn Company of West Germany. The design is rather unusual having a nonrotating bolt locked at the rear of the receiver by three retractable locking lugs actuated by the rotating cam on the bolt handle. It is said to be smooth and fast-operating although I've never tried it. An unusual feature is the action's split receiver. After the barrel is threaded into the split receiver ring, two transverse machine screws torque into position and lock the receiver around the barrel. The theory is that this method of attachment results in the barrel and receiver acting as one solid unit of steel. Considering that the rifle has been produced successfully in calibers ranging from .25/06 through .375 H&H and .458 Winchester magnum says quite a bit for its locking capabilities.

Another highly successful method of locking in both shotguns and rifles is the *tipping-block* system as used in the Browning Auto 5 and the Browning automatic rifle, better known as the BAR. The latter was introduced in 1918 and gained worldwide fame because of its strength, reliability, and automatic-fire capabilities.

The hammer pin is slightly in advance of the connecting link pin. Initial rearward movement of the slide moves the hammer rearward without movement to either the attached bolt lock or bolt for the first twenty-thousandths-inch of travel. This allows high breech pressures to subside to safe limits. As unlocking begins, the link revolves around the hammer pin moving the bolt lock downward out of the receiver hump and starts it rearward. This travel of bolt and bolt lock is accelerated as the lock disengages from the hump, clears the locking recess, and locks the shoulders in the receiver. Bolt lock placement

prevents it from revolving up from below the line of rearward travel of the bolt, ensuring that all other moving parts must continue backward movement in a straight line.

During this unlocking sequence a cam surface located on a slot in the bottom side of the bolt lock engages another cam surface on the firing pin lug, drawing it away from the bolt base. Meanwhile, the circular cam surface on the lower part of the bolt lock engaging the rear shoulders of the bolt support creates a lever action to loosen the cartridge case. The slide and its moving parts continue traveling rearward, carrying the empty case held in its seat in the bolt face by the extractor positioned on the right side of the bolt.

Just before the slide reaches its most rearward position

ROTARY BLOCK LOCKING SYSTEM

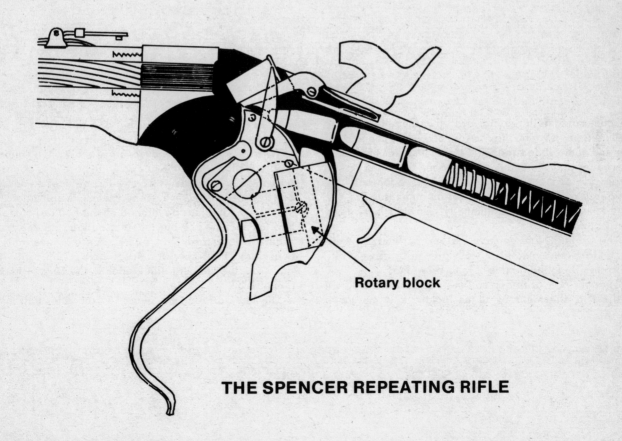

Rotary block

THE SPENCER REPEATING RIFLE

WINCHESTER MODEL 1873
TOGGLE BLOCK LOCKING SYSTEM

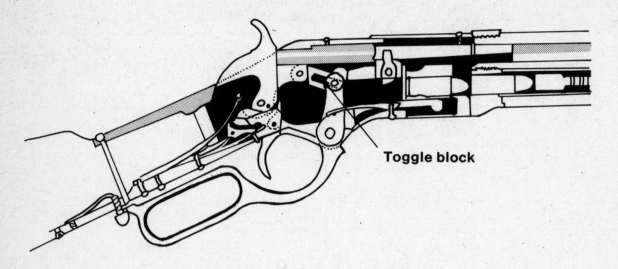

Toggle block

the case contacts the ejector located on the left side of the bolt feed rib, pivoting the case out of the ejection port. At the end of the slide's rearward travel it strikes the end of the buffer and the sear nose engages the notch on the underside of the slide, holding it in position until the trigger is pulled. If the rifle is set on automatic fire, the sear nose is depressed continually, allowing the slide its forward motion.

The tipping block locking system, particularly well-suited to semiautomatic and fully automatic rifles, is one more tribute to the genius of John Browning.

The *turn-bolt* or *rotary-bolt* system is of the greatest interest to riflesmiths of all the locking systems, since most of the work in customizing and modifying rifles to sporters is performed on the turn-bolt action.

With this system breech closure is achieved by moving a breech block or bolt in line with the bore. It is operated by using a bolt handle with camming surfaces on both the bolt handle root and in the receiver to lock and unlock the action. Locking lugs positioned on the bolt are cammed into lug recesses in the receiver making an extremely secure locking arrangement. Peter Paul Mauser may be considered the father of modern bolt-action center-fire rifles, but the concept dates back to the Dreyse needle gun of 1838.

The last variation of concern to the riflesmith is the

interrupted-thread locking system, which is employed on semiautomatic rifles such as the Remington gas-operated Model 742 and their slide-action Model 760.

With the Model 742 system, operation of the action is automatic. It utilizes the energy available from high pressure gases from the cartridge to unload and reload the rifle. The loaded cartridge is seated firmly in the chamber and supported at its head by the face of the breech bolt which is locked securely in the barrel extension, while the extractor is engaged in the extractor groove of the cartridge case. The hammer is in the cocked position, held by engagement of its notch into the sear notch. The disconnector has pivoted into engagement with the action bar holding the action from opening, at same time permitting the connector to fall into its lower position so the front surface of the connector, right, may engage in rear notch on sear.

When fired by pulling the trigger, the connector is actuated by the trigger, causing the sear to pivot on the sear pin. As the sear pivots, the sear notch disengages the hammer notch. The hammer is urged forward by the hammer spring plunger due to energy in the hammer spring until it strikes the firing pin. Just prior to striking the firing pin, the hammer spring plunger contacts a striking surface on the action bar lock; this causes it to rotate and lift the connector away from the sear, thus disengaging trigger. This rotating of the action bar lock also disengages it from the action bars. The firing pin strikes the primer and firing sequence is completed.

Gases act to rotate the bolt for unlocking. Cam pins in bolt carrier engage cam track in the bolt and translate rearward linear motion of action bar assembly into rotary motion in bolt. The bolt rotates approximately forty-five degrees, at which point lug of bolt lines up with openings in barrel extension and further rotary motion stops allowing bolt to be moved rearward. By this time primary extraction has been accomplished. There is more to the cycle of operation, but it is this rotation of the bolt that allows the interrupted threads to lock and unlock in the barrel extension.

This locking system is quite adequate for standard high-pressure smokeless cartridges, but is not designed for heavy magnum calibers as a general rule.

There are many other locking system adaptations, but those listed are the major locking systems riflesmiths are likely to encounter.

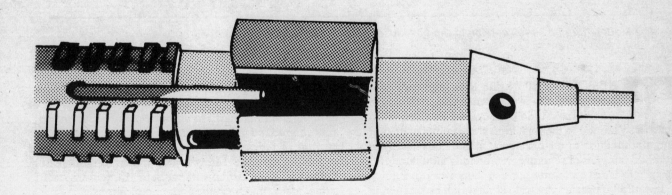

INTERRUPTED THREAD LOCKING SYSTEM

Bolt-Action Rifle Designs Are Favored The Most By Custom Riflesmiths

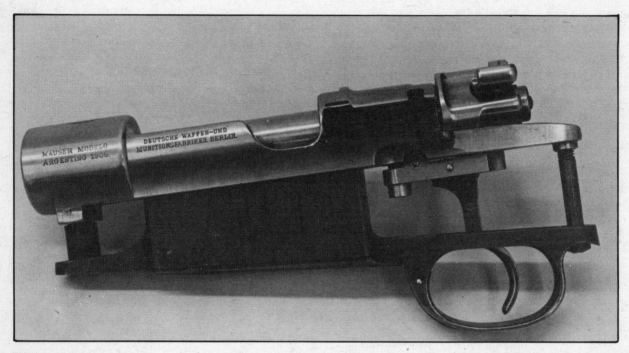

The Model Argentino 1909 version of the 98 Mauser action still is a favorite today with riflesmiths.

THE BOLT-ACTION rifle is far and away the most popular type of sporting rifle in the world today. The models discussed here must be limited to the best from standpoints of design and modification to custom status. Space does not allow detailed analysis of several commercially manufactured models that are quite adequate in their own rights.

It would be presumptuous to state which bolt action is the strongest, or best overall, since I've been in this business only nine years professionally. However, I have enlisted the assistance of many top riflesmiths for their opinions. I have also studied Stuart Otteson's outstanding, *The Bolt Action,* and recommend this meticulous, detailed tome.

It would be almost sacrilegious to begin this section without initial mention of the Mauser action, the father of them all. The Model 98 is easily the best of the military actions for conversion to sporter. However, certain vari-

eties such as the Argentino model 1909, the Peruvian, Polish, and the lightened Model 33/40 were made better than the German wartime efforts. Some European Mausers sporterized in Europe having deep dovetails cut into the top of the receiver ring weakened the action and should be avoided. Many highly engraved models from Europe were annealed without being re-heat-treated. In some cases, this has made them dangerous.

The 98 Mauser design is excellent, featuring a strong breech system. Escaping gas is eliminated safely through gas ports and the receiver raceways. The large claw extractor is perhaps the strongest type in existence. Hunters of dangerous game prefer this extraction system to all others. The large bolt locking lugs coupled with an additional safety lug make it one of the safest systems in the world. It has a strong positive ejection system. The rather sleek and streamlined receiver design lends itself with little modification to custom conversion.

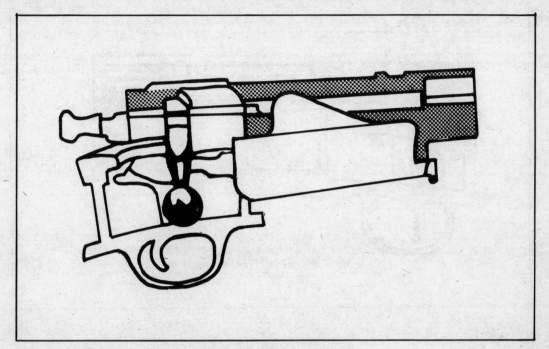

*Artist's rendition of the 1898 Krag-Jorgensen rifle illustrates
some of the reasons why it lends itself to customizing.*

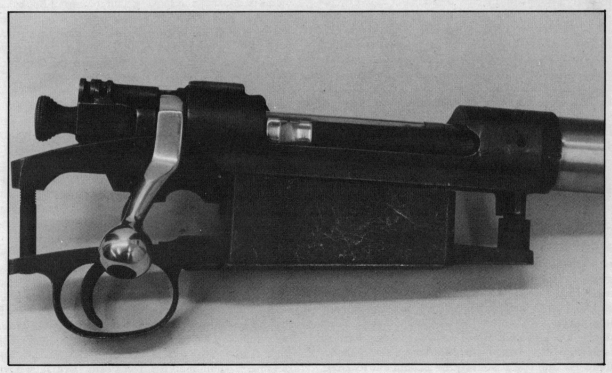

The venerable 1903 Springfield action appears crude at first glance, but it can be dressed up beautifully with work.

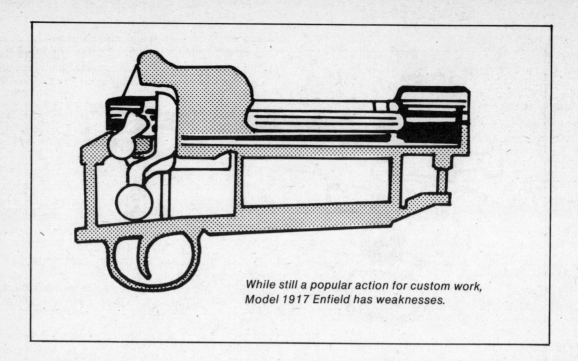

*While still a popular action for custom work,
Model 1917 Enfield has weaknesses.*

No action is perfect and the Mauser does have some drawbacks. Although the military safety is quite effective, it is not compatible with the addition of a low-mounted scope. A notched siderail and slender tang reduce receiver strength and rigidity. Straight bolt handle types must be altered if a scope is to be installed. Only thirty percent of the case head is encircled by the bolt-head rim when the cartridge is seated in the chamber. The military-type trigger does not lend itself well to adjustment modification and should be replaced with a Timney or Canjar. Lock time is considerably slower than with the more recently designed Remington 700, Winchester Model 70, Weatherby MK V, Savage 110 and Sako Vixen. Cartridges must be loaded through the magazine only.

The more desirable Model 98 Mauser actions continue to escalate in price as surplus inventories dry up. As mentioned, the Model 98 is still one of the top choices for custom conversion and definitely first choice among all military actions.

The U.S. Model 1898 Krag-Jorgensen — better known simply as the Krag — can be converted to sporter status, but does not have the strength, lines or some desirable features of the Mauser or Springfield. With its 43,000-pound-per-square-inch (psi) safety limit, it should not be converted to modern high pressure cartridges. However, it will safely handle the excellent 7x57 deer-size cartridge. Its single locking lug system and overall frail action make it a poor choice for the shooter who can afford only one custom rifle. The box-type side-loading magazine gives the rifle an awkward appearance, but is quite functional. The action is quite smooth due to excellent workmanship of the time, but probably is better left in original condition as a collector piece.

The U.S. M1903 Springfield lends itself to custom con-

version, although it is less desirable than the 98 Mauser. The Springfield is basically a Mauser-type rifle incorporating many design features and styling from its predecessor, the Krag. It is the best U.S.-made military action for sporterizing, however. Due to improper heat-treating, Springfields from the Springfield Armory under serial number 800,000 and those manufactured at Rock Island under 385,507 are considered unsafe. Also, just prior to World War II Remington and Smith Corona manufactured 1903A3 and A4 models that are quite strong, but they do not have the workmanship. They are quite rough, and should be avoided for sporter purposes.

The 1903 Springfields do have exceptionally smooth actions due to excellent workmanship and require little work by the riflesmith. The Mauser-type extractor works well, although the safety must be replaced if a low-mount scope is to be installed. Ejection is quite strong and the locking system is adequate, but the overall action lacks the strength of the Mauser. The direct-pull trigger should be replaced. Floorplates usually require bending when restocking for sporter use, the firing pin is rather weak and the lock time abominably slow compared to the Mauser or modern commercial rifles.

Made in the United States, the Model 1917 Enfield was a modified version of the Pattern 1913, a British modification of the Mauser. It ended up being sort of a bastard child that, like Rodney Dangerfield, never got no respect.

In spite of the fact that the final version of the 1917 Enfield was derived by borrowing a bit from the Mauser 98, a little from the 1903 Springfield, a dash from the Lee-Enfield, and a few scoops from the 93 and 95 Mausers, it didn't turn out all that bad. To be sure, the task of removing the cumbersome and ugly ears and the need to fill in the hole left in the bridge are time-consuming, but the gun does have several good points. Its more-than-adequate

The pre-World War II Winchester Model 70 action may well be the all-time favorite for building a custom rifle.

locking lugs and Mauser-type extractor make a strong action with an excellent two-position safety that is compatible without alteration to low-mounted scopes. It has a positive ejector, although the ejector springs tend to be quite weak. Its interior dimensions allow conversion to magnum cartridges better than any other military standard-size action.

Still, its poor gas-venting system does not match that of the Mauser. Firing pins are particularly susceptible to breakage due to gas pressure from blown primers. There are those who argue for its cock-on-closing principle, but the majority of riflesmiths prefer the Mauser cock-on-opening system. The direct-pull trigger should be replaced and it has an extremely deep magazine which should be modified for streamlined custom sporter rifles.

A majority of custom riflesmiths prefer to customize the pre-'64 Winchester Model 70 over any other commercially manufactured action. It has several design features desired in a custom rifle. Its low-profile, streamlined appearance is enhanced when fitted to a custom stock and it has gained immense popularity over the years with both collectors and shooters.

The Winchester Model 70 evolved from the Model 54. It retained the best features of the 54 and did more than a creditable job of correcting its weak points. The Model 70 was first offered to the public in 1936 and the rifle is still going strong. A segment of the gun purists insist pre-'64 models are superior to those currently manufactured, but I prefer not to enter that feud.

The Pre-'64 Model 70 action has a Springfield-type breech. Although this type of breech is said to be not as strong as others, the rifle has proven its strength in the field with extreme reliability for nearly fifty years in a wide range of heavy-caliber chamberings. The receiver is quite strong and rigid with the receiver ring, walls and bridge contoured to a low, graceful line. Its large recoil lug surface permits extremely stable bedding in the stock, while the large locking lugs and safety lug make for an outstanding locking arrangement.

The Model 70's large non-rotary (claw-type) extractor rivals that of the Mauser 98 for strength and reliability and the safety is probably the surest and most convenient ever designed for a sporting rifle. The adjustable override trigger can be adjusted easily by an amateur down to 2½ pounds and is one of the best commercial triggers in

use today. The rifle has a fine ejection system and overall has an exceptionally smooth action. The rifle's lock time is much faster than any of the military actions listed and rated higher than most other commercially manufactured sporting rifles.

Early Model 70s had a cloverleaf-shaped rear tang that had a tendency to chip the stock at the tang recess. It was restyled after 1947 so that the outer edge had an overhang to eliminate this problem.

The Model 70 also has a two-piece trigger guard and floorplate assembly that is of questionable design value. The rifle's gas-handling escape system has been considered suspect, but after questioning several riflesmiths no problems have been reported. The only real vocal complaint heard pertaining to the pre-'64 Model 70 to this writer is that there aren't enough of them around for sale and the ones that are have huge price tags.

Springfield followers and bolt latches are interchangeable with the Model 70. Enfield extractors also fit Model 70 bolts.

With the close of World War II the Remington Model 700 Series was introduced, an entirely new action designed under the leadership of Mike Walker. The goal was to build a rifle that would combine performance, strength and accuracy at a reasonable cost to compete with Winchester's Model 70. Thus, the Model 721 was born. It was an excellent rifle exceeding all expectations but one: appearance. It was dressed up and modifications included the 721B, 722B, 721BDL, and finally the 725 in 1958. In 1962 a modified version of the 721 with a tang more streamlined for aesthetics and an altered and checkered bolt handle emerged as the Model 700. Acceptance by the shooting public was immediate and it has sold extremely well ever since.

The Remington 700 has an extremely strong breech system. It if isn't the strongest, it certainly runs a close second. Stuart Otteson explains it best in *The Bolt Action,* saying, "Remington's Model 700 breech recesses the cartridge base into a deeply counter-bored bolt head, which in turn fits a counter-bore in the barrel. These are surrounded by the receiver ring and, as so often noted in Remington advertisements, the cartridge head is encircled by three steel rings. More important than the resulting structure itself, the close bolt-nose fit can confine case-head failure and limit gas escape back into enlarged, and thus more susceptible, portions of the receiver.

The Remington Model 700 rifle action boasts clean lines.

Author describes the Weatherby Mark V as neither fish nor fowl for customizing, as it has many custom features.

"The basic counter-bored breech was not an entirely new idea with this Remington action — the Japanese used it in the military Type 38 — nor is it exclusive with Remington today. It is used currently by several others, including Weatherby and BSA in England. Remington did, however, bring it into widespread commercial use and developed it to its purest form. Because of the solid Remington bolt-face rim, and the deep (about .15-inch), close-fitting nature of its bolt-nose encirclement, there probably isn't a more effective turnbolt shrouding system."

The Remington Model 700 is increasing in popularity with custom riflesmiths. Its cylindrical receiver design is exceptionally strong, has rigidity, can be bedded securely in a custom stock and boasts clean lines and a low profile. It has a positive safety that remains inconspicuous but convenient for the shooter. The Remington 700 has an excellent fully adjustable trigger. It has a much better than average lock time. The extractor, although quite small compared to the Mauser-type, has proved itself reliable in the ultimate testing arena, the field.

Although a reliable rifle by any standards, the position of the extractor can cause empty cases in certain calibers to bind in the right raceway as the bolt is pulled rearward. Altering the bolt handle or changing the knob must be accomplished without heating the soldered joint between bolt root and bolt body or it will fall off. The recoil lug is also a spacer between receiver ring and barrel detracting from the traditional "classic" look. The recoil lug system can be altered as described elsewhere in this book.

The Remington 700's design and streamlined appearance has not gone unnoticed in custom riflesmithing circles. A new machined trigger guard and floorplate assembly is now being offered by Pete Grisel of Bend, Oregon. A Winchester Model 70-type safety is available from Ken Jantz of Sulphur, Oklahoma. Such custom options do much to bring the Model 700 up to custom standards.

The Weatherby Mark V is one of the finest hunting rifles ever made and is a favorite of big-game hunters worldwide. Compared to other military and commercial actions that lend themselves well to modification and customizing, the Weatherby is neither fish nor fowl. The Weatherby is a production factory rifle, but is more expensive than many other commercial models due to the fact that it has many custom touches and better-than-average wood straight out of the box.

The Weatherby breech system is exceptionally strong, rivaling that of the Remington Model 700. The receiver is a nickel-chrome-moly forging that starts life as a cylinder and is machined completely to tolerances. It features a counter-bored breech similar to that of the Remington Model 700, the bolt head being shrouded by the barrel. The Weatherby has a bit more bolt-face depth — approximately three-thousandths — but the 700 has an internal extractor. The bolt is best described as massive with an integral handle adding to its strength. Its smaller locking lug surfaces allow for shallower recesses in the receiver to increase rigidity. This receiver structure also aids in producing an effective gas-handling system. The safety is direct-acting and quite convenient for the shooter. The rifle has good lock time that is a bit faster than the pre-'64 Winchester Model 70 and slower than the Remington 700.

Although the Weatherby Mark V has distinguished itself repeatedly in the field, chambered in the heavy magnum caliber range, I've never been sold on the nine-locking-lug theory that more is better. If the bearing surface — the most important factor in locking — of two large locking lugs equals or surpasses the total amount of nine combined lug surfaces, what has actually been gained?

Attempting to gain maximum bearing surface of nine lugs compared to two comes out to be about 4½ times more difficult. The only true way to get them all to seat is by firing the rifle until the bolt lugs set back. Hopefully all will contact the lug recesses in time.

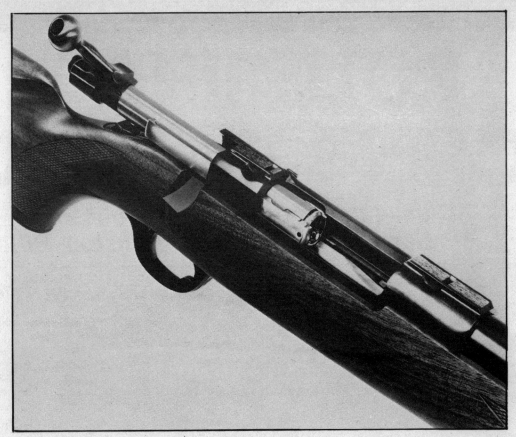

Author considers stocking on Ruger's Model 77 as a tribute to the late
Lenard Brownell, who designed the stock, trained factory stockmakers.

The bolt is designed with Mauser-type camming, but actually rotates less, reducing camming strength. The final closure of the bolt is a bit hesitant due to having to get the cartridge pushed past the extractor recessed in the bolt head and into the bolt-face counter-bore.

The Weatherby Mark V has earned an excellent reputation as a big-game hunting rifle. The action is strong enough to handle magnum calibers and is quite reliable. Because it does carry a bit higher price than many other commercial rifles, Weatherby rifle owners generally prefer to keep them in their original condition.

The Ruger Model 77 has been a growing favorite among custom stockmakers. Bill Ruger has a reputation for engineering genius and the long line of excellent handguns, shotguns and rifles he has produced constitutes a credit to the man and the shooting industry as well.

Ruger designed the Model 77 as a turning-bolt action incorporating a recessed bolt head, but it is partially enclosed to retain the Mauser type extractor, thus allowing the recessed feature for more than half the bolt head's perimeter. It might appear that the extractor doesn't have much room to engage the cartridge, but this system has been in use for several years on rifles such as the Remington Model 740 and has proved satisfactory.

The Ruger 77 innovative recoil lug setup has a front guard screw at a rear and downward forty-five-degree angle. This three-screw bedding arrangement pulls the recoil lug firmly into contact with the mating surface in the stock mortise. It works quite efficiently. The Model 77 may also be ordered with integral scope ring bases located on the bridge and receiver ring. This custom feature generally is found only on the better European sporting rifles.

The Mauser-type extractor and spring-loaded plunger-type ejector are strong and positive. The safety is located in the tang, which makes it extremely convenient to reach for a hurried shot in the field. The rifle also has an excellent adjustable trigger, hinged floorplate and guard bow floor plate release.

The Model 77 is a smooth-functioning rifle with a clean, low-profile design that custom riflesmiths look for in an action. Although a custom-made stock in exhibition grade wood will enhance any rifle, the Model 77 is probably the best stocked — including inletting, checkering and finish — of any factory rifle. That is a tribute to the late master stockmaker, Lenard Brownell. Ruger hired him to design the stock for this rifle and to teach others at the Ruger plant.

Chapter 3

POLISHING & HONING THE ACTION

Glass-like Smoothness Should Be A Standard Feature On Every Custom Rifle

A custom rifle should not only look better than a factory rifle but it should also function better. This beautiful pre-1964 Model 70 Winchester was executed by Dale Goens, with custom metalwork by Tom Burgess and engraving performed by John Warren. The cartridge for which it's chambered is 7x57mm.

MANY CUSTOM rifles are built upon military actions. Springfields, Enfields and many of the surplus Mausers require polishing and smoothing of the actions to improve bolt travel and improve overall functioning and feel. However, many military actions are a bit sloppy and the emphasis should be on eliminating rough spots, burrs, and machine marks rather than polishing each internal part to a mirror finish. It is more a matter of smoothing the metal than eliminating it. Fortunately, in the case of many Mausers such as the FN, Argentino 1909, the Polish Radom and Peruvian model the actions were pretty smooth straight from the factory.

The first part to polish is the bolt. Since a new barrel will be fitted to the action, the bolt must be worked to give eighty percent contact between the locking lugs and the lug recesses in the receiver. As the lugs are lapped they also will be polished by the lapping compound. This operation should be accomplished using a fine-grit silicone carbide lapping compound. Be certain to clean all parts thoroughly with kerosene or solvent after polishing

as the silicone carbide breaks down into smaller particles and can continue to cut metal if not removed. Do not use valve grinding compound, as it is too course.

The extractor collar groove on the bolt should be checked for rough edges and polished, using a Dremel Moto-Tool and jeweler's rouge on a small buff. If the bolt is rough or scratched, it may be hit with a 500-grit polishing wheel to remove light scratches, then buffed to a mirror finish on a 600-grit wheel. Remember, buffing only displaces metal while polishing removes it. The bolt may be jeweled later, giving it a custom appearance.

The final step in polishing the bolt — in this case a 98 Mauser — is to stone all contact points carefully. Remember that every bearing surface must be checked for roughness and polished to eliminate drag. A hard Arkansas stone or the super-hard ruby stones do an excellent job of polishing hardened steel surfaces.

Begin by honing the top and bottom surfaces of the locking lugs to eliminate drag as they pass back and forth over the receiver ways. Next check the guide rib, safety lug and the extraction cam located on the forward edge of

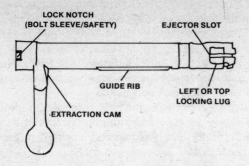

Top view of a Mauser Model 98 bolt, with callouts for the important features for consideration.

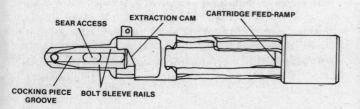

Top view of the Mauser Model 98 receiver.

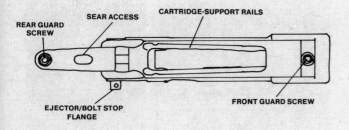

Bottom view of the Mauser Model 98 receiver.

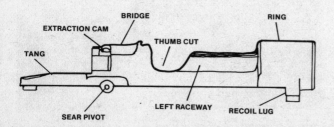

Right-hand side view of Mauser Model 98 receiver.

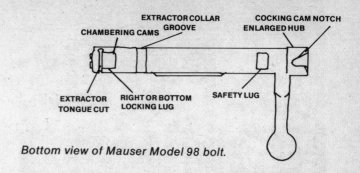

Bottom view of Mauser Model 98 bolt.

Dremel Moto-Tool with abrasive-impregnated rubber bit is quite useful for polishing receivers, particularly in areas such as the feed ramp.

the bolt handle and hone them accordingly. The cocking-cam notch and even the lock notch for the bolt sleeve and safety locks should be inspected for burrs. Again, we are attempting to only eliminate drag; if too much metal is removed we will be left with a sloppy fit which can result in the bolt grabbing in the receiver during its cycle of operation.

The extractor, especially the front portion where it engages at the extractor tongue cut in the bolt, should be inspected carefully. Any wear marks should be stoned to reduce friction as the bolt is opened or closed. The sides of the extractor also should be jeweled if the same work has been performed on the bolt. This step will hide any minor pitting, reduce reflected light in the field and help eliminate rusting as the jeweling retains oil better than an unjeweled metal part.

The big job in polishing and honing an action is the receiver. Besides the various stones and a Dremel Moto-Tool with abrasive-impregnated rubber wheels, there is a need for specially cut hardwood mandrels to fit inside the receiver to aid in polishing the ways and interior walls. The first hardwood mandrel should be shaped to fit into the receiver through the bridge. The diameter should be just a bit less than that of the bolt, allowing it and the wet-or-dry paper to pass through. The second may be fashioned from a square or rectangular piece of hardwood with each side radiused to effectively polish the receiver's internal walls, especially the left raceway.

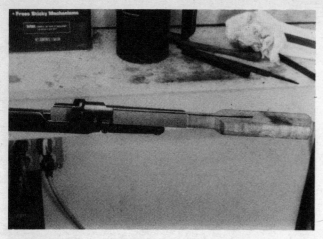

The hardwood mandrels should be made just undersize of the bolt diameter to allow wet-or-dry paper to be wrapped around them, entering the receiver through the rear of the bridge.

Begin polishing the receiver by starting on the underside. Its flat bottom should be draw-filed smooth to eliminate machine marks. It promotes a better bearing surface when the receiver is inletted into the stock for optimum bedding and should not be neglected on a custom rifle just because it won't be seen by the owner.

The polishing may be started at the rear of the receiver with the bolt sleeve rails. Machine marks should be removed with round hard Arkansas stones and polished with 240 through 400-grit wet-or-dry paper. Do not neglect the recessed flat region. This is the cocking piece groove and should be polished with small stones to eliminate machining marks. The hole in the cocking piece groove is the sear access. Check to make certain no burrs exist around its edges.

The internal walls of the receiver now may be polished using the round hardwood mandrel as a backing for the finishing paper. Be sure to check the slot on the internal section of the bridge that allows the guide rib on the bolt to pass through. If there are any battered edges, they must be removed using a knife edge stone. The left raceway

Draw-filing the underside fo the receiver is necessary to true up the area and aid in proper bedding of the action to the stock.

Bottom of the Mauser Model 98 receiver as well as lug and guard screw are also cleaned and trued up.

just ahead of the thumb clearance cut into the receiver is particularly noticeable when the bolt is opened. It should be polished with the second mandrel radiused to fit the raceways.

The side rails must be polished absolutely smooth to allow the bolt lugs to travel back and forth without drag. The edges of the rails should be trued up to aid in smooth cartridge feeding.

The cartridge feed ramp also should be polished smooth to eliminate drag as the bullet nose rides over it and into the chamber. A Dremel Moto-Tool and abrasive-impregnated rubber wheel are especially handy to complete this task. Be careful not to run the tool at too high a speed as it will have a tendency to bounce, creating high and low spots in the ramp. This region should be smoothed up, but not re-contoured which could adversely affect feeding.

The extraction cam located on the top rear portion of the bridge should be checked for burrs or rough spots. A

Bolt sleeve rails have been polished to approximately eighty percent completion. Cocking piece groove and sear access must also be polished to eliminate drag and improve appearance.

Internal walls of the bridge should be polished and guide rib slot checked to allow guide rib on bolt to travel easily. If the receiver is drilled and tapped for scope mounts, be sure to check for any rough edges at the bottom of the holes. Also make certain the tips of the base screws do not protrude through the receiver. Should they do so, it is necessary to grind the screw tips flush with inner surfaces, polishing as needed.

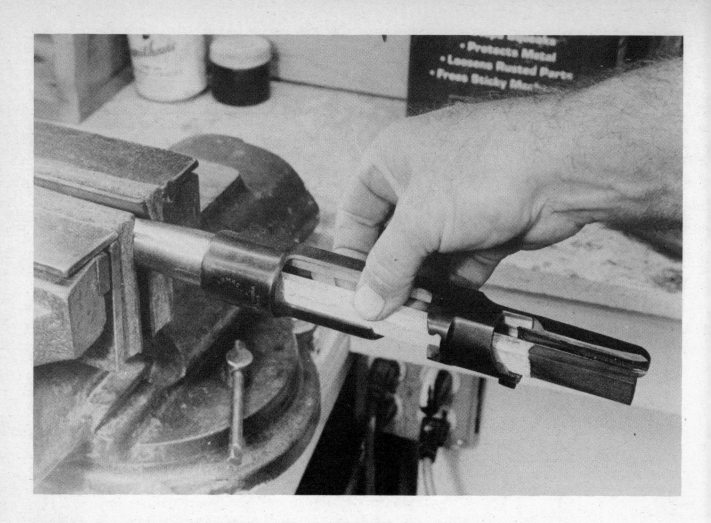

Receiver raceways are best polished using a piece of hardwood radiused to mate, supporting a piece of wet-or-dry paper. In the photo below, the left raceway has been polished to a 240-grit finish. Note the uneven edge on the left siderail. It will have to be trued up with hard Arkansas stone.

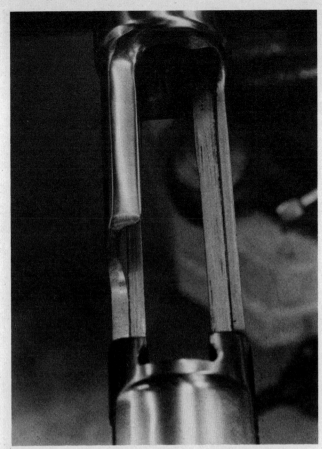

Although stoning has begun on the siderails, marks are still visible. It is necessary to eliminate such marks without removal of any more metal than is absolutely necessary to avoid sloppy fit between parts.

Final step is polishing of the external surface. Take great care not to round any edges or "run" the stamped lettering since that is considered highly unacceptable in custom work.

bit of stoning will help in smoother opening and closing of the bolt.

Virtually every piece in the action requires inspection and some polishing. However, the result of this additional work is immediately noticeable when the rifle is assembled and functioned. It is the difference between factory and custom.

The last polishing is on the exterior of the receiver. It may be done on a conventional polishing wheel setup. However, care should be taken to not round any edges or ruin any lettering; the mark of the amateur.

Above, a view of the Mauser Model 98 feed ramp before polishing with the rubber-impregnated bit in the Dremel Moto-Tool; compare to photo at right.

Here, the polishing of the feed ramp has begun, revealing high and low spots as well as a surface that is somewhat battered, needing more polishing.

Chapter 4

THE BIG BEND

Altering Bolt Handles For A Custom Look Can Become An Art In Itself

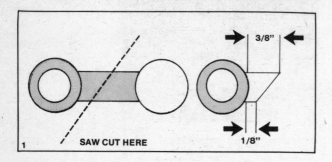

SAW CUT HERE
3/8"
1/8"

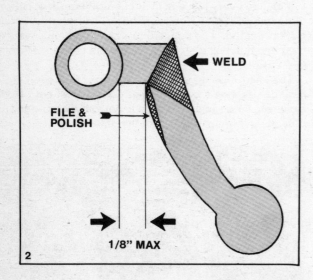

WELD
FILE & POLISH
1/8" MAX

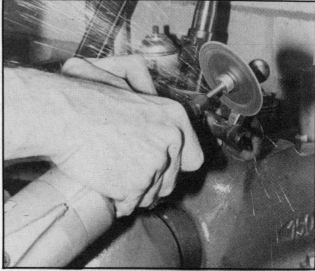

A 3-inch abrasive wheel and hand grinder for cutting bolt handles are indispensible. Hacksaws will not cut properly hardened steel handles, the author has found. Such an effort with a band saw simply ruined the blade.

R IFLESMITHS ARE required to perform alterations or even replace bolt handles on the majority of bolt-action rifles they receive for customizing. Most popular military rifle actions used to build custom rifles have either straight or curved handles that are not compatible with installation of a low-mounted scope. Military bolt handles also are rather unattractive. Customers often will request bolt handles on commercial actions be altered or replaced for functional or cosmetic reasons.

Altering the bolt handle on a military bolt may be accomplished by first cutting the handle, heating it with an oxyacetylene torch to the proper angle and welding it back in place. Another method is to use a bolt-bending jig along with heat from the torch and a hammer to bend or forge the handle to the correct angle. The former method

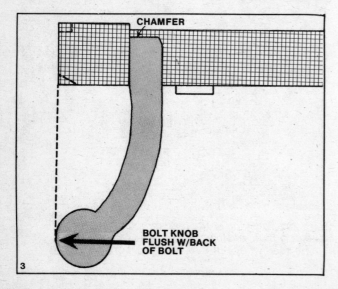

CHAMFER
BOLT KNOB FLUSH W/BACK OF BOLT

Left: 1. Altering military Mauser bolt handle to the custom configuration is accomplished by measuring ⅜ inch from bolt body along top of handle. A 45-degree cut is made with abrasive wheel; leave ⅛ inch at the bottom of bolt handle stem for welding of new handle. 2. New or altered bolt handle must be welded on top, bottom for strength and proper engagement to receiver. 3. Most riflesmiths prefer new or altered Mauser bolt handle knobs to line up with rear of bolt. Contention is that it offers better functioning with new cosmetics.

The abrasive wheel makes a sharp, clean cut. Note the location of the cut approximately 3/8 inch away from the bolt body. It is made at a downward angle of 45 degrees. Leaving handle attached makes welding easier.

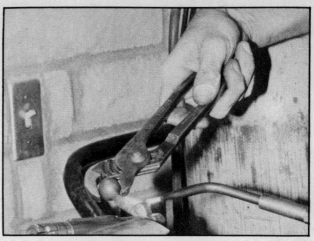

Torch is used to maintain cherry red color on the part of the bolt handle that is being bent to proper angle.

is a much better way than the latter for reasons that will be discussed.

Replacing military or commercial bolt handles with custom handles seems the most popular alternative among custom riflesmiths today. There are a number of excellent-quality custom handles available. Pete Grisel of Bend, Oregon, makes one and Brownell's carries some fine ones in their catalog. Installing a replacement handle requires that the riflesmith run a perfect weld for optimum strength.

All aforementioned methods of bolt handle alteration and replacement require an oxyacetylene torch. They all require heating with a torch, even the process using bending blocks. During the bending process beating on the

The uncut portion of the bolt handle is heated to a cherry red, bent to proper angle using hammer as lever. Work is begun with the handle in perpendicular position. It is necessary to use bolt plug to prevent warpage.

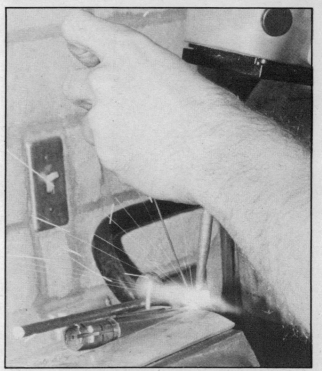

Temperature maintained on the bolt handle is critical during the welding operation. Riflesmith Joe Reid is one who favors deep weld penetration. He begins the weld with #5 tip, uses smaller tip after the build-up.

After the welding phase has been completed, the handle is reheated, contoured to a custom shape with pliers.

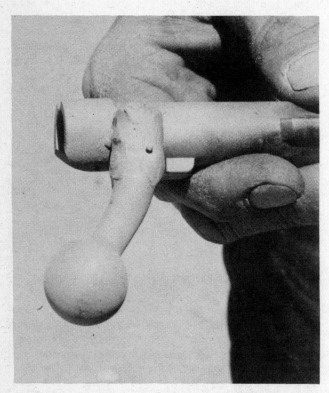

After cutting, bending, welding and initial shaping, the Mauser bolt handle must be shaped, trued, polished.

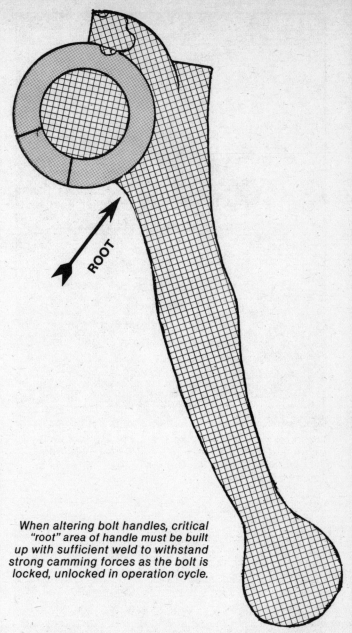

When altering bolt handles, critical "root" area of handle must be built up with sufficient weld to withstand strong camming forces as the bolt is locked, unlocked in operation cycle.

ROOT

bolt handle can upset the metal on the bottom side of the bolt handle where it joins with the bolt body. Since this area is critical to bolt handle strength, it must be welded, ground and polished to tolerance as with the other methods.

Anything less than a perfect weld in bolt handle alteration or replacement spells failure. It is not enough to simply build up the area with weld. There can be no slag, impurities, or pits left in the weld or the handle is likely to break. Having the bolt handle break when a hunter is after dangerous game could mean his life.

One might think that, even with an imperfect weld, the chances of snapping off a piece of steel handle approximately one-quarter-inch thick is unlikely. However, turn-bolt designed rifles have powerful camming surfaces on the bolt and receiver that increase the leverage ratio. For example, the Mauser action — due to certain features such as bolt handle length and camming surfaces — has an eight-to-one leverage ratio. All this simply means is

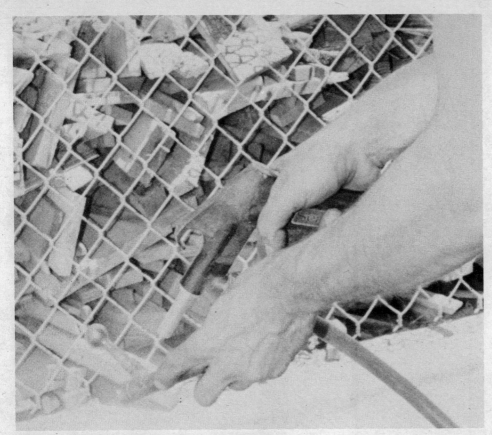

Tucson riflesmith Joe Reid uses a sandblaster for the removal of scale from the altered bolt handle before grinding off excess weld and truing the surfaces.

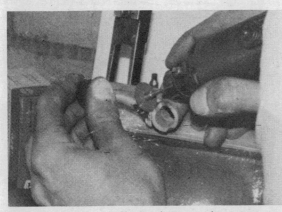

Dremel tool and cut-off wheel are used to remove excess weld from underside of bolt handle shank where it joins the bolt body. This area, called the "root," determines overall strength of bolt handle and should be inspected closely for evidence of flaws or possible pits in weld.

that even forty pounds of pressure exerted on the handle (certainly reasonable for an adult male) would exert over three hundred pounds of pressure through the handle, down the bolt to the extractor and finally to the stuck case rim.

The type of weld employed during most bolt handle alterations or replacements is the common tip weld. This weld is accomplished by heating the metal of both parts to the melting point of each and they actually begin to flow together. The weld then is built up by adding metal from a welding rod of compatible nature until both pieces and the welding rod are combined into a single homogeneous state.

A key factor in making a perfect weld is in having a neutral flame. After the torch is first lit with the acetylene valve open, you will notice a yellow, rather dirty looking flame. The oxygen valve is turned on slowly until the yellow flame disappears and a light blue inner cone with sharp edges emerges. If this inner cone is not perfect, moving the molten puddle during welding without blowing the bead of weld is next to impossible.

Altering a military bolt handle such as that of the Mauser 98 can be completed by cutting, bending and welding. With a bit of grinding and contouring it rivals most custom handles in function or aesthetics. The method used by Joe Reid and Sterling Davenport is the best way I have seen for altering a military handle.

Before beginning bolt handle alteration they remove the bolt sleeve, striker assembly, extractor and extractor collar. Applying heat to the bolt handle or bolt body without removing these pieces would anneal and ruin them.

The first step in their method of bolt handle alteration is for Reid and Davenport to put on their safety glasses; for safety's sake follow their example. It is necessary to cut almost entirely through the handle approximately three-eighths-inch out from the bolt handle body. The cut is begun on the top portion of the handle, cutting downward at a forty-five-degree angle until there is about one-sixteenth-inch of metal remaining to hold the handle on. The cut should be made with an abrasive cut-off wheel. A hacksaw blade will not cut bolt handles well as the steel is too hard. If it does cut easily the bolt is too soft and should not be used. Attempting to cut bolt handles with a band saw will ruin the blade.

Abrasive wheels are an excellent investment as they make a very smooth cut. Cutting almost through the bolt

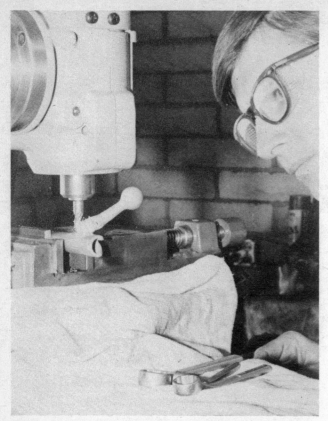

Using a milling machine with an endmill cutter can be invaluable for truing bolt handle camming surfaces. The job can be accomplished with hand files and lots of hours.

Curved military bolt handles are altered in the same manner as straight handles, except that the handle is straightened, then cut to gain added length desired.

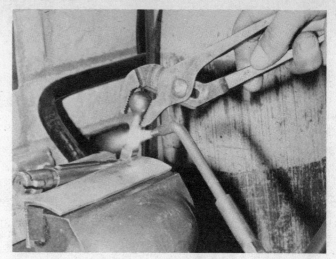

The curved handle of the Mauser bolt action rifle can be straightened with heavy pliers when heated properly.

handle, then heating it with the torch in the prescribed manner, actually adds length to the Mauser handle. This is important as Mauser handles are a bit short to begin with.

After the initial cut has been made make sure that a bolt plug is inserted in the bolt to prevent heat from warping it. Before using pliers or a hammer to bend the bolt to the desired angle, the area to be bent is heated to a cherry red. The bolt should be securely held in a vise during the bending operation.

Not cutting off the bolt completely with the abrasive wheel makes the bending process easier. Having to heat only the uncut region to a cherry red reduces the possibil-

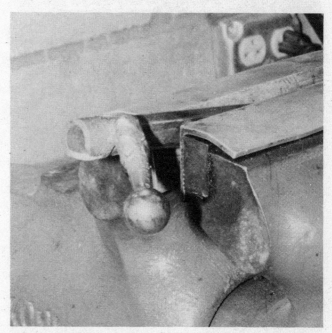

After the straightening operation has been completed, the bolt handle is cut, bent to the proper angle, then contoured for the custom look, shaped, final polished.

Bolt bending blocks marketed by Bob Brownell are used to hold the Mauser bolt during bending and forging.

Bending blocks draw off heat as bolt handle is heated; this reduces chance of bolt warpage. The blocks are set in a vise, should be touching, not crushing the bolt.

then switches to a smaller tip to accomplish the final buildup of weld. After the weld is completed the handle is reheated and a pair of pliers used to put desired contours or cosmetic sweeps into the handle.

All slag is removed from the bolt handle weld using a bench grinder and hand files. If there are any pits the work must be re-welded. If not, the handle is finish-shaped using either files or a Dremel Moto-Tool with a cut-off wheel. The underside of the bolt handle — the bolt root where it joins the bolt body — determines the strength of the entire project.

After the weld has been cleaned and the bolt handle contoured, the bolt root, the front extractor cam (front side of bolt handle where it joins bolt body) and rear portion of the bolt handle must be trued up. Although this can be done with hand files, a more accurate method is with a mill

Heat should be applied to the area of the bolt handle that protrudes immediately from the blocks until the color is cherry red. To direct heat otherwise could upset metal in the critical root area during bending.

ity of overheating and potentially warping other areas of the bolt body as there is much less material to bring up to the proper heat condition.

With the bolt handle standing straight up out of the vise and heated to the proper red, it is bent downward with either pliers or a hammer. The bolt handle should be bent downward from its original position about forty-five degrees. To check for the proper angle allow the metal to cool and place bolt in the receiver. With the bolt in the closed position it should stick out at a forty-five-degree angle between 1 and 1¼ inches from the right receiver wall.

With the bolt handle bent to its proper angle, it is time to begin welding. To get good penetration in the weld a large welding tip should be used to heat up the work quickly. Joe Reid prefers a #5 tip for this phase. When the work is properly heated he begins the initial welding,

Heat is applied continuously to the bolt handle during forging or bending with use of a hammer. Blows with the hammer must be struck at slight angle toward knob.

Bolt handle alteration is rather expensive, as it takes time as well as skill in welding, machinist knowledge, and some hard work with hand tools.

A second method of altering military bolt handles employs the bolt bending block. In this instance we use a forging process. Bolt-bending blocks, which can be made from cold-rolled steel or purchased through Brownell's, greatly reduce the possibility of warpage to the bolt should it absorb excess heat. However, this method of handle alteration does have a few drawbacks.

First, you do not gain additional length on Mauser handles as you do with the first method described. Second, it is likely that in heating the bolt root and handle the root area will be upset requiring some welding, since this region determines the strength of the bolt handle. Also, because Mauser handles require so much lowering, a notch must be cut in the receiver tang.

and end mill cutter. The exact angle of the extractor cam is important.

With the bolt handle finished it is necessary to cut a notch in the receiver tang. The notch should be cut just deep enough to allow the military safety to be turned to the fully locked position. If the notch is not deep enough, the bolt will not be completely closed. If the notch is too deep, the bolt will have a tendency to jump when the firing pin falls. Work slowly when cutting this notch going only deep enough to get the safety to fully lock.

This system of altering military bolt handles is popular with gunsmiths, because it is strong, allows handle contouring, and adds length to the handle. However, care should be exercised to prevent heat from running down the bolt body to the locking lug area. This can be checked by watching the colors run toward that area during the welding operation.

After the bolt handle has been bent flush with contour of the bending blocks, it can be roughly contoured to the desired angle or sweep that the customer wants.

Riflesmith Sterling Davenport uses a home-made belt grinder to remove scale from bolt handle and to rough shape it.

Nonetheless, bolt-bending blocks do make bolt handle alteration a much simpler job. After removing the extractor, collar, striker system and bolt sleeve, the bolt is placed into the blocks. It is important that the blocks be touching to effectively draw off excess heat, but not so tight as to injure the bolt.

Sterling Davenport prefers a #5 welding tip to quickly heat the bolt root and the handle to the required shade of cherry red. He then uses a large hammer to forge the handle down to mate with the contour of the blocks. After ini-

tial bending has been completed and the handle is still in the cherry red state, any final bending or contouring is completed. After allowing the bolt to cool any scale is removed and the bolt handle is contoured and shaped to personal preference. Careful inspection should be made of the bolt handle root, checking for crack or pits. If any are found, this area must be rewelded.

The preferred method of converting military bolt handles to custom configuration is replacement of the military bolt handles with custom handles. As mentioned

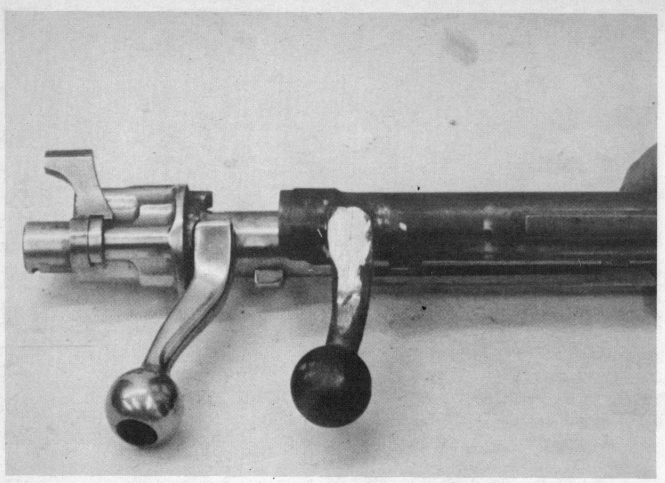

One drawback encountered in using the bending block system of alteration as opposed to the cutting and welding technique is resulting shortness of the bolt handle. This possibility is especially notable in reworking a Mauser.

This Mauser 98 military bolt handle has been cut off at a 45-degree angle ⅜-inch from the top and will be replaced with a handle made by Pete Grisel.

The new Grisel replacement bolt handle is ground at the mated edge to give deep penetration at the outset of the welding operation necessary in replacing the handle.

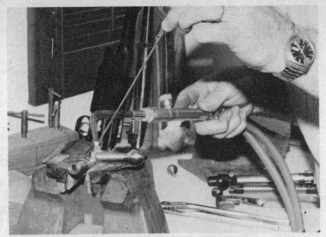

A #5 welding tip is utilized to bring the temperature of both the handle and bolt shank to the critical heat quickly, welding rod is ready to use as metal starts flow.

As the weld is allowed to cool, inspection is made to ascertain that the top section of bolt is fully filled.

earlier, two excellent replacement handles are offered through Pete Grisel and Brownell's. Both have the length, contour and quality steel that are sought after by custom riflesmiths.

Replacement of a handle begins in the same manner as the first method described in alteration except the entire military handle is cut off with an abrasive wheel. The cut is made approximately three-eighths-inch out from the bolt body, angling downward at forty-five degrees. The new handle then is taken to a bench grinder where the end to be welded to the bolt body is tapered. This allows for a deep penetration weld. Next, the bolt body — with the bolt plug inserted — is placed in a vise. Davenport uses the soft jaws on the vise to set the new handle at the proper angle. Once the weld on this side is completed the bolt is flipped over in the vise and the bottom weld made. The bolt is replaced in the vise in the first position and any bolt handle bending is completed. A #5

The Brownell bolt-welding jig holds the bolt handle and bolt body at a proper angle to make the welding operation much faster, simpler.

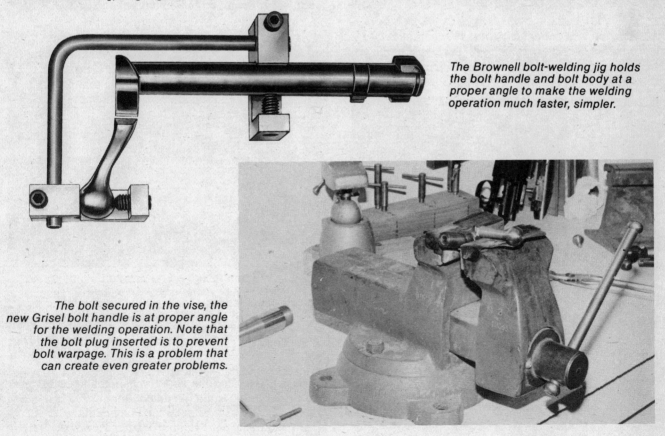

The bolt secured in the vise, the new Grisel bolt handle is at proper angle for the welding operation. Note that the bolt plug inserted is to prevent bolt warpage. This is a problem that can create even greater problems.

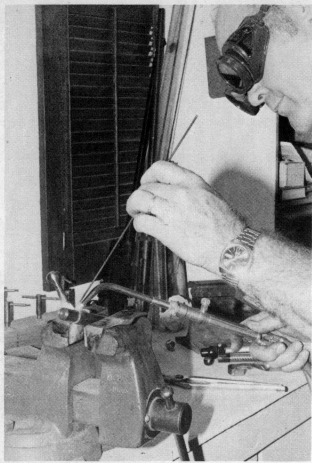

After the top side of the handle has been welded to the bolt shank, it is turned over, critical root area welded.

Final shaping of the new replacement Grisel bolt handle is done with hand files by Davenport for custom lines.

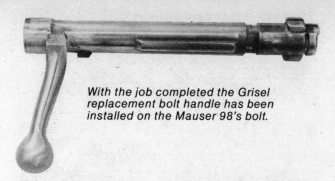

With the job completed the Grisel replacement bolt handle has been installed on the Mauser 98's bolt.

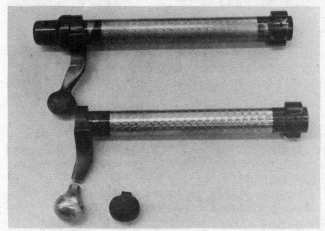

An unaltered Remington Model 700 bolt is shown at top for sake of comparison. Beneath, the factory-installed knob has been cut off for replacement by custom knob.

The bolt from the Remington Model 700 is held firmly in the vise, the new replacement knob held at the precise angle required for the initial welding job.

welding tip is used to get the work heated quickly and the welds completed. A smaller tip is used after all of the scale is removed to fill in tiny pits.

As suggested earlier, one commercial action favored for custom rifles is the Remington Model 700, but many riflesmiths prefer to replace the bolt handle knob with a more traditional pear-shaped version. However, altering this handle knob adds a new problem to the riflesmith.

The bolt handle on the Remington Model 700 is silver-soldered to the bolt body. During welding of the new knob

After welding of the new bolt knob to the Remington 700 handle, the piece is turned over to complete welding. A container of water should be close at hand for this.

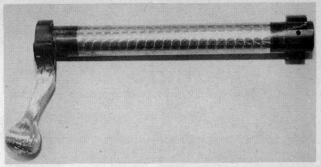

The replacement bolt handle knob from Brownell's has been installed on the Remington 700 bolt and is ready for final polishing for a custom appearance, bluing.

if heat runs up the bolt handle it can melt the solder. If the handle should fall off, replacing it in exactly the right position may be difficult and, at the least, time-consuming. The way Sterling gets around this problem is to wrap wet paper towels around the area where the bolt body and the bolt handle are joined by the silver solder. It's a good idea to keep a container of water close by during the welding process keeping the towels soaked.

After the initial weld is completed on the top, the bolt is flipped in the vise and the bottom portion is welded. Contouring and polishing require grinders and hand files and finally the polishing wheel.

Altering or replacing bolt handles requires gunsmithing experience and skill. Unless the amateur is capable of running a perfect weld, it should not be attempted.

Wet paper towels have been wrapped around the Model 700 bolt prior to welding on the new knob. Purpose of this move is to prevent heat from destroying silver-soldered joint that connects the bolt handle to body of the bolt.

Chapter 5

BARRELING THE ACTION

Fitting, Chambering, Headspacing — Each Is An Individual Challenge

STANDARD 98 MAUSER

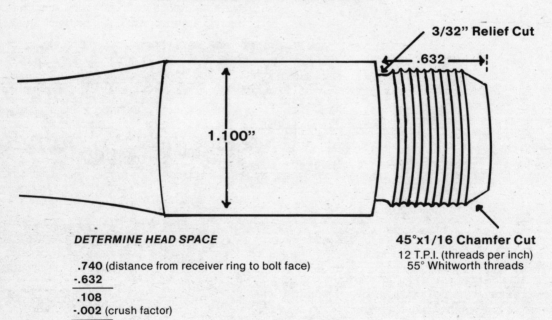

3/32" Relief Cut

.632

1.100"

DETERMINE HEAD SPACE

.740 (distance from receiver ring to bolt face)
-.632
‾‾‾‾‾
.108
-.002 (crush factor)
‾‾‾‾‾
.106

45°x1/16 Chamfer Cut
12 T.P.I. (threads per inch)
55° Whitworth threads

THREADING, chambering and headspacing a barrel to an action requires special equipment and experience. It is not a task recommended for the novice gun enthusiast. However, the amateur should have basic knowledge of the amount of work, and the professional expertise required to complete this critical phase of riflesmithing. Barrel threading, chambering and proper headspacing are among the most essential factors in building a rifle.

Threading a barrel is performed by cutting threads with a lathe for connection of the barrel to the action or receiver. Done correctly, the barrel can be screwed to the action with no gaps and be absolutely true with the axis of the bore.

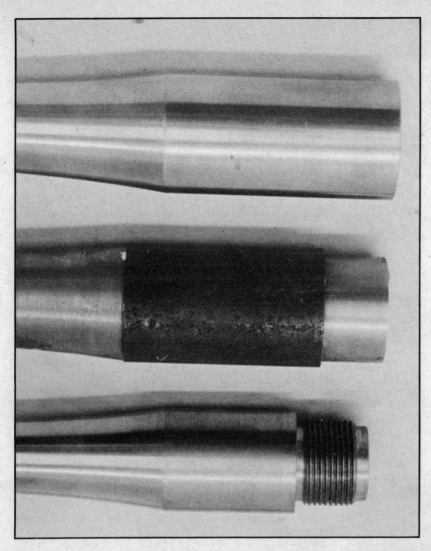

Top barrel is a turned blank as it comes from Douglas Barrels; center is barrel that has been turned on a lathe to major diameter; at bottom is barrel that has been threaded to fit the action of the subject rifle.

After determining whether barrel will have a long or short shank, it is secured in a power hacksaw and the excess metal is thus removed.

Chambering consists of reaming out the breech end of the barrel with special chambering reamers. They enlarge the barrel to accommodate a particular cartridge with precise tolerance between barrel and bolt face. There are three types of reamers employed: roughing, finishing and burnishing. The chamber must be reamed to allow a standard cartridge to fit and operate within safety standards of both a minimum and maximum size.

Correct chambering is critical to both safety and accuracy. It is essential to give maximum shooting life to the barrel. It is necessary to ensure smooth, efficient extraction of fired cases. Chambering is directly related to barrel threading and gauging of proper headspace.

During the chambering operation the barrel is also "throated." The throat is that portion of the barrel forward of the chamber that tapers to correct bore diameter. The term may be better understood by saying it is that part of the barrel reamed for the bullet seat. Target rifles are built with less throat than sporting rifles. On many target rifles the throat is so minimal that, when a cartridge is inserted into the chamber, there is so little distance between the front tip of the case to the beginning of the lands and grooves that if the cartridge is extracted the rifling will show on the bullet nose. Although this type of target throating is used to increase accuracy, it also increases

chamber pressures and will wear out barrels much faster than those of rifles throated for conventional sporting rifles.

During my student gunsmithing days we were taught to cut the throat a distance equal to the diameter of the particular cartridge on standard caliber rifles. I have since learned that riflesmiths have differing views on how much

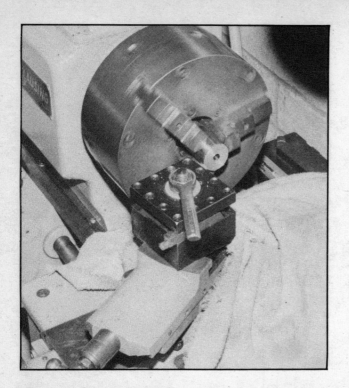

The chamber end of the barrel is faced off in a lathe while being held in place by 3-jaw or universal chuck.

throat should be used. The general feeling is that the farther a bullet travels from the case mouth to the beginning of the lands and grooves of the barrel the greater the possibility of it "jumping" into the bore and causing bullet deformity that results in poor accuracy. Yet, I recently read an interesting study involving early Mauser rifles that had been found with a much longer amount of throat with a lesser angle of entry into the lands and grooves than standard-issue Mausers. In many cases the latter were more accurate.

Probably the best way to determine amount of throat cut into a custom rifle barrel is through experience and experimentation. Custom riflesmiths experiment with each rifle on the range to determine optimum accuracy for that particular firearm. If it does not perform up to their individual standards the rifle may need to be rethroated.

Barrel is set up in the lathe so the barrel shank can be cut to its major diameter. In the case of the Model 98 Mauser this is 1.100 inches.

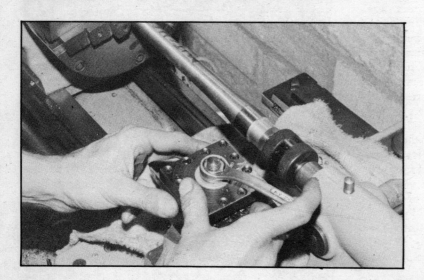

Length of the barrel shank will be .632 inch — distance from receiver ring to the inner shoulder — so the barrel will mate with the receiver.

Fifty-five-degree Whitworth threads are cut into barrel shank. Each thread is cut in shape of perfect inverted V.

Correct headspace is accomplished while fitting the barrel to the action. It simply means that the chamber must hold the cartridge snugly against the bolt face, at the same time supporting both the primer and cartridge against the bolt face during firing. Headspace for rimless cartridges may be defined as the distance between the angle on the shoulder of the case against the angle on the chamber shoulder to the bolt face.

Measuring tools called, *go* and *no-go* gauges are used to determine headspace. The latter gauge slightly exceeds the standard maximum allowable amount of headspace. To use the gauges the bolt first is stripped and extractor removed. The go gauge is inserted into the chamber and with gentle pressure on the bolt handle the bolt is closed to the locked position. It then is removed and the no-go gauge is placed in the chamber. If the

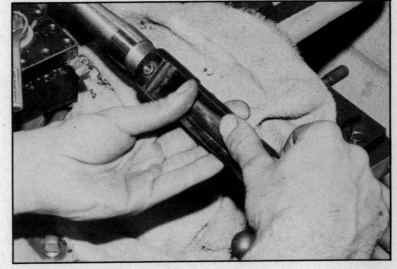

When threads have been cut close to proper depth, lathe is stopped and riflesmith Joe Reid attempts to screw the action into the barrel in what is termed a Class Four fit.

Mauser action requires that a relief cut of 3/32 inch be made to mate the barrel to receiver. Special cut-off tool is used.

In order to chamber the barrel, it must be set up in a steady rest with jaws to support work.

With the jaws placed on either the shank or threads, Reid can face off shank to precise length.

firearm does not have excessive headspace the bolt handle will stop approximately one-half inch before arriving at its locked position. This test is made with only gentle pressure.

Before going through the twenty-seven steps required to completely barrel an action, a word of caution is urged. A lathe, like any power tool, can be quite dangerous if the rules of safety are not observed. I have seen experienced gunsmiths fall into the old familiarity-breeds-contempt syndrome while working with power equipment only to be seriously injured. I have been guilty of it myself and paid the price. Fortunately, I have lived to be older and hopefully wiser. I suggest the following rules be prominently displayed in every gunshop or home workshop:

1. Always wear safety glasses.
2. Don't wear long-sleeved shirts.
3. Watch your fingers. There are a myriad of cutting edges and possibilities of catching a finger while turning metal.
4. Put handles on all files. The tang of a file can cause serious injury.
5. Don't attempt to remove chips of metal from the lathe by hand. Use a brush.
6. Keep the lathe chuck wrench in a secured position.
7. Never start the lathe without checking for the whereabouts of the chuck key. If left in the machine and the lathe is turned on, it can fly

out at dangerous speeds.

8. Be especially wary of coming into contact with lathe dogs and jaws.

9. Never strike the tool bit with the hand to remove or change its angle.

10. Never wear rings or watches. You could lose a finger, or worse.

Some actions are more difficult to rebarrel than others. Enfield, Springfield and Winchester Model 70s require a cone being cut into the rear of the barrel shank leading up to the edge of the chamber. An extractor slot also must be cut. On Model 70s an extractor slot must be cut in conformity with the radius of the cone, the opening of the rear chamber and the shape of the extractor hook. This additional work is more difficult and time consuming, therefore, more expensive to the customer. Also, properly headspacing smaller-caliber cartridges is more difficult than larger-caliber cartridges due to the more critical dimensions involving headspace. If a .22 caliber action is headspaced under acceptable dimensions the gun can fire accidentally when the bolt closes in the action pinching the rim. Excessive headspace can lead to over-expansion of the rim during firing causing a cushioning effect which softens breech pressure; this results in reduced velocity and poor accuracy.

The action enjoying the most popularity today for custom rifle conversion is the Model 98 Mauser. It is one of the strongest actions ever designed and has aesthetically pleasing lines admired by gun purists.

Joe Reid, an excellent gunsmith in Tucson, Arizona, and I have chosen a 1909 Argentinian Model 98 Mauser and a McGowen premium barrel to explain the methods of rebarreling. Many riflesmiths develop their own unique procedures for barreling an action and our methods serve simply as a guide. The following procedures for

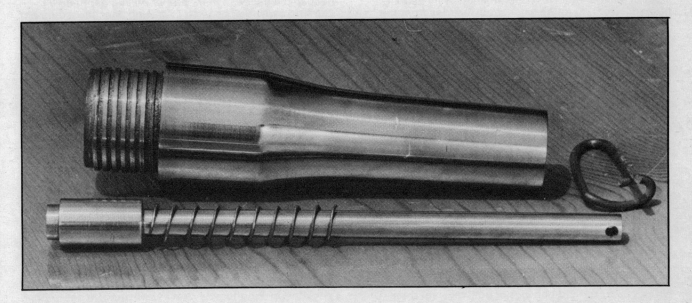

This jig was made by the author for use in lapping bolt lugs for 80 percent contact with the action. The jig is screwed to the action, lapping compound applied to the bolt locking lugs, then the bolt is opened and closed under jig spring tension until the desired amount of contact is achieved. An old barrel can be used to create jig.

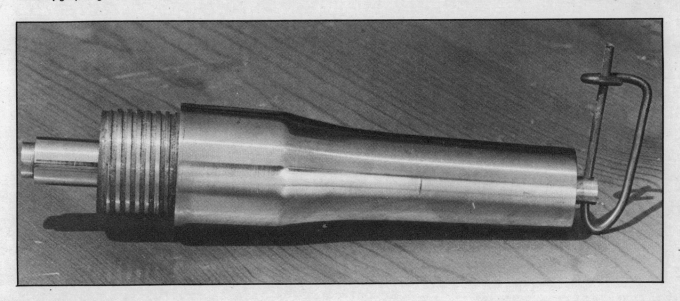

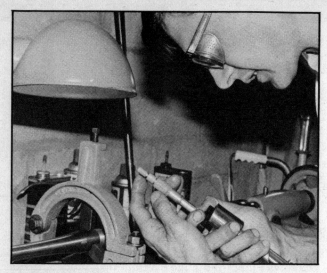

Joe Reid determines exact headspace measurements with a depth micrometer. This is determined by measuring from receiver ring to the inner shoulder, then from the receiver ring to the bolt face, using extreme care.

Reid uses a drill bit as a roughing reamer. He uses a headspace gauge to mark proper drilling depth on bit. Extreme care must be used in making each measurement.

obtaining correct headspace measurements, barrel threading, chambering and polishing techniques, reaming, headspacing, throating, chambering and final polishing of the chamber have been learned through first-hand experience. Each step must be performed with the utmost desire for precision if optimum accuracy and reliability are to be expected.

THE TWENTY-SEVEN STEPS

1. Clean all rifle parts completely to make accurate measurements with a depth micrometer. Make a detailed diagram and record all measurements. Any dirt or foreign matter can throw off critical dimensions enough to require doing the entire job over again.

2. Examine the action and barrel for worn, damaged or cracked parts. Be especially wary of oversize firing pin holes, cracks around bolt lugs or front receiver rings. The bolt lugs also may be worn or even set back due to firing cartridges with excessive pressures. Check springs and

the color of the metal to determine if the gun has ever been in a fire. If reworking a used barrel check that the lands are sharp with little or no pitting. Inspect for bulges or rings inside the barrel. Don't assume that a new barrel blank is not defective or bent. The action or receiver ring is subject to burrs where it butts against the shoulder of the barrel. They must be removed to obtain accurate measurements when rebarreling. Minor dents around the muzzle may be disregarded since it will be recrowned.

3. If rechambering a standard-caliber action to magnum, the bolt face must be opened. Gauges should be made for each caliber in cold rolled steel and stamped accordingly if volume work is anticipated. Since bolt faces often are quite hard, it may be necessary to draw back the steel to a medium blue with an oxyacetylene torch to permit cutting. If this step is necessary, be sure to pack the locking lugs to prevent warping. When setting the bolt between centers in the lathe never run the lathe with the tailstock center in the firing pin hole. Instead, set

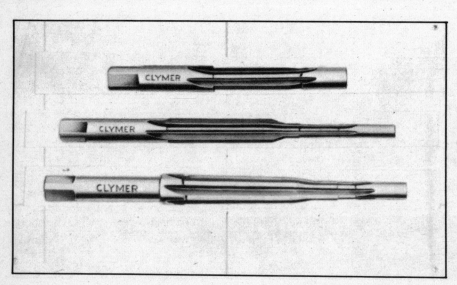

Practicing gunsmiths should have a selection of roughing and finishing reamers in popular calibers as a part of shop equipment. Brownell carries a wide selection of these.

it up between centers using a lathe dog and drive plate and a steady rest. The steady rest should not be positioned too closely to locking lugs or gas ports on Mausers.

4. Perform any bolt handle alterations. (This is discussed in another chapter.) If the bolt is overheated during this phase it may become warped, requiring replacement.

5. Heat treat the action if required after all shaping, drilling and tapping have been completed. Be sure to remove any burrs after tapping.

6. Check the locking lugs for approximately eighty percent engagement with locking recesses in receiver. If engagement is not sufficient the bolt must be relapped. A special jig may be used to accomplish this task. The receiver is screwed to the jig containing a spring-loaded metal projection. The projection presses against the bolt face which pushes the locking lugs back against the locking recesses. The bolt is then opened and closed with lap-

A maximum 3/8-inch cut is made with each pass. The drill bit or reamer should then be removed and both chamber and bit cleaned to prevent chips from causing rings.

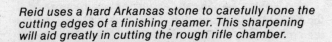

Reid uses a hard Arkansas stone to carefully hone the cutting edges of a finishing reamer. This sharpening will aid greatly in cutting the rough rifle chamber.

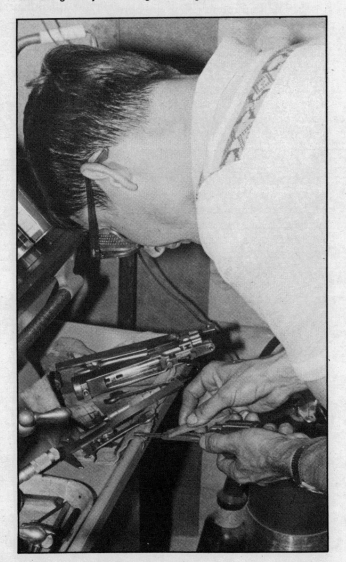

ping compound packed between the locking surfaces. The amount of engagement is checked by applying Dykem to the engaging surfaces prior to lapping. This operation must be performed with the extractor removed from the bolt. Also, be careful to prevent lapping compound contacting other areas which can result in a sloppy fit in other areas of the bolt and receiver.

7. Measure the receiver to determine barrel thread extension length and headspace. This measurement must be extremely accurate and taken with a depth micrometer. When the barrel is tightened to the action using an action wrench and vise the barrel engaging shoulder is actually crushed. This is known as the "crush factor" and an additional .002-inch must be considered in measurement tabulations. To obtain the measurements the depth micrometer is held flush across the front ring of the action measuring down to the inside front shoulder. The measurement for the Mauser illustrated is .632. To get the other measurement, Joe Reid measures from the same front action ring to the bolt face which has been stripped of internal parts and extractor and locked in its closed position. Our Mauser shows a distance of .740-inch. We now subtract .632 from .740 to get .108 inch. We also subtract the .002 inch for crush factor to get .106. This is the amount our go headspace gauge must protrude from the chamber breech to rest against the bolt face and achieve proper headspace. We also know that we must cut exactly .632 as the threaded portion on the barrel to fit the action to its inner ring.

8. Cut new centers in the barrel with piloted center drill .001 inch under bore diameter. This leaves both ends true to the bore. If you are working with a new rifle blank the shank length of the barrel must be determined. The shorter the shank, the lighter the rifle, but consideration to aesthetics also must be considered.

9. True the outside of the chamber area by making a

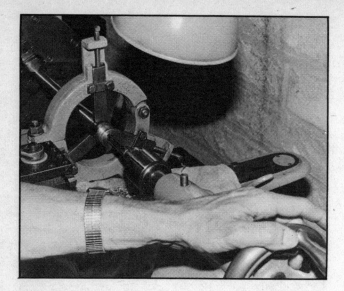

Joe Reid uses a dial gauge on the tailstock in order to ream to exact depth. Lathe should be turning slowly; max speed should be about 40 revolutions per minute.

clean-up cut. This is an area prone to chatter and must be watched closely.

10. Turn the major diameter for threads between centers. The major diameter on Model 98 Mausers is 1.100 inches.

11. Make a necking cut if required. In the case of our Mauser a relief cut of 3/32 inch is necessary. It is made with a cut-off cutter forward of the threads on the barrel at the shoulder edge. The depth should be approximately .003 inch deeper than the minor diameter of the newly cut threads. This cut allows the action to be screwed up flush with the barrel shoulder with no gap.

12. Cut a 45°x1/16-inch chamfer in the breech end of the barrel. This cut allows for smooth feeding and extraction of cartridges.

13. Thread and fit the action by hand to a class 4 fit. This is best described as a hand-turned snug fit. This is done while cutting the threads. (With the Mauser, this was done with a 55° Whitworth metric cutter, although many gunsmiths use a 60° V-form cutter. Both have twelve threads per inch (tpi). As we see the cutter turn the threads to the desired inverted ⋀ position we try to screw the action on to check for snug but not sloppy fit. This cutting to full depth of the threads should be done slowly with great concentration.

14. Contour the barrel if needed to custom shape. With the barrel turning in the lathe, this is done using cutters, then a lathe file.

15. File and rough polish the barrel. The lathe file or smaller file is first used to eliminate scratches. Next, strips of aloxite are held apart above the work during polishing. Don't wrap the strips around the turning barrel or you could lose a finger, or worse.

The headspace gauge is inserted into the chamber and checked for protrusion to determining the particular degree of headspace that is required for the rifle that is being worked on. Each riflesmith develops his own techniques.

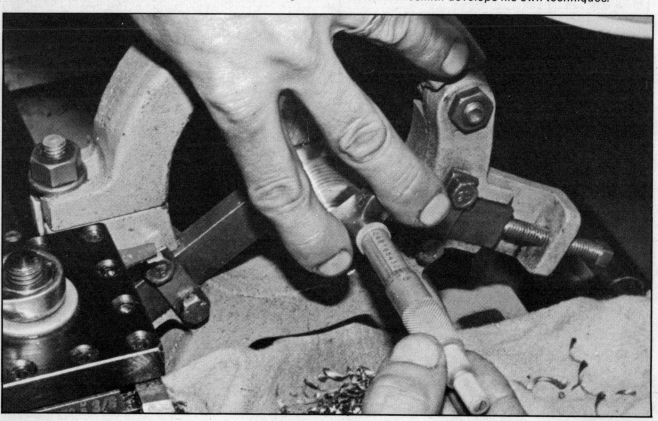

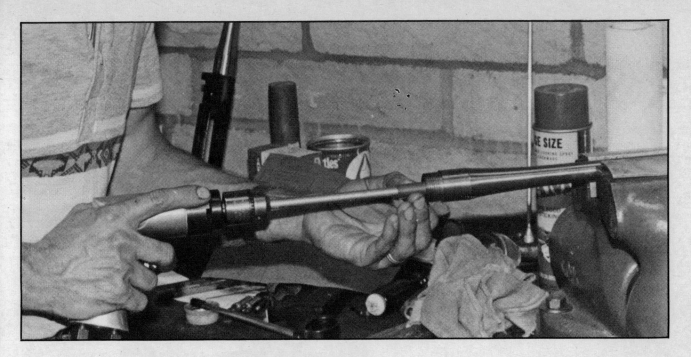

After completion of the headspace operation, the chamber is polished with hand drill, mandrel, wet-or-dry paper.

16. Set the lathe's steady rest on the shank section of the barrel or its threads. Face off the thread extension to required length after measuring with a depth micrometer. This operation allows the receiver to be screwed to the barrel tightening up to the inner shoulder without any gap between barrel shoulder and receiver ring.

17. Rough chamber to proper depth using a roughing reamer. Maximum three-eighths-inch cuts are permissible during the first few cuts. A proper size drill bit may be used if no roughing reamer is available. Joe Reid subtracted .025 inch from the smallest diameter on the shoulder of the cartridge to determine which size drill bit is acceptable. He then placed a go gauge beside the drill bit as a measuring gauge and marked a spot about .0125 inch less than the length of the gauge on the drill bit. If you are using a roughing reamer, use the headspace gauge from the edge of the reamer shoulder, mark a spot approximately one-sixteenth inch back from the base of the gauge. A finishing reamer can be used instead of a roughing reamer or drill bit, but it is susceptible to breakage or wearing out. Since reamers are quite expensive, chambers should be rough chambered first. By using finishing reamers strictly for finish reaming you will also have ultimately smoother chambers.

To rough chamber the barrel it is placed muzzle-first into the lathe's three-jaw chuck. The steady rest holds the chamber end resting on the threads or just forward on the shank. A center is used to true the barrel as it turns at a slow speed, usually 30 to 40 rpm, then is removed. Next the center is removed from the tail stock. The roughing reamer is attached to a T handle with the reamer shank extending approximately one inch through the T handle. A three-jaw Jacobs chuck is inserted into the tail stock. The protruding roughing reamer shank can now be secured to the chuck and rough chambering begun. A washer also may be placed between chuck and T handle to aid in chambering at the correct angle.

Before making each pass, thoroughly coat the roughing reamer with Brownell's Do-Drill or a good commercial grade of cutting oil to the bore. No more than three-eighths-inch cuts should be made initially and both bore and cutter should be cleaned thoroughly to remove metal chips after each pass. If both cutter and bore are not cleaned each time, metal chips will cut rings into the chamber and ruin the job. Should the reamer ever catch in the bore, release the handle immediately and let it rotate with the barrel until you can turn off the lathe. Attempting to hold on to it can result in a broken reamer or ruined chamber.

18. When the chamber has been rough-reamed to

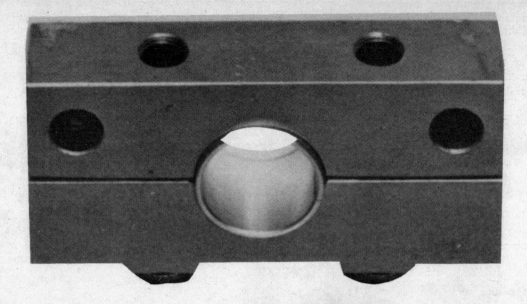

To secure the barrel properly to the action and achieve proper fitting, a good action wrench (left) and barrel vise (above) are necessary tools. As barrel shoulder mates with receiver ring, .002 inch of metal is crushed.

the depth mark on the reamer, the bore is ready for finish reaming to proper headspace. It also must be necked and throated. Before finish reaming carefully inspect the reamer for any sign of burrs. Joe Reid makes it a practice to hone the edges of the finish reamer to help eliminate any possibility of a rough chamber. A sharp cutter also helps the riflesmith to determine whether any chips are catching on the reamer's cutting edges.

The finishing reamer is used until chips begin showing on the shoulder of the reamer. It now is time to begin inserting the headspace gauge into the chamber and measure its protrusion accurately with the depth micrometer. Subtract the desired amount of headspace — in our case .105 inch — from the reading just taken with the headspace gauge inserted into the chamber. In order to remove just enough metal to get our desired .105 we use the dial gauge on the tailstock taking small cuts and checking headspace protrusion until we reach .105 inch. Be certain to continue to clean the finish reamer and chamber after each of these small passes.

19. Polish the chamber and round feeding edge with 400- and 600-grit wet-or-dry paper. Joe Reid wraps the paper around a mandrel attached to a hand drill to polish out roughness and burrs in the chamber. However, a novice should be careful not to over-polish as an oversize chamber could result.

20. To fit the barrel to the action a barrel vise and action wrench are used. During the tightening the shoulder of the barrel will be crushed against the shoulder of

the action by approximately .002 inch, but this amount was pre-calculated into our figures earlier. When tightening the barrel to the action be sure to use a good lube or grease on the barrel threads to prevent the threads from seizing in the action.

21. Back off the barrel vise and action wrench a few times before final seating. This will help the barrel to seat properly.

22. Check the bolt for free travel. Insert the stripped bolt and attempt to close it in the action gently. It must close without hitting the end of the barrel extension.

23. Check headspace using the go and no-go gauges. *Never use live ammunition.* To accomplish this place the bolt, sans internal parts and extractor, into its locked position in the receiver. Place the go-gauge into the chamber and attempt to close the bolt. The bolt should close fully with no pressure. Remove it and place the no-go gauge into the chamber and gently attempt to close the bolt. It should stop no more than one-half inch from its final locked position. *Never force it.* This will ruin the chamber.

24. Mark the extractor location if required. Extractor slots can be made with a fine-tooth hacksaw blade, Swiss files and a Dremel Moto-Tool, using cut-off discs. The slot then is polished with either wet-or-dry paper or emery cloth. Extractor slots may be located by applying inletting black to the forward surface of the extractors and bringing the bolt up against the barrel shank face with the

Cutting the barrel to the desired length can be done quickly with a power hacksaw. If a barrel is being cut to the minimum legal length, one should allow about one-quarter inch additional for the final finishing job.

The first step in crowning the muzzle of the barrel is for riflesmith Reid to set the barrel back into the lathe and to secure it in a steady rest. Crowning is demanding and can have a decided effect on accuracy of the firearm.

new barrel turned into the action and properly headspaced. It now is standard practice to assemble the bolt and check for firing pin protrusion. A maximum of .050 inch is acceptable in high-powered rifles.

25. Punch an index mark on the barrel and receiver should the barrel be removed for any reason, it can be replaced in precisely the proper location by lining up the marks. After indexing, clean the barrel and action in preparation for test firing. Be sure to use factory loads for test fire examination. After firing, check the case for rings, tears or bulges. Check also to make certain the primer is not protruding, which would indicate excessive headspace.

26. Stamp the caliber designation on the left side of the barrel above the stock line. This is a federal regulation. Stamping techniques are described at the end of this chapter.

27. Cut and crown the barrel. The barrel length is measured from the bolt face forward. Minimum legal barrel length for rifles is sixteen inches and twenty-six inches overall. If cutting a barrel to minimum length, always leave at least one-fourth inch extra on barrel. The type of crown will be determined by intended use of the firearm and customer preference.

The entire operation of threading, chambering and headspacing a rifle is exacting work requiring specialized equipment and an experienced riflesmith. As all are directly related to strength and safety as well as accuracy of the firearm, the customer should seek out reputable smiths for this work. Riflesmiths should work carefully, measuring everything twice while taking pains to keep the work as clean and free of metal chips as possible for best results.

There are several ways of creating the muzzle crown for a rifle. The rifle above has been crowned for hunting, while the inset crown pictured below is designed for use on a rifle that will be used primarily for targets.

Open 'er Up! Bolt-Face Changes
Often Follow The New Barrel

OPENING THE face of a bolt on a standard bolt-action rifle to accept a magnum cartridge case is not a difficult operation for a gunsmith with access to a lathe. Tucson gunsmith Joe Reid completed the operation from start to finish in a little more than fifteen minutes.

Reid began by measuring the diameter of the standard case of the 8mm Mauser which he found to be .472. He then measured the .338 Winchester magnum case and came up with a diameter of .532. To determine the exact amount the bolt face must be opened he subtracted .472 from .532 and arrived at .060 (sixty-thousandths).

Knowing the amount of metal that must be removed,

By subtracting the diameter of the rifle's present caliber from the desired magnum caliber diameter, the riflesmith is able to determine how much metal must be removed from the rim that surrounds face of bolt.

Reid places the bolt in the three-jaw of the lathe with the shroud end of the bolt held by the three-jaw. He next sets up the "Steady Rest" attachment contacting the bolt in front of the locking lugs. To insure that the bolt is centered he must bring up the tail stock and center it on the firing pin hole. He now tightens the Steady Rest to hold the bolt precisely in position and removes the tail stock.

With the bolt face in position on the lathe Reid will use a special cutting tool (available from Brownell's). Reid actually accomplishes two operations with this cutter. He opens up the bolt face, but also cuts slightly into the bolt face enough to true it up. This should be done on any bolt face that may be somewhat burred or peened due to heavy use.

Using a lathe with a non-direct reading Reid turns on the lathe and faces off the bolt face until he makes contact with the bolt rim. Since he wants to remove a total of .060

he will move the measurement dial a total of .030 (thirty-thousandths). This cuts .030 off each side for a total of .060.

After cutting the bolt rim the required amount Reid slips a .338 Win mag case into the bolt face to check its fit. It is important that he removes about .003 (three-thousandths) extra gap, which is necessary to insure that the cartridge will align with the chamber after all work is completed.

The bolt is now removed from the lathe and held securely in a vise. At this point the cartridge will not feed up into the bolt face until we cut away the excess material on either side of the rim. The excess rim metal is removed with a Dremel Moto-Tool and a carbide cutoff wheel.

We are now ready to fit the extractor. Approximately .030, which is one-half of the diameter we opened the bolt face, is removed from the extractor with a Dremel Moto-Tool and small grinding wheel. A proper test to determine whether the extractor is properly fitted is to place a cartridge into the bolt face and hold the whole arrangement in your hand. The extractor should hold on to the cartridge. This is a matter of feel. The cartridge should not fall out, but should not be held under too much pressure either, or feeding problems will result.

To allow the cartridge to feed smoothly we now remove the extractor and polish the bearing surface on a buffing wheel. This also helps to prevent damaging of cartridges.

The amateur gun tinkerer is not likely to have access to a lathe or to be barreling any actions, but hopefully will appreciate the time and precise measurements using very expensive machinery the riflesmith goes through to accomplish these tasks.

To true up the bolt between centers, it is placed in a 3-jaw lathe, tail stock centering on firing pin hole.

1.

In order to perform the operation successfully, the riflesmith uses special cutter to open up bolt face.

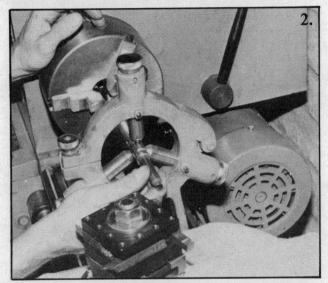

2.

After removing .060-inch from the rim of the bolt face, riflesmith Joe Reid checks work with .338 Win mag case.

3.

Excess material on either side of the slot in the rim that allows cartridge to move up into position in the bolt face must be removed. A Dremel tool works well.

4.

After removal of excess material from either side of rims, Joe Reid uses a magnum case to check the fit.

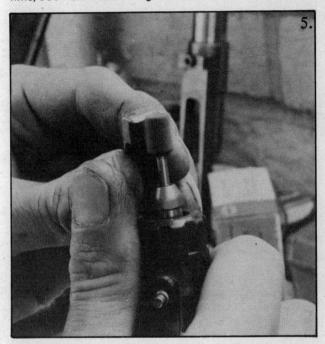

5.

With .030 removed from each side of the bolt face rim, .030 will also have to be removed from extractor claw. Dremel tool with small grinding wheel is fast, efficient.

6.

Of the two military Mauser bolts, one on the left has been opened up to accept .338 Winchester magnum case.

Chapter 6

STAMP OUT

REPRODUCTION

When A Rifle Is Rebarreled, You Have To Have The Numbers; Here's How To Do It Professionally

Twenty-seven piece letter stamping set is made of high-grade precision steel, hardened to Rockwell 62C.

Simple but efficient nine-piece number metal stamping set from Young Bros. Stamp Works. Number 9 is turned upside down for number 6; all in drilled wood holder.

AFTER BARRELING up an action the caliber must be stamped on the new barrel. It's a federal regulation. This regulation may be found in "Commerce in Firearms and Ammunition (part 178 of title 27, Code of Federal Regulations), Subpart F — Conduct of Business, Section 178.92, Identification of Firearms." Written in long-winded legal jargon only a lawyer could decipher, the part we're concerned with states, "Shall legibly identify each such firearm by engraving, casting, stamping (impressing) the caliber or gauge."

The simplest method of complying with this regulation is stamping. Stamping sets in either figures or letters may be ordered through Brownell's. These sets are available in the standard one-sixteenth- and three-thirty-seconds-inch sizes or the one-eighth-inch, which is a bit large for stamping rifles. The nine-piece figure (numbers) set sells for around $11 while the twenty-seven-piece letter set goes for about $33.

Each stamp must be hand-cut and taper-ground as well as hardened to Rockwell 62C to prevent chipping or battering. They are a necessary investment for any gunsmith and pay for themselves after the first few rebarreling jobs.

The trick to stamping barrels is in getting each number or letter to line up with the others. B-Square of Fort Worth, Texas, helps to eliminate this problem with their Steel Stamp Guide. It serves as an aid and positions the individual stamps with blanks used as spacers. The guide is secured with a sturdy clamp to any barrel up to 1½-inch diameter. Since a botched job of stamping results in having to file off the numbers or letters and do it again, the B-Square Guide is a handy addition to the toolbox. Without a guide the riflesmith must stamp the caliber on the barrel by eyeball and feel. I learned a great deal in watching Joe Reid stamping the .22-250 caliber figures on a Douglas Premium barrel just fitted to a 1909 Argentine Mauser action.

B-Square Stamp Guide, below, is a handy device which is used to align steel stamps in position on barrels.

The first step to ensure that each number lines up at the right height is to use a piece of masking tape as a guideline. The strip of tape is placed parallel on the barrel to the lowest lettering on the receiver as this lettering is normally above the stock line and we want the caliber markings to be visible. In this case the lowest lettering on the

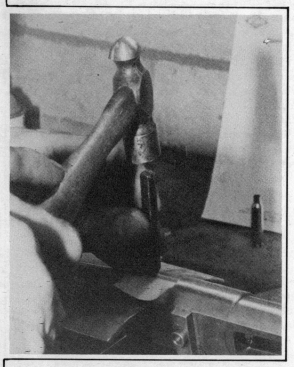

Before the gunsmith begins stamping selected letters or numbers, masking tape is applied to help line up stamp. Steel stamp must be vertical to surface, positioned to appear just above stock wood line.

receiver is *ARGENTINO 1909*. With the first stamp held in a vertical position to the barrel it is brought to touch the tapeline. With the stamp barely resting against the tape the top of the stamp is angled a bit closer to the riflesmith.

Reid offers a gentle tap with the hammer and removes the stamp to check for location. All he has done is lightly impress the bottom of the letter, in this case the lower portion of the number two. He then carefully places the stamp back into position using the first impression as a reference point and gently begins tapping the stamp with the hammer. With each succeeding tap he rolls the stamp away from him insuring even depth of the number two at top and bottom. Any high or low spots are corrected by gently tapping the stamp from the proper angle. If the riflesmith wants the number to move slightly to the right or left he merely angles the stamp in that direction and taps it.

The location of the caliber stamping is generally placed two to four inches from the reciver ring. Just make sure you allow yourself enough room to accommodate all stamping before running into the receiver.

It is better to stamp the figures or letters deeply and uniformly. After the stamping is complete high points left by the stamp are filed away. By using a file and either aloxite or wet-or-dry paper the new caliber designation should be of uniform depth and rival the best factory stamping.

Remember to stamp each figure or letter slowly, using several medium taps with the hammer. This is a job not done by lining up the stamp and attempting to give it one hard belt. Stopping periodically and checking each figure for depth and trueness will insure professional results.

Once position of letter or number is determined, stamp is lightly and continuously hammered as stamp is rolled across barrel surface, as below.

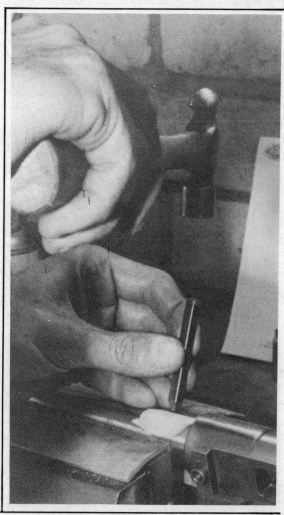

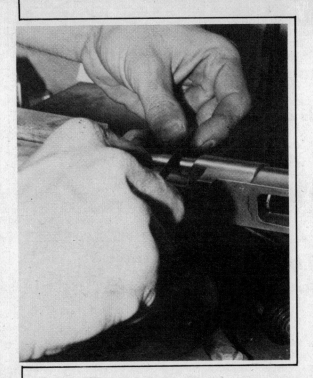

Stamping is done purposely deep and riflesmith then lightly files off any high edges or surfaces to desired depth. Stamping depth should be uniform.

File marks may be removed using aloxite 100-grit paper in shoeshine motion across barrel stamping.

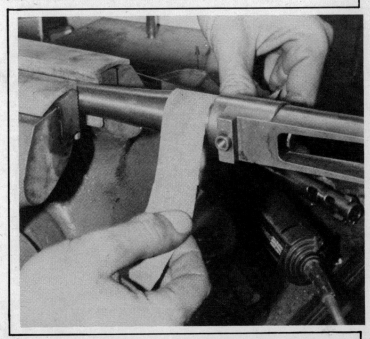

New caliber designation stamping completes barreled action work; job is now ready for final polishing.

Chapter 7

JEWELING RIFLE BOLTS

The Fine Points Of Creating The Pattern Of Small, Overlapping Circles On Bolts And Similar Brightwork

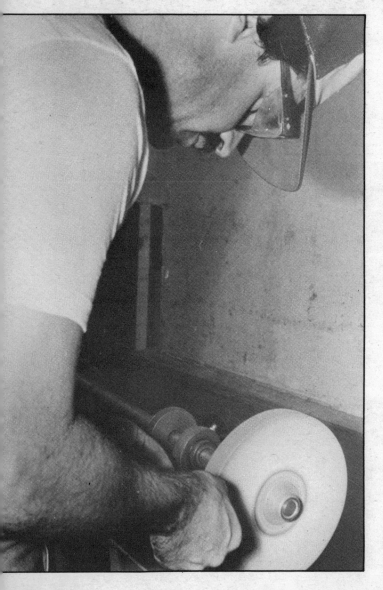

BOLT JEWELING is both decorative and functional. It is one of the simpler gunsmithing tasks, but monotonous, time-consuming, and certainly not the best money-making proposition for the full-time riflesmith. It takes almost 1½ hours to jewel a Model 98 Mauser bolt, but is generally only a $20 charge to the customer. However, the process should be understood by the amateur and professional as it has been around for many years and will probably be requested by customers for years to come.

Bolt jeweling, damascening, or engine turning are one and the same. The word, *damascening* is a bit vague. R.A. Steindler in his *The Firearms Dictionary* describes it as, "the decorating of metal with another metal, either by inlaying or attaching in some fashion. Damascene is often confused with Damaskeening or engine turning."

When polishing bolt, avoid contact between polishing wheel and any camming surfaces of the bolt, polishing only portion to be jeweled. Metal removed from camming surfaces can cause improper functioning.

Before jeweling operation is begun on bolt, bluing is removed with naval jelly, then polished on a 400-grit wheel and finished on a 600-grit wheel for a mirror finish. Preliminary polishing makes the big difference in final appearance of bolt after jeweling is completed.

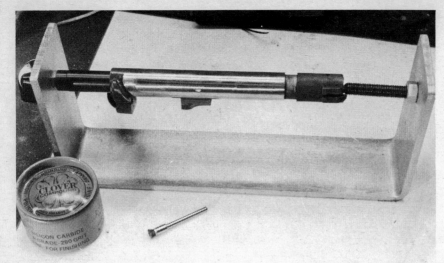

B-Square jig holds bolt between arbor and center. Turning handle at left allows bolt to be rotated for further rows of jeweling to complete job.

Just to be sure I checked with good old Mr. Webster and he says, "to decorate (iron, steel, etc.) with wavy markings or with inlaid patterns of gold or silver." Now I'm really confused. Many engravers inlay gold or silver into steel firearms. Damascus-type steel has wavy patterns. Perhaps it would be best if you and I just stick to calling it jeweling.

We aren't going to be doing any inlaying, nor wavy lines either. Instead, we are going to place overlapping straight rows of small circular burnishing marks on a rifle bolt. They may also be applied to bolt stop springs, floorplates, extractors, the sides of triggers, and any other piece of metal your heart desires.

Bolt jeweling can be accomplished with a portable electric hand drill and even a Dremel Moto-Tool, but to do it right requires a drill press, a B-Square bolt jeweling jig, a small circular wire brush, and lapping compound, preferably 400 grit.

Jeweling seems to be most often requested by customers because it's pretty. However, it does add certain functional advantages to the shooter and hunter. During the jeweling operation high and low spots are created in the metal. These low spots hold oil or lubricant making for a smoother action. Jeweling also acts to break up reflected light which is important to a hunter in the field. Jeweled metal seems to resist rusting more than unjeweled metal. It is also an excellent way to hide any pitting.

The most important factors in successful jeweling are to have each circular burnishing mark the same uniform size and each row of marks dead straight. In order to accomplish this a bolt jeweling jig is necessary. B-Square

A square is positioned on drill press table and secured with C-clamps as guide for jeweling rig.

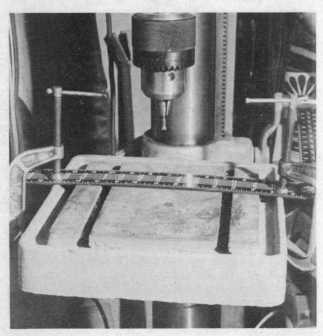

To achieve desired jeweling pattern, work must be directly centered beneath the jeweling brush.

A jeweled surface retains lubricants better than a plain one. Author jeweled both bolt and extractor on this custom Enfield to smooth action, add to looks.

makes an excellent jig that gives results superior to any other method I have heard of.

The tool that actually imprints the circular burnishing mark is a small circular wire brush. I have tried other markers such as wooden dowels and pencil erasers, but the wire brush does a much more precise and finer job. The brush is more flexible and cuts better on rounded surfaces.

An abrasive compound is necessary to cut the marks into the bolt or other metal part. Many riflesmiths use 240-grit lapping compound, but I prefer 400-grit for a more highly polished result.

A drill press will give better results than any other tool. The press should be run at about medium speed. Practice will teach you how much pressure should be applied on the wire brush. If too much pressure is exerted, the bristles on the brush will squash and go out-of-round destroying the circular pattern. If too little pressure is applied the circles will be too faint.

As a student at gunsmithing school I was taught to hold

Jeweling can be performed on surfaces other than bolts. Here, modified bolt stop spring has been jeweled to add a further distinctive embellishment.

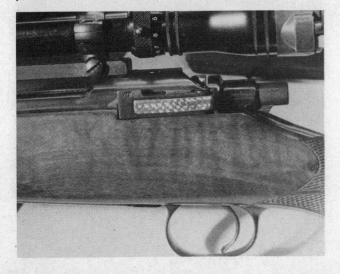

the brush down on the work and count to ten. The brush would then be lifted and moved to the next spot. After several attempts I found that the most distinct burnishing marks were created if I held the brush down for a count of fifteen (approximately fifteen seconds).

The wire brushes will have a tendency to wear and deform. It is a simple matter to fix them. Just use a bench grinder to cut off any stray ends and to true up the bottom of the bristles. Two brushes come with the B-Square jig, but it's a good idea to order some extras to avoid having to wait for them if they are ordered at a later time.

The B-Square jig is a tool that holds the bolt body between an arbor inserted into the rear of the bolt and a center pressed gently into the firing pin hole. The bolt may be seated facing in either direction to allow running the jeweling in either direction on the bolt.

To produce perfectly shaped circular burnishing marks the bolt and jig must be positioned directly under the brush in the drill press. Therefore the jig must be squared to the brush. This is accomplished by placing a straight edge in the exact position by jockeying the jig around on the press table until it is directly under the brush. The straight edge is then placed flush with the bottom edge of the jig and held in position by C-clamps at either end to eliminate any chance of movement.

With the work correctly positioned we are ready to begin jeweling. First, the lapping compound must be applied to the bolt or piece to be jeweled. Use a brush and apply plenty of compound. Cover the entire piece to be jeweled with the compound. Do not use harsh brush strokes when applying the compound as it is an abrasive and will scratch the metal.

The pattern may be begun at either end of the work. However, each succeeding row must also be started at the same end to produce the best pattern. After counting to ten or fifteen to yourself to get the desired burnishing circular effect lift the brush and move the jig just enough that the succeeding circle will half-cover the previous one.

After completing one row the jig has an indicator dial which is turned to the one-half spot mark. The next row is started from the same end as the preceding row. The marks should also overlap the burnishing marks in the row just finished. The process is continued until the entire bolt body is jeweled.

Remember to check the brush periodically to make sure the bristles are not spreading. If they are, remove the brush and squeeze the bristles back to shape with a pair of pliers and remove any irregular bristles on a grinding wheel.

After the entire area has been jeweled the lapping compound must now be removed. It should *not* be wiped off with a cloth. Remember, the compound is abrasive and will scratch the work. Remove the compound by running a strong jet of hot water over the bolt body in the sink, flushing away all excess compound. The bolt should now be oiled thoroughly and is ready to be reassembled and returned to the customer.

The B-Square jig, two brushes, and compound may be ordered at: B-Square, P.O. Box 11281, Fort Worth, TX 76109. Cost of the jig kit is $21.95, subject to change without notice.

Chapter 8

BOX MAGAZINE MODIFICATIONS

The Long, The Short And The Tall Require Changes That Are Demanding But Not Difficult

Here is a box-type magazine proportioned to fit the .30/06 Springfield cartridge immediately above it. A .375 H&H magnum cartridge is just above the .30/06 and you can see its additional length, requiring an additional elongation of the space to allow .125-inch of nose-room for the nominal 3.600-inch magnum round.

THE TWO most common magazine box modifications are shortening or lengthening them. The modification becomes necessary when rebarreling an action for either a shorter or longer cartridge. It is not a difficult gunsmithing operation and can be accomplished easily by the amateur riflesmith who follows certain guidelines. The only tools required are a hacksaw, welding torch, files, hammer, scrap steel and either a bench grinder or Dremel Moto-Tool with grinding points. The entire modification should take less than an hour to complete.

Magazine boxes may be broken down into four categories: The smallest is the short cartridge box measuring 2⅞ inches in length. It will accommodate the .22-250, .220 Swift, .225 Winchester, .243 Winchester, .257 Roberts, 6mm Remington (.244), .250 Savage, .284 Winchester, .300 Savage, .30-30 and .308 cartridges. The next size box is the .30/06 and short magnum box 3⅜ inches in length. It

is made for 6.5x55, .270 Winchester, .30/06, .30-40 Krag, 7mm/06, 7mm Remington, .300 Winchester magnum, 7mm and 8mm Mausers, .303, .308 Norma, 8mm/08, and .458 Winchester. The 3⅝-inch box is made for the standard magnum calibers such as .300 H&H, .300 Weatherby, and .375 H&H. The large magnum magazine box measures four inches to handle the .458 Ackley, .450 Watts, .416 Rigby, .475 A&M and .505 Barnes.

While the short cartridge and .30/06-length boxes allow approximately one-sixteenth-inch clearance from bullet nose to the front edge of the box, the latter two should have about one-eighth-inch clearance. Attempting to modify boxes for the .17 Remington, .22 Hornet, .218 Bee, and .222 require additional modifications in the action and should not be attempted by the amateur riflesmith.

Popular U.S. military surplus actions like the Enfield and Springfield originally were chambered for the .30/06

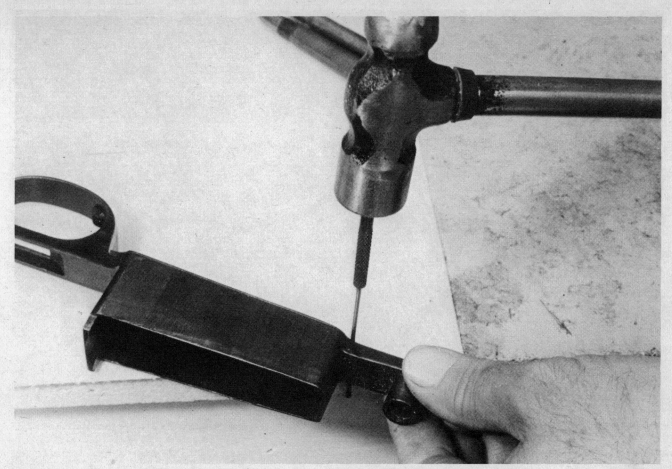

The commercial Mauser trigger guard assembly has a pin that must be driven out to remove the floor plate.

A hacksaw is used to cut sides and bottom of front wall of magazine box. A Dremel Moto-Tool with a carbide cutoff wheel likewise works well for this.

with an overall cartridge length of 3.340 inches. The 98 Mausers in 8mm measure out to 3.350 inches. Changing these actions to a magnum round such as the .375 H&H with an overall cartridge length of 3.600 inches must be accomplished by cutting the front wall of the magazine box and lengthening it sufficiently to allow a one-eighth-inch gap between bullet nose and front wall.

The task of lengthening or shortening a magazine box can be done with minimum time and effort as shown in the accompanying illustrations of Sterling Davenport lengthening a .30/06-size magazine box to accept the .375 H&H. He begins by driving out the pin holding the floor plate. (Military-style Mausers do not have this pin.) A hacksaw is used (an eighteen-tooth-per-inch blade will cut best)

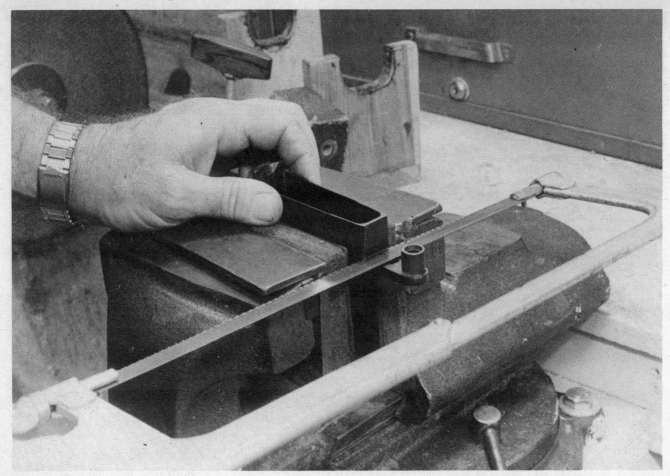

To cut the bottom of the front wall, hold the hacksaw blade flush with the upper surface of the trigger guard.

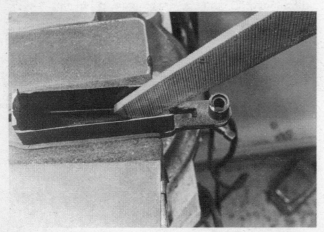

Davenport uses files to cut bevel on each sidewall to eliminate any sharp edges that may catch on bullet.

to cut away the front wall of the box. He cuts on each side of the front wall where it meets the side walls. The hacksaw then is placed flush with the upper side of the floor plate to cut the remaining section that holds the front wall.

After removing this front wall, Davenport uses a file to bevel each inner side of the box that will be joined with the new extended front wall. Be careful while doing the file work not to cut yourself on any sharp edges. The reason both areas are slightly beveled is to allow the cartridges as much additional room as possible when loaded into the magazine.

After checking that each side wall of the magazine box is exactly the same length, a piece of scrap one-sixteenth-

Using a ball peen hammer, the new front wall is bent precisely at the scribe marks.

inch steel is cut to act as the new front wall. Davenport allows about a one-quarter-inch excess material to remain above and beyond the diameter of the new wall surface. He carefully scribes the scrap steel where it meets each side wall. A hammer is used to bend the steel at each scribe line leaving enough excess material on either side to overlap each sidewall, insuring a strong weld.

To determine the additional length of the new front wall the riflesmith uses a .375 H&H cartridge as a guide. The new front wall extension then is placed in its proper location allowing an additional one-eighth-inch gap between bullet nose and wall. The front wall extension diameter is still less than that of the floor plate, an essential to proper inletting.

A piece of .0625-inch steel is used as new front wall for the magazine box.
A scribe is used to mark position so that it will mate to the sidewalls.

A chamfer is cut on each inner side of the new front wall to eliminate sharp edges and assure strong weld.

A .375 H&H magnum cartridge is held in box and used as a measuring guide to position the new front wall.

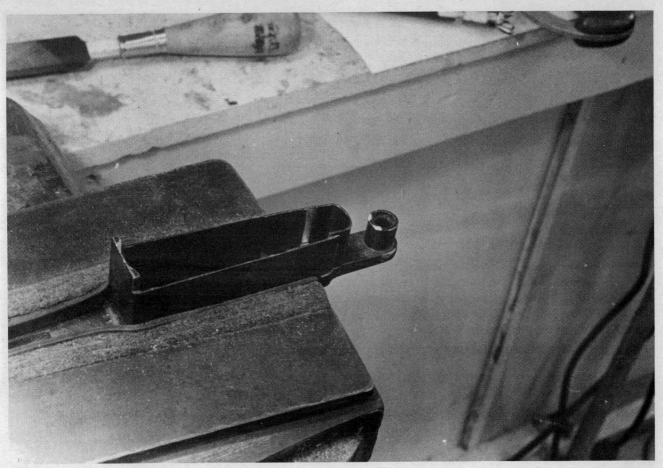

The sides of the new front wall are positioned inside the sidewalls to prevent overlap which would cause problems when inletting the trigger guard.

By keeping the sides of the new front wall extension bent just enough to be placed in position, final adjustments can be made with the new extension holding itself in place for measuring and welding.

The new front wall extension may be silver soldered, brazed, or welded in place. Davenport prefers welding to eliminate any possibility of solder or braze lines after the magazine box and floor plate are blued. A small welding tip should be used, as the steel is thin and does not require as much heat to weld as, say, a bolt handle.

Be certain during the welding operation that the weld covers the mating of the new piece with the sides of the box both inside and outside. No gaps or pits should show after the work is cleaned up.

Excess weld is removed by first hitting the work on a bench grinder. Final grinding on the outside and especially on the inside is accomplished with a Dremel Moto-Tool and grinding bit. When the extended front wall is absolutely flush with both the inner and outer walls of the magazine box, it is final polished and ready for the bluing tanks. However, it should be checked in the action to

Davenport prefers welding new front wall in place over soldering to eliminate possibility of solder lines showing after bluing. A small tip should be employed during the welding operation.

All gaps, both inside and outside of box must be filled with weld. Slag and outside surface can be cleaned up easily on bench grinder or by filing.

make certain the upper edges of the box mate perfectly with the receiver to prevent feeding problems later on. At the same time the follower and spring should be checked to make sure the firearm feeds properly.

There are other steps in converting .30/06-size magazine boxes to magnum calibers, depending on the size of the magnum round selected. The feed ramp on the receiver may have to be altered to accept the longer round as well as alteration of the follower and receiver siderails recontoured. However, modification of the box itself is as simple as cutting, filing and polishing.

When converting actions to the large four-inch magnum box the Enfield is better suited than the standard Mauser. For the Enfield the box is stretched by cutting off both the front and back walls of the box, then welding new walls in place.

During the welding phase it may be a good idea also to

The total time to lengthen the .30/06 magazine was just over thirty minutes. Final steps consist of polishing and bluing.

weld small cartridge guides in place in the magazine box to avoid deformation of soft-pointed bullets. The guides are simply supports positioned in the insides of the box just forward of the shoulder of the cartridges to hold them in place and prevent them from being thrust forward against the front wall of the magazine box during recoil. The guides may be fashioned from any small half-round strips of steel and welded just forward of the cartridge shoulder. If guides are placed on the sides of the box the follower will have to be notched to prevent the follower from catching on them. A better method is to narrow the follower from a spot just behind the guards forward.

Modifying the magazine box is an essential task in converting a barreled action to that of a magnum. The bolt face also will require being opened up, the follower must be changed, and the receiver rails and feed ramp changed to accept the new larger cartridge. Dummy rounds should be used as a final step in checking the feeding characteristics of the altered rifle.

Final contouring is best performed with a Dremel and grinding bit; quite handy for cleanup inside box.

Chapter 9

CUSTOM ALTERATION OF THE REMINGTON M700 RECOIL LUG

A Gain In Good Looks Without Slightest Sacrifice In Strength Of The Rifle

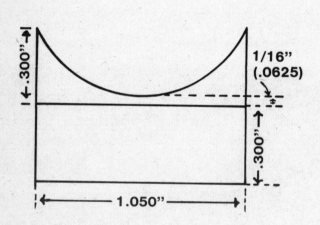

THE REMINGTON Model 700 center-fire rifle is one of the finest bolt-action rifles ever produced. The design of the action is strong, reliable, and has established a reputation for its smooth feeding characteristics. It has a fine trigger mechanism which lends itself well to both hunting and target shooting. Made in ADL, BDL, Classic, Varmint Special, and 700C Custom grades it can be ordered in a myriad of caliber preference from the .17 Rem, through .458 Win magnum. It is one of the most popular rifles in the medium-priced field because of its proven performance and outstanding overall design features.

Although manufactured by Remington Arms as a sporter rifle, the military has taken note of its toughness and reliability. There are many modified M700s in service today used as long-range sniper rifles. Gale McMillan, a gunsmith based in Phoenix, Arizona, has obtained excellent results building special one-thousand-yard sniper

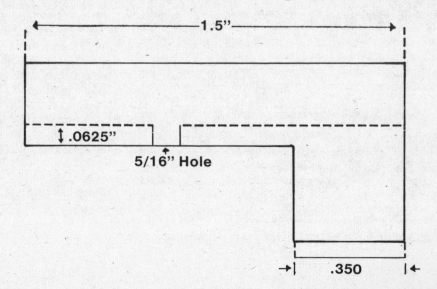

Changing the recoil lug system on the Model 700 to that of the Mauser requires machining a steel block to match radius of the 700's receiver. Front portion of underside of block is cut away to leave a Mauser-type lug. A hole is drilled to allow the guard screw to pass through the lug for attachment to the 700 receiver.

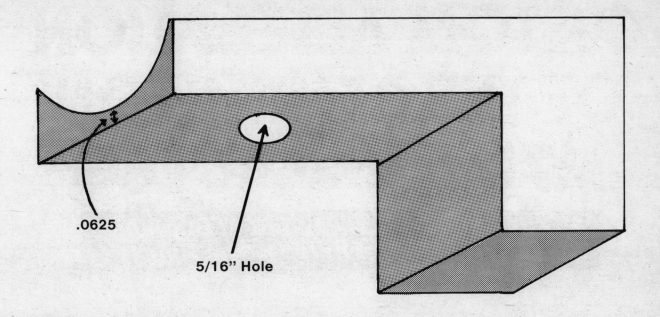

.0625

5/16" Hole

Sterling Davenport's Mauser-type recoil lug alteration on the Remington Model 700 is accomplished without a loss in bedding strength and it allows the new barreled action to take on more traditional classic lines often desired.

rifles for the military for the past several years. It is one of the few actions that commands a place next to the legendary Mauser Model 98 and the Winchester Model 70.

The Remington Model 700 is quite popular within the inner circle of top custom riflesmiths. Generally speaking, when customizing the 700 certain custom accessories are added. Most riflesmiths prefer to restock the gun, add Jantz Model 70 type safeties, machined triggerguards and floor plates, and possibly classic-style bolt handles. Additional smoothing of the action is also standard procedure for conscientious smiths. This work, however, is performed on all factory rifles, regardless of manufacture, to bring the firearm to a custom state-of-the-art level.

During one of my frequent visits to Sterling Davenport's shop in Tucson I spied a most unusual-looking Model 700 barreled action on his bench awaiting re-stocking. Instead of the factory spacer ring between receiver and barrel,

which also acts as the recoil lug, this particular action featured a much thicker recoil lug, more resembling a Mauser lug system.

This 700 hybrid intrigued me. After a bit of questioning Sterling was quick to point out that the Remington recoil lug system was quite sound. Any rifled action chambered for the .458 Win magnum had better be. However, Davenport preferred building custom 700s without the spacer ring between receiver and barrel more for cosmetic reasons. He felt his system resulted in producing a gun more along the accepted classic lines of the Mauser and Model 70.

Although Sterling emphasized the fact that he altered the Remington 700 recoil lug system more for looks than anything else, it was obvious that his much thicker recoil lug system should be a least equal to that of the factory-type lug.

Davenport also mentioned that a few other custom riflesmiths employed this custom feature on Model 700s

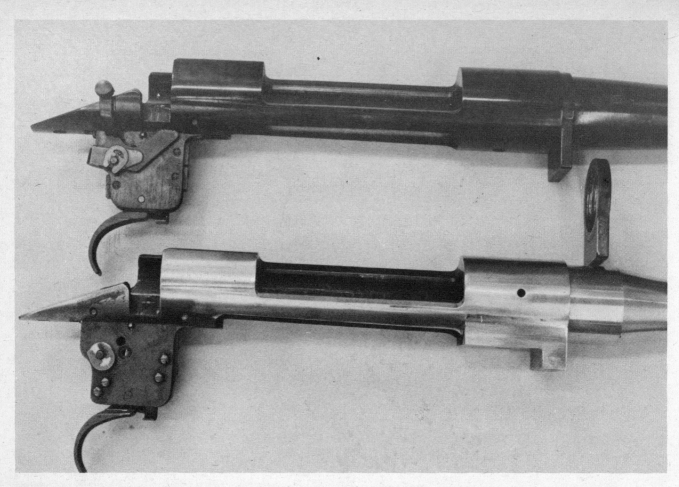

Above: Action at top is standard Remington 700 with its factory spacer ring lug. Beneath it, action is installed with new Mauser-type lug. Custom 700 has new barrel with classic-style barrel shoulder butting the receiver ring. (Below) End mill cutter was used to cut radius in steel block. Note increased bearing surface of Mauser-type lug.

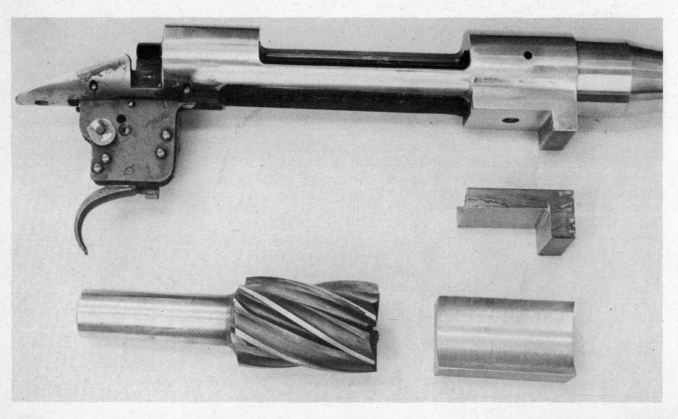

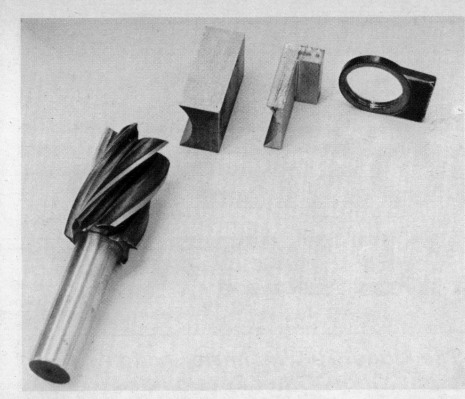

A 1-23/64-inch mill cutter is used to contour the block of steel to mate with bottom receiver ring. The block is further machined, heli-arc welded in place to complete the custom lug alteration.

and deferred from taking credit for this excellent innovation.

I like it. Although I've conducted no comparative strength tests between Remington's factory recoil lug and Davenport's Mauser-type, common sense and just one look at the massive lug leads me to believe it has to be extremely strong. Also, like Davenport, I feel getting rid of the spacer ring improves the overall looks of a custom 700.

Sterling feels that this Mauser-type recoil lug system looks and works better when fitting a new barrel to the Remington 700 action. If the spacer ring were to be removed and the same barrel used it would be necessary to cut off an amount from the chamber end of the barrel; an amount equal to the diameter of the spacer ring, re-thread, chamber, and headspace it to fit. Since the factory Remington barrel has a small shoulder to begin with, you would actually be losing the aesthetic appearance we are trying to gain.

It is best to fit a new barrel with a larger shoulder to the action. It will make for a stronger receiver-barrel relationship and enhance the rifle's custom lines.

Fitting a Mauser-type recoil lug to the Model 700 involves radiusing a solid block of steel to mate with the bottom of the receiver. The block is then cut to desired lug configuration, drilled to allow the guard screw to enter the receiver, heliarc welded to the receiver, and sent out to be checked and re-heat-treated if necessary.

Davenport begins by truing up a solid piece of steel to 1.5 inches long by 1.050 inches wide by .625 inch deep. It is then placed on a mill and the top radiused using an end mill cutter. To determine the proper size cutter the diameter of the Model 700 receiver ring is measured. It is 1.355 inches in diameter. A 1-23/64-inch (1.3594) cutter will work quite well. The cut is made approximately .300-inch deep.

After radiusing the block is then repositioned on the mill to cut the flat on the bottom of the block. By removing .300-inch depth a length of 1.150 inches we will be left with a lug surface approximately .350 inch in diameter by .300 inch deep. This large amount of bearing surface against the stock will guarantee an exceptionally strong recoil lug system.

The next step is to measure the distance from the front receiver ring back to the center of the guard screw hole in the receiver. This hole accepts a ¼-28NF screw. We now measure this same distance back on our Mauser-type machined lug from the front edge of the lug and mark the spot with a punch. The hole should be drilled oversize to allow the guard screw to pass through into the receiver without binding. A 5/16-inch drill bit or larger will suffice.

A ¼-28-tpi-threaded screw is now employed to hold the new recoil lug piece flush to the bottom of the receiver. The unit is now heliarc welded together for a permanent bond.

After all welding has been completed, the work is ready to be cleaned up and shipped off to check hardness and be heat treated again, if necessary.

Replacement of the factory spacer ring recoil lug arrangement with this Mauser-type lug system requires considerable amount of machining, time, and expense. If re-heat-treating is necessary that will have to be borne by the customer. Since the original recoil lug system has proven quite satisfactory in the field, even in the heaviest of magnum calibers, the purpose of this operation is definitely slanted toward cosmetic appeal. However, any customer having his favorite Remington Model 700 converted to full custom mode may wish to consider this unique custom option. It does result in a rifle with a more traditional classic appearance with an extremely strong recoil lug system.

Chapter 10

SHORTER CAN BE BETTER

Shortening The Model 70 Winchester Action Reduces Weight, Offers Other Possibilities

A FELLOW gun writer questioned why a riflesmith would want to modify a perfectly good action when all you really had to do was install a magazine block to accommodate a smaller cartridge.

Actually, there are a number of reasons to tackle such a project. The modified action will be lighter by about four to five ounces and features a shorter bolt-throw. Shortening the Winchester Model 70 action results in a unique,

custom rifle built on one of the finest actions ever designed. And it allows the riflesmith to experiment and perfect his craft. It could even end up as a prototype for a whole new breed of short-stroke, lightweight Winchester Model 70s!

All work on this modification was performed by Joe Reid, an immensely talented gunsmith residing in Tucson, Arizona. This particular Model 70 action is being chambered for the popular 7mm/08 Remington cartridge. This cartridge, based on the .308 Winchester case,

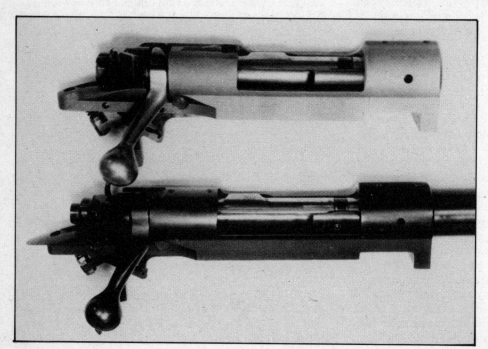

The unique custom-shortened Model 70 action, top, still in the white, with a standard Model 70 action for comparison.

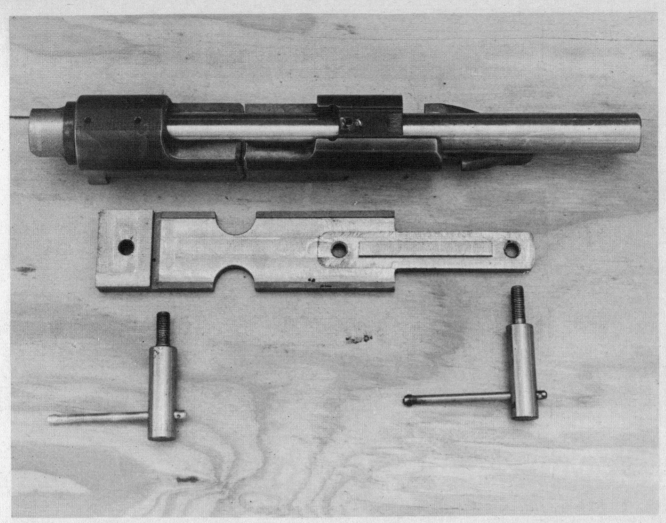

Mandrel is inserted through receiver ring. It is threaded in front of the shoulder at 16 threads per inch (tpi) at a major diameter of .975-inch for a length of .800-inch and screwed into threads of the receiver. The shaft diameter is .700-inch, enabling it to slip past the receiver ring and bridge inner walls. The portion of the mandrel butting against the receiver is tapered with flat sides machined into it to assure good holding power in the three-jaw lathe chuck. It is approximately 1½ inches from shoulder edge to tip and the entire mandrel is about ten inches in length, allowing it to be set between centers on the lathe. The guard screws have been threaded ¼-32 tpi. The jig is seven inches long with holes for guard screws to match shorter action. The half-moon notches allow welding while entire unit is held in the jig to prevent warping or misalignment.

has been found outstanding for metallic silhouette competition and a more than adequate big-game round. After all metal work was completed it was stocked by Sterling Davenport for his personal collection.

Shortening the Model 70 action involves cutting and shortening the receiver, bolt, firing pin, firing pin spring, as well as the magazine box and floor plate. Neither the ejector nor extractor require shortening. All parts requiring shortening are cut down exactly one-half-inch.

It has always been much easier for me to learn how to do something by standing over someone's shoulder and watching him do it first. Reading a lot of technical data invariably puts me to sleep. I guess that means I'm visual-minded, but most of my gunsmithing associates feel the same way. Hence I have photographed each step in performing this task. Appropriate instructions are included for those who would like to attempt this particular job. Similar techniques can be employed to shorten other popular actions like the 98 Mauser.

The pre-1964 Model 70 action with special mandrel inserted through the bridge and receiver to assure accurate alignment during the shortening process.

The mandrel-mounted receiver is secured in the lathe with the three-jaw headstock chuck holding the jig shoulder and the tailstock in the counterbore in the bridge end of the mandrel. The initial cut will be made at the point of the inner shoulder on the wall of the receiver. This shoulder prevents cartridges from shifting forward and deforming the bullet tips during recoil. By making the cut here, it greatly simplifies later cleanup and helps to make the traces of the modification less obvious, perhaps even undetectable.

A second mark is scribed .500-inch to the rear of the first, as above.

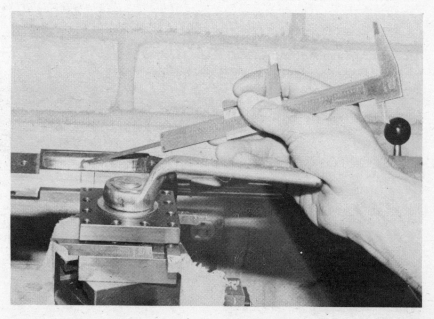

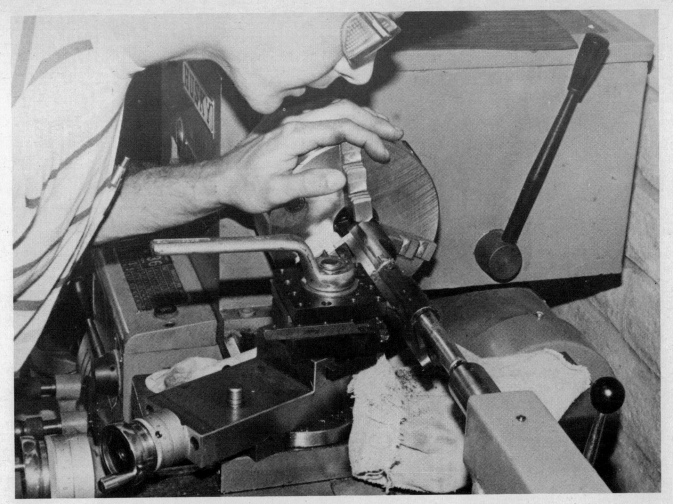

The parting of the two side rails is performed with a cut-off tool bit. The lathe should be operated at a slow speed; either first or second speed in back gear. Reid does not cut all the way through the receiver, but leaves about 1/16-inch of material to be removed at final separation as depicted later here.

Cutting oil is applied liberally during the parting operation. It is important to keep the cutter progressing through the steel receiver to prevent it from work-hardening and dulling the cutter.

After the first cut has been made, Reid uses vernier calipers to establish the mark for the second cut precisely .500-inch from the first cut. If steel is too hard, it can be cut with abrasive wheel; a safer approach than annealing the area.

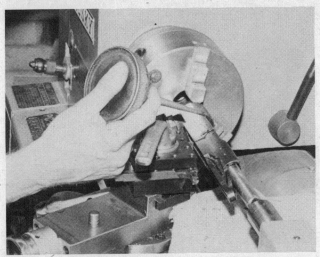

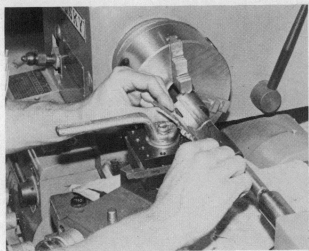

Both cuts have now been made. The second cut was widened slightly to achieve an exact .500-inch dimension. The towel serves to catch chips and simplify subsequent cleanup of the lathe bed area.

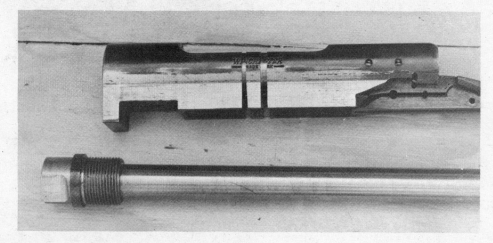

After initial slotting, workpiece is removed from lathe and the mandrel is taken out to permit the final cutting of the receiver.

This particular Model 70 permitted use of a power hacksaw. If steel is too hard, it can ruin the blade. In such instances, an abrasive cut-off wheel can be used for final cutting.

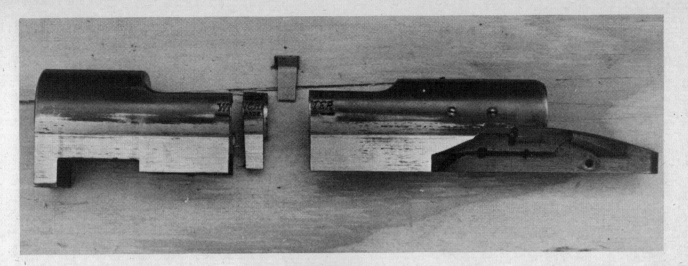

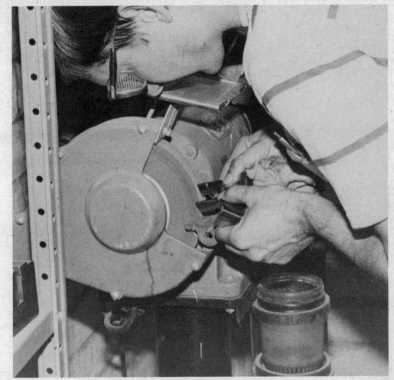

Photo above shows .500-inch sections of receiver walls removed. Right, a grinding wheel is used to remove rough edges after cutting. The sides are trued up and a deeply beveled angle is ground on both pieces to assure ample weld penetration during that phase.

Unfortunately, the location of the Winchester trademark makes it a casualty of the modification. Note the deep bevel of receiver edges. A perfect weld must be made to assure maximum strength of the finished receiver.

Joe Reid has put both halves back on the mandrel and has attached the jig to the underside of the receiver. This arrangement assures perfect alignment between the two halves for the welding operation. The mandrel is removed after having served to align halves for the securing jig to bypass welding problems.

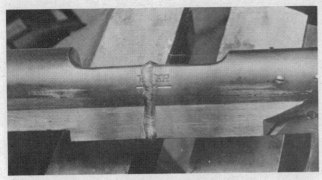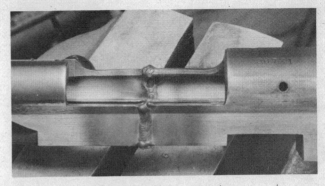

In the two photos above, the inner and outer walls of the receiver after heli-arc welding. Areas not to be welded should be wrapped with wet cloths to prevent overheating and softening of metal in lug recesses and similar critical places. Heat-Stop, a product from Brownell's, works effectively to prevent problem. Reid recommends using either 4120, 4130, or 4140 mild steel welding rod for this operation. It will accept bluing better, showing no telltale weld lines. It is important that weld be perfect with no low spots.

Here Reid is using 4130 welding rod to fill in the remaining letters of the Winchester trademark on receiver.

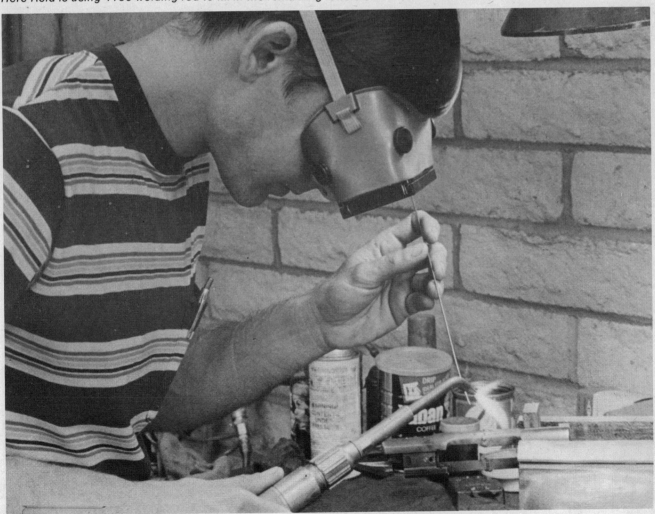

A grinding wheel removes excess weld from sides of receiver. Wearing safety glasses is mandatory!

After welding, first step is to clean welding scale from the receiver, using a sandblasting setup.

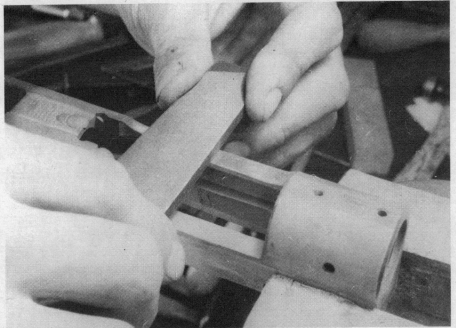

External surfaces are trued up, using a file, as here.

Hold work solidly in vise for finish filing. As filework brings weld down flush with receiver, any wobble will cause scraped receiver surface and that will entail additional work later.

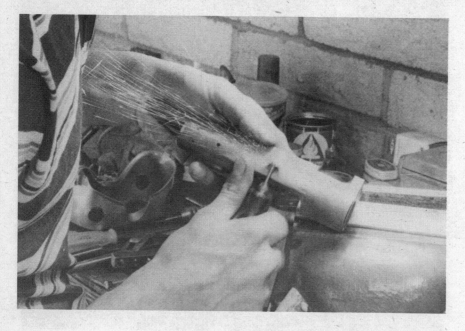

After filing, Dremel Moto-Tool and carbide cut-off wheel at an angle cleans and trues up welded surface.

The carbide cut-off wheel is indispensible for removing the high spots, as here.

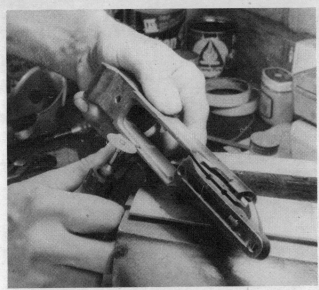
Inner surfaces of receiver walls are also first cleaned up with cut-off wheel in the Dremel Moto-Tool.

There is no avoiding hand work. Small three-sided file is employed to remove weld along left siderail.

After all of the weld is cleaned up, Reid sets the receiver up in the milling machine. He levels work in a vise, using square measured off flat underside of receiver and recoil lug. The bottom sides of the receiver are trued up with end mill cutter.

Here, the flat sides of the receiver are being trued up in the milling machine.

A special tool is used to recut the ledge that supports the cartridge shoulder in the magazine. The tool is a radius cutter, available from most industrial outlets. It would be best to take the receiver to the outlet to measure the existing shoulder to determine exact specifications needed for the cutter on the given rifle.

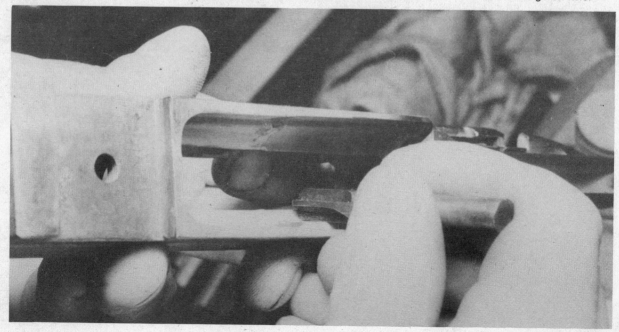

Above, with the radius cutter chucked up in the mill, the receiver wall shoulder is recut. Left, final contouring of shoulder is done with Dremel and carbide deburring tool bit.

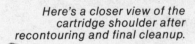

Here's a closer view of the cartridge shoulder after recontouring and final cleanup.

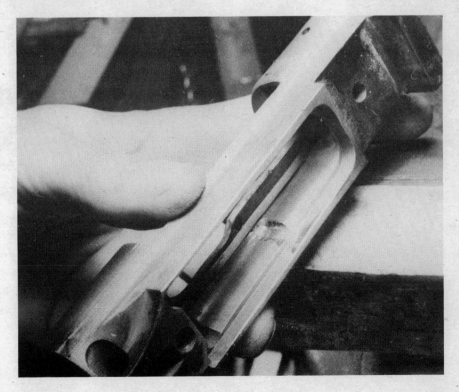

Reid uses a portable drill with a strip of 180-grit Aloxite attached to the shank for final polish of shoulder.

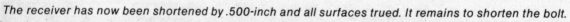

The receiver has now been shortened by .500-inch and all surfaces trued. It remains to shorten the bolt.

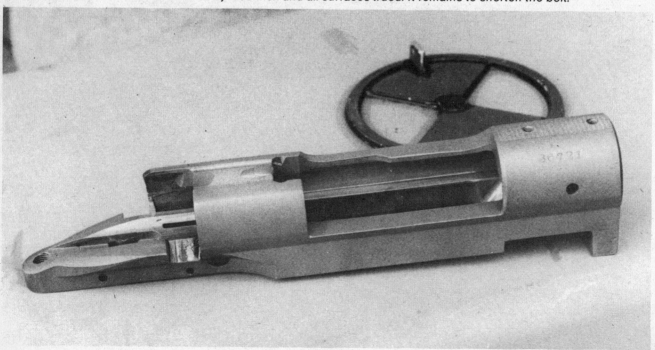

THE GUN DIGEST BOOK OF RIFLESMITHING

Here are the bolt and firing-pin assemblies, both of which must be shortened by precisely the same .500-inch dimension, then rejoined by the use of hi-temp silver solder in perfect alignment.

The bolt is secured in the lathe headstock, using a bolt plug. The plug is held in the three-jaw chuck, with the tailstock centered in the firing pin hole. Since the bolt face will be faced off later, as standard practice when rebarreling to a new caliber, there is no need to worry about damaging the hole. Vernier calipers are used to measure from the edge of the extractor collar slot closest to the bolt handle back exactly .500-inch and marked with scribe. Reid simply turns on lathe and lets caliper points drag to establish the lines. Cutting this area is best because it's back from the lugs. It avoids drawing lug temper when rejoining. Also, bolt diameter is greater behind lugs than in front. Gas port is in the segment removed and that necessary feature will be replaced at a later point in the operation.

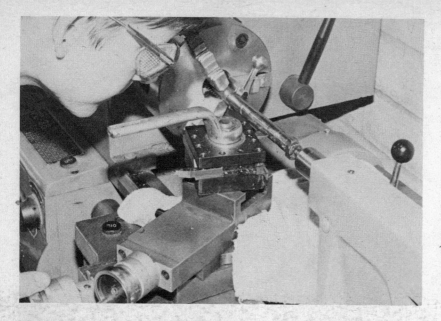

Index line is made with sharp tool bit with bolt in lathe. Motor is not turned on, but headstock is rotated by hand to establish first mark, then a second line is made a trifle more than .500-inch to the rear of first line. The front of the extractor collar slot is locating point for the first line.

Diameter of extractor collar slot is .618-inch. Reid begins by cutting bolt down to this diameter between the two lines, then uses a cut-off tool to cut the bolt almost through.

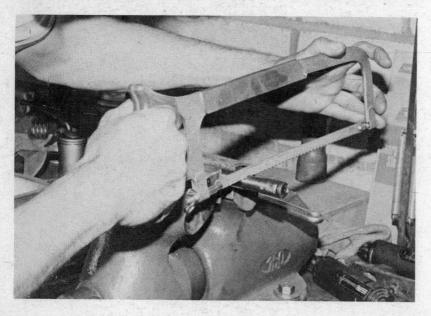

After removing bolt from lathe, final parting is done with hacksaw.

After parting, main body is held in headstock with bolt plug and a steady rest positioned about one-half inch from other end. Rough edges and tool marks are trued, edge squared and ready for internal cut to be made.

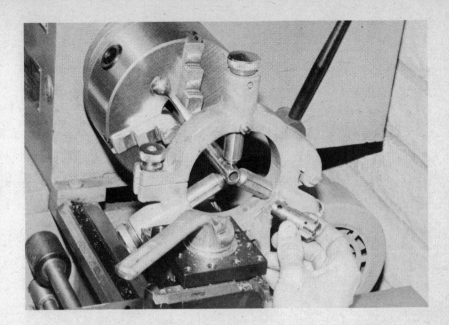

A boring bar is used to bore the end of the bolt to a diameter of .618-inch plus approximately .0005-inch more for easier fit of the two pieces. Depth of inner cut is exactly .5100-inch. The additional .010-inch allows for silver solder used in joining.

The bolt body is continuously checked with a feeler gauge until exact inside diameter has been cut with the boring tool bit.

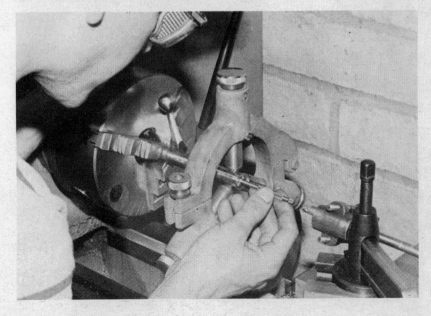

A closer look at the two parts of the bolt to be joined together after being shortened by one-half inch. Note index marks on both pieces to assure perfect realignment. After hi-temp soldering, the gas port hole will be recut, using a .125-inch drill bit for the starting hole and a carbide deburring tool to enlarge the opening back to the original 3/16-inch diameter.

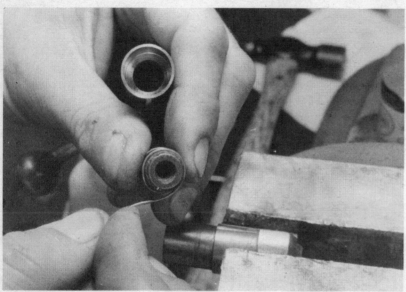

The Model 70 bolt is now ready for hi-temp soldering. Reid uses a mandrel smaller in diameter than the .618-inch body hole, making it easier to place the coiled solder in the bolt body cavity, as here.

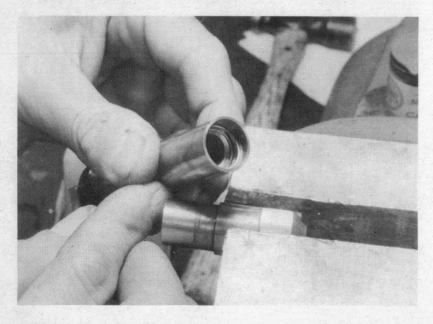

The coiled hi-temp wire solder is placed in the bolt body cavity, taking particular care to get one complete coil flush with the inner edge to assure maximum bonding strength between the two pieces.

With the coil of wire solder in place, flux is applied with a brush to both surfaces being joined.

After sliding front part into main bolt body, extractor collar is used to verify proper diameter of the new extractor collar slot.

Take pains to assure perfect alignment of the two index lines. This is important in getting parts to fit the receiver.

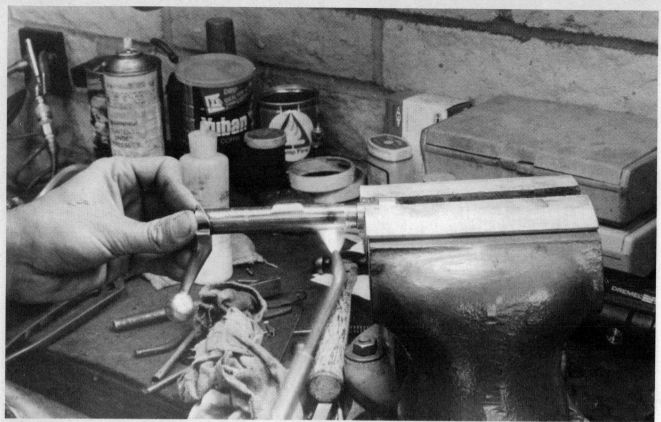

Reid applies heat from welding torch to main bolt body to solder both pieces into a permanent bond. If Brownell's Heat-Stop compound is not available, make certain both bolt lugs are seated in the vise with aluminum or brass soft jaws in vertical position during heating. The jaws act to draw the heat away, thus avoiding heat damage to the locking lugs. Solder will run from its seat to edge of the extractor collar slot. A line of solder will be visible entirely around the juncture if a perfect solder job has been achieved. Below, before removing bolt from vise after soldering, check straightness of the job, using a straightedge. Top edge of bolt, guide lug and edge of recoil lug should be in line and entire bolt straight as a plumb line. If this is not the case, it will be necessary to reheat and realign until these conditions are met.

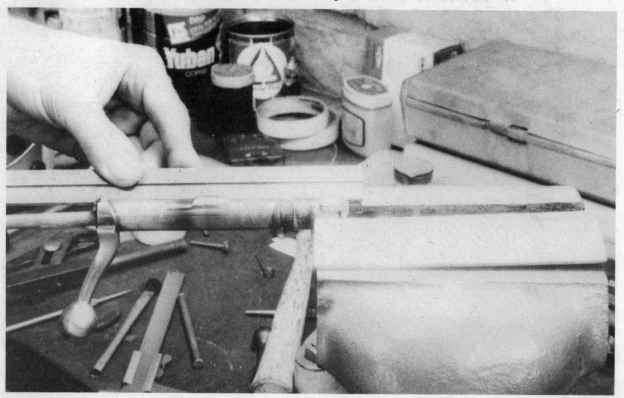

After soldering and alignment are accomplished, the inside of the bolt must be cleaned up to remove any high spots created by solder at joining edges. This is easily accomplished using portable drill and shank with 180-grit Aloxite paper.

The bolt is then placed back in the lathe. Reid uses a bolt-facing tool — available from Brownell's — to true up the bolt face. This guarantees the face will be perfectly perpendicular to the bolt and bore axis.

Here's a better look at the bolt-facing tool from Brownell's, as removed from tool post of lathe.

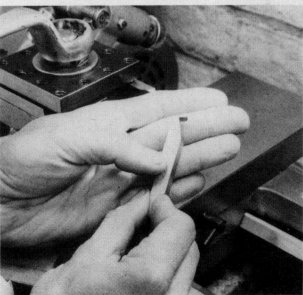

With the bolt positioned in the lathe, the extractor collar slot and leading edge are cleaned of excess solder.

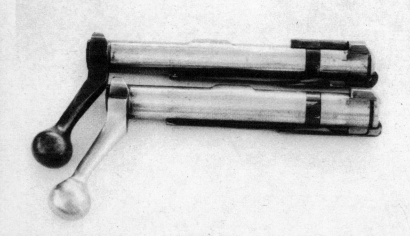

Bolt of the Model 70 has now been shortened. It's shown beneath an unmodified bolt for comparison.

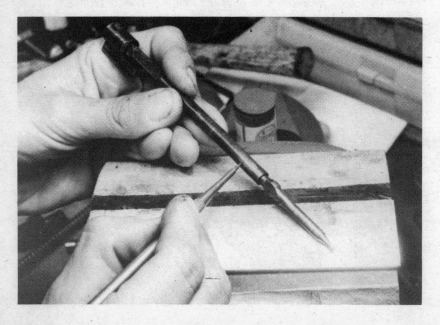

The next step is the shortening of the firing pin by the same half-inch distance. Measurement is taken from the edge of the small-diameter ring located behind the mainspring detent, as indicated by scribe tip.

The firing pin must be shortened ½" in length. The pin is cut to a minor diameter of .212" matching the diameter of the firing pin spring detent on the firing pin. The cut is begun at the rear edge of the spring detent.

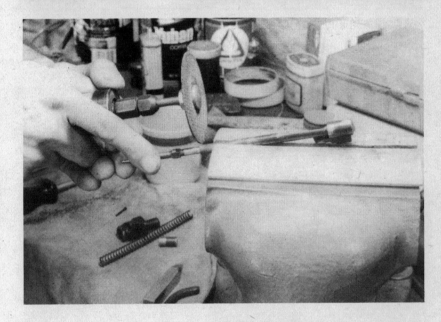

The steel in the firing pin is quite hard but a carbide cut-off wheel cuts it easily.

After cutting, it's obvious the main body needs to be put in the lathe and faced off.

The steel in the firing pin proved to be too hard to cut the inner diameter of the main body to fit the front portion of the pin and it had to be annealed.

Since it's important the metal cool slowly, Reid lays a piece of pine wood on the vise with the pin on top of it. He heats the pin to dull red, also heating the wood, with suitable fire precautions.

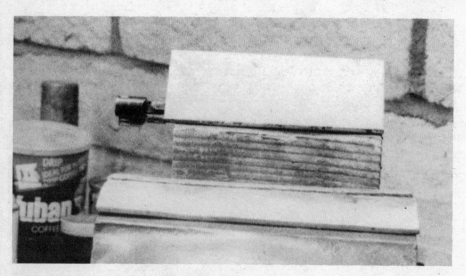

A piece of angle iron is placed over the pin to aid in retaining heat and delaying its cooling.

During cutting the .212-inch inner diameter in the firing pin main body, lathe is run slowly and a sharp bit is used. Bit must be advanced into the work continually or steel will work-harden, resulting in an undesirable dulling of the bit.

Cut end of the smaller piece must be beveled for easier insertion into the main body of pin. Mating surfaces are fluxed and solder is coiled and inserted in main body cavity to its leading edge.

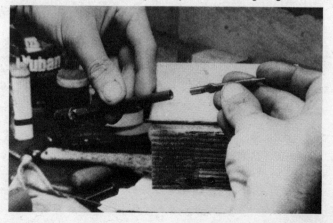

A good way to check exact shortened length of pin is to take overall length before alteration, join parts and do another check, shifting small piece slightly as needed. Indexing lines as on bolt body aren't needed since firing pin needn't be rotationally realigned. Here, welding torch is being used to apply needed heat.

Here's the completed project beneath an unmodified Model 70 action for comparison. It is also necessary to shorten the floorplate and magazine box. Magazine box alteration is illustrated elsewhere here. Box, however, should be cut at the rear, shortened by one-half inch and the back side placed back into position and welded in place. Altering the floorplate is quite simple. Just cut off the rear tang portion closest to the trigger guard by .500-inch. The finished result after cleaning up the work will make the floorplate similar to the custom straddle floorplates currently enjoying some degree of popularity.

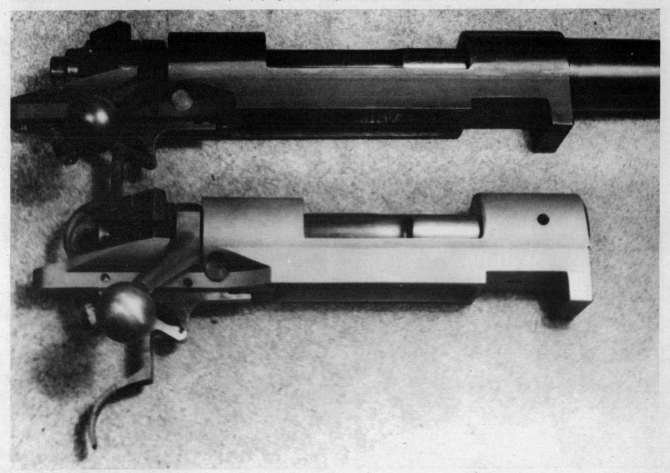

Chapter 11

METAL CHECKERING

This Technique Offers Functional And Aesthetically Pleasing Additions To Any Custom Rifle

METAL CHECKERING is a job frequently required in custom riflesmithing. A checkered bolt handle knob affords the shooter a better grip than an uncheckered knob, while metal checkering the receiver bridge or a front ramp sight greatly reduces reflected light. Pistolsmiths checker the mainspring housing and frontstrap on the .45 ACP for a more secure grip. It is also an eye-appealing custom option desired by the majority of the shooting fraternity.

Metal checkering, like wood checkering, requires experience and practice, but is a task that can be mastered by the amateur. Of the two popular styles, the first method involves cutting parallel lines in one direction with the crossing parallel lines made at a ninety-degree angle to create hundreds of pointed squares. The second method is similar to wood checkering as the second set of parallel lines are cut across the first at about a thirty-degree angle making pointed diamonds. Bolt handle knobs and other rifle parts involve a much smaller area than wood checkering, so there is less possibility of getting off track with increasingly curved lines destroying the overall appearance.

The square-cut pattern is easier for the amateur, as the work can be set up in a vise at the proper angle just below the surface of the top of the vise jaws. The metal checkering file then may be set against the inside wall of the jaw and used as a secure guide. It is the initial lines that deter-

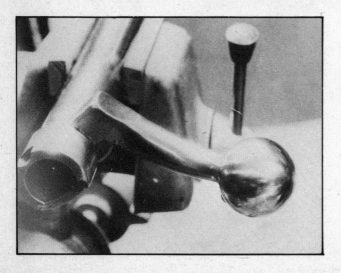

Bolt should be polished carefully prior to checkering.

Dykem is applied to bolt handle and a circle pattern is drawn, using a scribe.

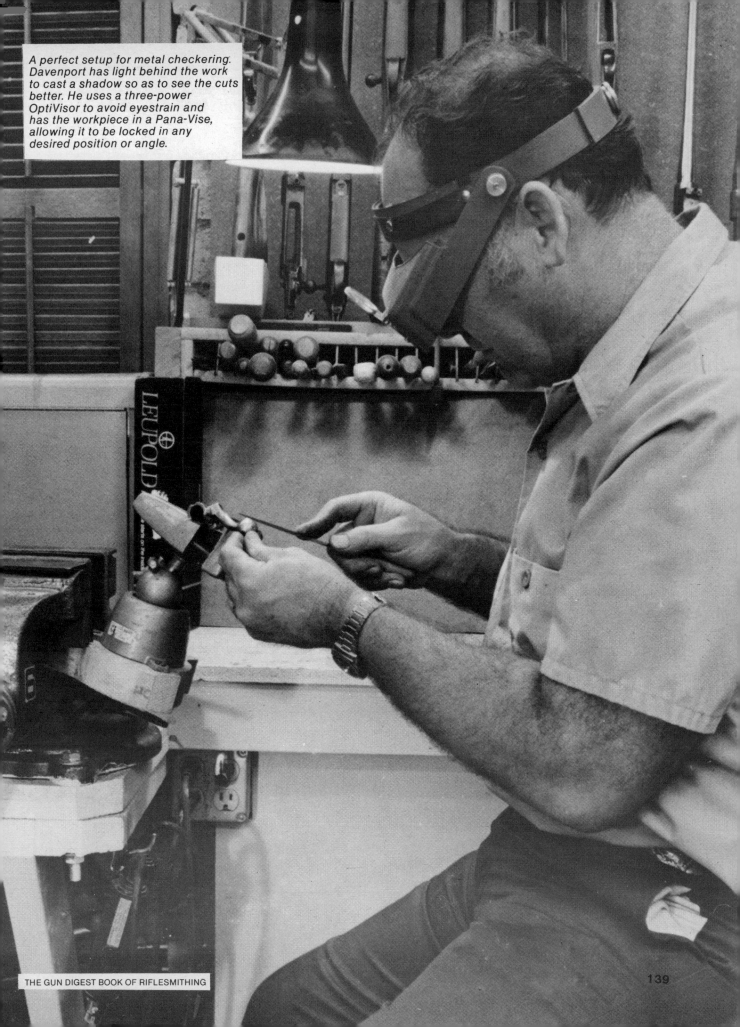

A perfect setup for metal checkering. Davenport has light behind the work to cast a shadow so as to see the cuts better. He uses a three-power OptiVisor to avoid eyestrain and has the workpiece in a Pana-Vise, allowing it to be locked in any desired position or angle.

A triangular file is used to deepen the boundary to full depth. Take care to apply pressure on file into area to be checkered. Should file slip, scratches will not show after checkering is completed.

mine the overall straightness of the pattern. After cutting all the lines in one direction, the work may be shifted in the vise ninety degrees and the set of crossing parallel lines again may be cut with the inside of the jaw as a guide.

Metal checkering files may be ordered through Brownells to anywhere from twenty to seventy-five lines per inch. The more course the file, the better the gripping power. Any checkering over thirty lines per inch becomes more a matter of cosmetics, but still will reduce reflected light effectively.

It may be wise for the amateur to begin his metal checkering with the easier-to-use twenty lines per inch file. Wooden tool handles should be used with metal checkering files to eliminate the possibility of an accident with the tang of the file. The handle also affords a better grip for applying pressure for the file to cut faster.

A small triangular file also is necessary for metal checkering to cut each line to its full depth and to point up the diamonds or squares. It is a good idea to stone or grind smooth one face of the file. Thus both edges may be sharpened to permit a finer cut when pointing up the work.

A Pana-Vise or the new Versa-Vise from Brownell's can be invaluable when checkering curved surfaces. The work must be turned constantly and tilted to run parallel lines over a curved surface. It is much simpler to turn and tilt the vise than to attempt to move the work to accomplish the same purpose.

Metal checkering over a curved surface is more difficult than over a flat surface, but can be achieved with professional results if the craftsman takes his time. Each line should be cut carefully and checked for straightness

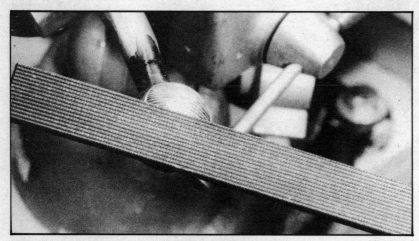

As each line is cut from the centerline toward the worker, the checkering file's top edge is used as a guide with the prior cut line to keep each cut parallel.

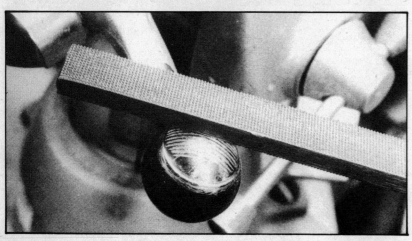

When making cuts away from the centerline and checkering the bottom, left edge of the file is used to make cuts and kept parallel with the prior cuts.

After the first set of parallel cuts have been made they are cut to depth and to the boundary line, using a triangular file.

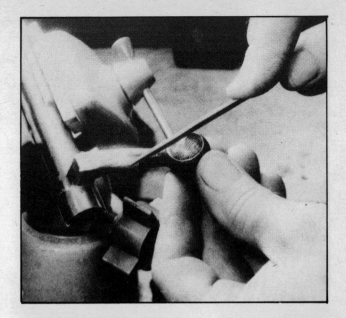

before moving to the next line. Sterling Davenport uses a three-power OptiVisor to better view the work, although a magnifying glass may be substituted.

Before checkering is begun on the bolt handle knob a purple-blue layout fluid called Dykem is applied to the surface and allowed to dry.

Davenport then uses a scribe to draw a circle pattern. If the amateur has trouble drawing a circle freehand, cutting a round piece of tape to be used as a template will work well. After outlining the desired pattern with a scribe the boundary line is cut with a triangular file. The line is cut with a short back-and-forth sawing motion. It is important to apply pressure inward toward the center of the circle during cutting. Until the line is cut to its initial depth the file will tend to slip on the smooth, rounded surface of the knob. Should it skip out of the line it may skid across the surface, but later checkering will erase any scratches.

To act as a guide, a piece of tape may be stretched across the center of the area to be checkered. The line then is cut using a triangular file. The tape then is removed and all parallel lines are cut within the circular pattern line. Do not attempt to cut to the edge with the checkering file. The lines will be extended using the triangular file and cut to full depth.

After the center-line has been drawn, Davenport revealed a trick to keep each line parallel when using the metal checkering file. Moving right to left from the center-line, Davenport makes each cut with the exact right-hand edge of the file. By looking at the preceding line already established and keeping the edge of the file parallel to that line succeeding lines are spaced more evenly. When cutting the lines from the center-line left to right he uses the left edge of the file.

After all lines have been cut in one direction the tri-

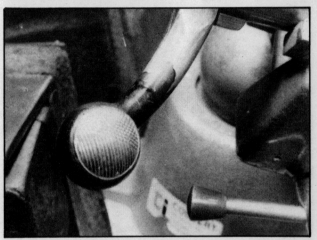

To establish the thirty-degree crossing master line, a piece of tape should be used as a guide. It is then removed and the checkering file is used to make cuts and kept parallel with the preceding cuts.

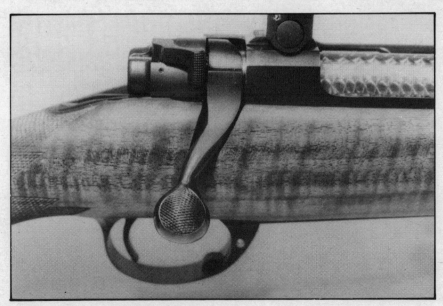

After checkering, the bolt may be blued or left in the white. The checkering does assist the shooter in getting a better grip on the bolt handle knob and adds a handsome custom touch to the rifle.

Bolt stop at left has standard release lever. Release lever at right is result of checkering a piece of cold-rolled steel then soldering and fitting it flush to the bolt stop.

Release lever for bolt stop is fashioned from piece of cold-rolled steel 3/32x¾ inches in cross-section and ground to contour of a right triangle.

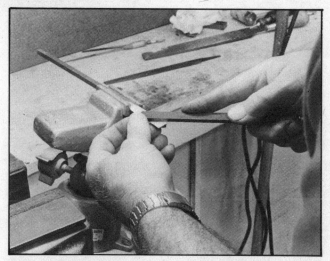

First series of parallel lines are cut at approximate thirty-degree angle with a checkering file.

angular file is used to cut to the boundary line. If one works slowly and carefully there should be no overruns. If a mistake is made, it can later be polished out and the line crossing the boundary recut.

To cut the parallel lines in the crossing angle, again lay a piece of tape across the first set of lines to act as a guide. The angle should be approximately thirty degrees. They then are cut to depth, using the same techniques described earlier.

It is recommended for both gripping and aesthetics that a matching circle be cut and checkered on the reverse side of the knob. Although checkering over a cur-

After cutting crossing lines with the checkering file, a triangular file cuts checkering to depth and points up the diamonds.

After checkering is completed, cut off the checkered portion about ¼-inch longer than necessary. It will be ground to fit later.

ved surface looks a bit difficult it is one of the simpler jobs for either amateur or professional and does add a custom touch to any rifle.

After learning to checker a curved surface doing the same on a flat surface is even simpler. Davenport alters Mauser bolt stops and metal checkers them as an option on many of his custom rifles. He begins by taking a piece of 3/32x¾-inch cold-rolled steel and grinds it down on one side until the metal is reduced to a right angle triangle in shape. He then makes a series of parallel lines at a thirty-degree angle beginning at the edge of the newly ground steel. It does not matter how far from the edge he continues the lines as it will be cut later to fit the bolt stop.

Using a piece of tape to cut the master line crossing the first set of parallel linnes again is completed, using a triangular file. After running all the parallel lines in the crossing diamond pattern with the metal checkering file (in this case a forty line per inch model) and finished with the triangular file to full depth we are ready to cut off the new custom bolt stop release lever with a hacksaw. The piece will be slightly under one-half-inch in length when we solder it to the top of the bolt stop, but it is better to leave it a bit long.

The old semi-circular bolt stop lever is ground off using a bench grinder. The top of the bolt stop then is filed to eliminate any high or low spots.

The new checkered lever is now positioned on the top of the bolt stop and silver soldered in place. Don't worry that it is a bit oversize. After soldering, it will be ground and filed flush on all sides to match the bolt stop. That's all there is to it.

This additional touch gives the rifle an added custom feature and is much more functional than the standard bolt stop lever. Davenport informed me that this style custom touch is called a Brno release.

The checkered Brno-style release affords secure surface for operating bolt stop and adds a pleasant custom touch to the completed rifle.

Chapter 12

RESTYLING TRIGGER GUARDS

With Care, Patience And The Right Equipment, A Resculptured Guard Can Add To The Elegance Of The Finished Job

STYLING OR recontouring a trigger guard is not a difficult gunsmithing task, but will do much to add to the graceful lines of a custom rifle. Styling military trigger guards will do much to improve upon their rather massive and squared design. The particular shape modification is up to the individual, but for the sake of strength and appearance one should have a good idea of what the final result will look like before he begins the project.

There is only so much metal that can be removed from a trigger guard from a strength standpoint. The guard does perform the function of guarding the trigger from external obstructions and damage if the firearm should be dropped against a hard surface. Therefore it is important to improve upon the lines without lessening its safety functions.

The tools required to perform the job of styling the guard are quite basic. A flat file, a half-round file, scribe, Dykem marking fluid, dividers, flexible straightedge or masking tape, a vise with soft jaws, and various grits of wet-or-dry paper will do the job. However, a Dremel Moto-Tool with two or three carbide cutoff wheels is excellent for cutting the guard to a new shape and for all initial rough contouring.

I do prefer to leave the front of the guard in its original width, only contouring the edges for a more streamlined appearance. The front of the guard is more apt to come in contact with branches in the woods or other objects so it should be left in as strong a state as possible. I also leave the rear base of the guard quite thick and gently contour the lines toward the center, also for purposes of structural strength. Military trigger guards are rather thick with ugly square sides. There is sufficient metal to reshape them into pleasingly curved surfaces without sacrificing strength characteristics. However, there should be no sharp edges.

One of the most popular contours for trigger guards is accomplished by gently curving the bottom of the guard

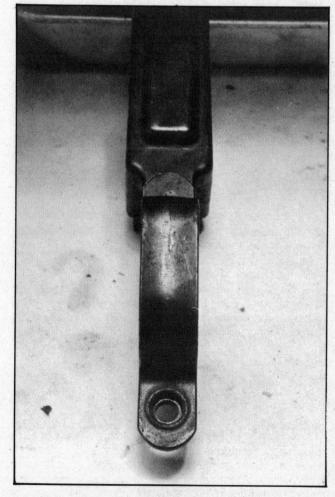

Less than an hour of time and a minimum of hand tools are all the riflesmith needs to transform military-type trigger guard such as this one from an old 1903 Springfield, to a beautiful custom job.

Basic set of hand tools includes flexible rule, dividers, scribe, and variety of files for styling work on trigger guard. Dremel Moto-Tool with carbide cutoff wheel reduces amount of hand cutting and contouring.

beginning at the front bow. The curve should continue to the back of the guard at the rear bottom row and then gently extend back out to the edges where it joins the flat of the guard.

The most critical aspect of contouring the trigger guard is removal of exactly the same amount of metal from each side. If more is removed from one side than the other the guard will immediately look off-center, the mark of shoddy workmanship. This is easily prevented by properly laying out the contour lines before any cutting or filing is begun.

The first step should be to completely polish the entire guard and remove the old finish. The guard is then positioned in a vise with soft jaws to prevent bending or crushing the sides. The bottom of the guard is then coated with Dykem marking fluid and allowed to dry. A centerline is then established. This is easily accomplished with a set of dividers. Just adjust the dividers to the exact width of the guard. Then measure that width with any accurate measuring device. Close the dividers to exactly half the original width. Now lay one edge of the dividers on either outside edge of the guard and slowly move it forward and back with the other divider tip scratching a line

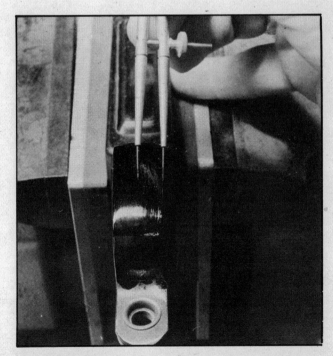

Dividers measure existing width of unaltered trigger guard and distance is halved. Dykem marking fluid is painted on guard and centerline is scribed as shown.

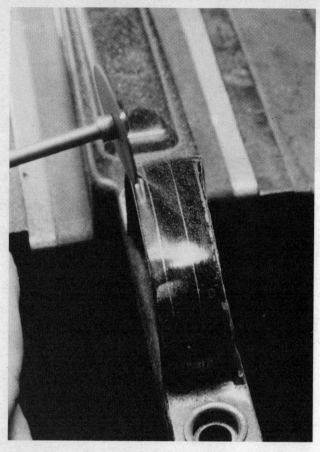

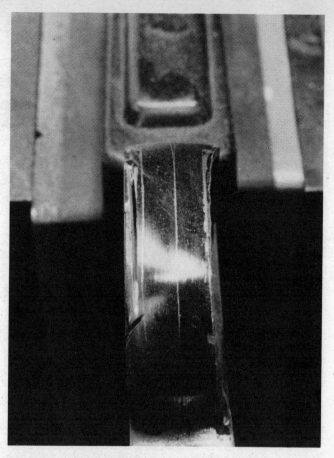

About one-third — a sixth from each side — of guard is removed with cutoff wheel chucked in Dremel Moto-Tool.

Carbide cutoff wheel makes short work of metal removal. Using the wheel as a grinder and holding it at an angle, guard is quickly rough shaped.

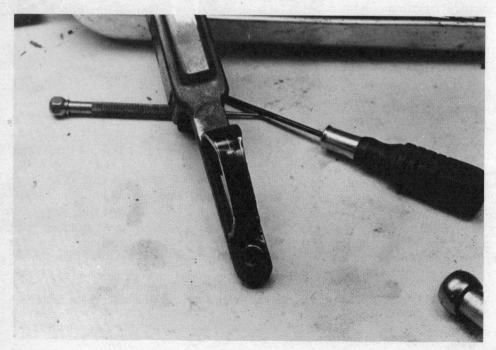

In this case, a pleasing appearance is formed by leaving the front of the trigger bow at full width.

Final shaping down to scribed lines is accomplished with flat and round files, then wet-or-dry sandpaper.

Moto-Tool with a carbide cutoff wheel. This arrangement not only makes short work of cutting off excess metal, but also quickly contours the edges as well when the wheel is held at a sharp angle to the work. It then acts as a grinder instead of a cutter. This power tool kicks up quite a bit of dust and tiny metal chips. Safety glasses and a mask should be worn for protection. The tool should be run at a fairly slow speed, which will save on the cutter and still effectively cut or grind the metal.

After all excess metal has been removed and the guard initially contoured it is time to final-shape the edges with small flat and round files. By taking your time and stepping back from the work to check each side against the centerline, it is rather simple to get each side perfectly balanced. During the final shaping the contour running along the back of the guard down to where it joins the flat

After rebluing, contoured trigger guard is lighter in weight and enhances rifle's custom appearance.

through the Dykem in the center of the guard. Now use a scribe and a flexible rule to establish the exact centerline along the entire outside length of the guard.

The amount of contour is up to the discretion of the worker. The 1903 Springfield trigger guard has a rather substantial width to begin with. I decided to remove a total of one-third the width, which would still leave plenty of metal for safety purposes, but give me a pleasing contour and sufficiently reduce unnecessary weight. In order to remove exactly one-third of the width I measured the entire width and set the dividers to one-third the width (one-third from each side of the centerline equals two-thirds of the total surface requiring that one-sixth be removed from each side).

Using the flexible rule laid along the centerline as a guide, the dividers now scribe a line on each side of the centerline to indicate the amount of metal to be removed from each side. If a flexible rule is not available, a piece of tape will do.

The curve is then outlined with a scribe in the Dykem marking fluid freehand from the front edge of the guard curve to the scribed outside lines. The curve should be gentle, reaching the lines just forward of the middle of the guard. Since we will be filing or grinding to these edges they need not be exact. The final judge of matching each curve will be done by eyeballing the work from different angles.

If only hand tools are available, it is time to begin filing the outside edges to the newly established outside edges. As you can see in the photos, I prefer using a Dremel

or bottom of the guard should be blended by removing metal on the outside edges toward the centerline. By removing metal in this area the curve will be less noticeable, but still leave plenty of metal for strength.

After the shape has been completely established the sides or edges of the guard should be gracefully thinned down to match the streamlined shape of the guard. The guard is then polished with wet-or-dry paper before bluing.

With a Dremel Moto-Tool, this job can be done in less than an hour. It takes close to two hours using only hand tools. The trigger guard is quite noticeable on any rifle and this simple modification will greatly enhance the overall appearance of any custom rifle.

Chapter 13

TRIGGER TOPICS

Wherein We Detail Types, Modifications, Installation And Adjustment

THE TRIGGER has one primary function. When pulled, it releases the hammer allowing it to move forward under spring tension to fire the gun. There are several types of triggers, most quite simple in design. Unfortunately, attempts to alter, modify or adjust them by the inexperienced tinkerer usually leads to problems. Triggers seem to fascinate the amateur. They are one of the most frequently altered mechanisms on a rifle, which usually renders them unsafe or inoperable. Trigger work is not difficult, but does require basic gunsmithing knowledge.

There are two-stage or double-pull triggers common to the military Mausers, Springfields and Enfields. Sporting rifles of modern manufacture feature quite efficient single-stage types. Semiautomatic rifles such as the M1 Garand and Ruger Mini-14 employ disconnect trigger systems. Single set and double set triggers are to be found on target rifles and occasionally in sporting rifles as well. A new era of electronically-operated triggers has arrived on the scene.

The sporting rifle is the type encountered most com-

monly by the riflesmith. Most of today's commercially manufactured rifles have single-stage triggers ranging from adequate to excellent. However, many sporterized military surplus rifles still can be found with the two-stage or double-pull trigger that should be replaced or altered. I recommend replacement with either the Timney or Canjar trigger, quite an easy job providing excellent results, but modification of a military trigger can be accomplished with a bit of work for highly satisfactory service in the field.

Anyone attempting to improve trigger pull characteristics should be aware of the features he does not want in a trigger, as well as those he does hope to obtain. There are several negative conditions that will adversely affect accuracy and safety: *Creep* — or *slack* — is the noticeable movement of the trigger during the pull before engagement between the sear and firing mechanism occurs until let-off is complete to fire the gun.

Most conventional triggers have some degree of creep. However, this factor was built into military rifles inten-

This two-stage Model 98 Mauser trigger can be altered to single-stage mode. Arrows point to areas requiring modification. See drawing at right.

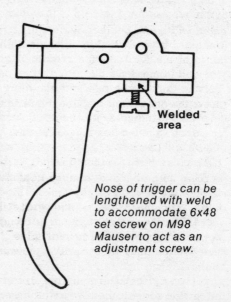

Welded area

Nose of trigger can be lengthened with weld to accommodate 6x48 set screw on M98 Mauser to act as an adjustment screw.

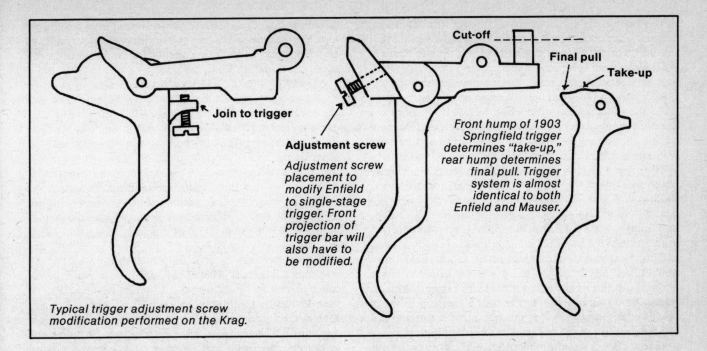

Join to trigger

Adjustment screw

Adjustment screw placement to modify Enfield to single-stage trigger. Front projection of trigger bar will also have to be modified.

Cut-off

Final pull

Take-up

Front hump of 1903 Springfield trigger determines "take-up," rear hump determines final pull. Trigger system is almost identical to both Enfield and Mauser.

Typical trigger adjustment screw modification performed on the Krag.

tionally. The double pull provided a greater area of contact for the sear, increasing the safety margin in the field. It eliminated possibility of the gun firing in a combat situation if the bolt was slammed closed. This greater amount of sear engagement required a much longer trigger pull. Thus, a hump was placed on the top of the trigger to create a sort of double fulcrum effect thus allowing initial pull to be quite light and distinct. After the soldier began pulling the trigger, it would move approximately one-eighth-inch (slack) before engaging the sear. Although this safety feature has proved its worth on the battlefield, it is undesirable for sporting rifles.

Backlash, backslap, or *overtravel* in a trigger adversely affects accuracy. Whichever name is used, it is the trigger movement immediately following the release of the sear. The trigger finger actually accelerates until the trigger is stopped at its rearward travel. This situation upsets the shooter's aim and hold, causing overall rifle movement before the bullet has exited the muzzle.

Rough triggers have no place in the field, as they create a heavy pull. Several factors can cause this problem. There may be burrs or machine marks on the sear, cocking piece or bearing surfaces surrounding them. Angles may have been honed improperly. With commercial single-stage triggers, they may have been adjusted incorrectly. The tip of the trigger could be contacting the trigger guard at the bow or it might be bearing against the guard where it comes out of the action. Sear or trigger pins may be bent or rough, increasing drag.

Light triggers can be quite dangerous. A trigger that is too light does not offer the shooter trigger control, often causing the rifle to fire before the shooter is ready. If sear angles have been improperly honed, engagement between the bearing surfaces can be reduced to the point that the gun will be inoperable or unsafe. These bearing surfaces are only case-hardened a few thousandths. If they are stoned through each time the rifle is cycled these parts will wear, worsening the problem.

Occasionally rifles will be brought into the shop after

attempted modifications by those that should have left well enough alone. The trigger shape may have been altered. The curved standard shape of a trigger is designed for function as well as looks. That curve mates with the natural curve of the finger allowing maximum control. It also increases the room in the guard area allowing the use of gloves on cold days. People sometimes polish off the serrations, giving the trigger a streamlined appearance, but reducing finger control.

A good trigger should have a smooth pull, but with enough resistance to allow the trigger finger complete control during movement. It should be light enough to allow easy let-off with no overtravel or backlash. A 2½- to 3-pound pull on a hunting rifle is fine. However, a five-pound pull is not too great to influence accuracy and is a bit safer, especially in the hands of the inexperienced hunter. Disengagement of the trigger should be clean and sharp. Trigger travel from the start of pull to let-off needs to be short and each step should be consistent with no variance.

Double-pull, two-stage or double-draw triggers, as they sometimes are referred to, are quite reliable and well suited to the use for which they were designed: the military rifle. It is possible to modify such triggers to improve their performance in sporting rifles.

Before discussing modification, it is important to understand how the trigger functions. The 98 Mauser trigger, as an example, is made up of five parts and is non-adjustable. The trigger and sear move together for a long pull. This long pull acts as an additional safety feature during combat conditions. It is accomplished in two stages, using a double-pivot mechanism, which allows the trigger pin to float and sear to pivot to the receiver directly. The humps located on the top of the trigger piece act sequentially as fulcrums underneath the receiver to cam the sear down and out of engagement. The first stage takes up the slack and initial sear engagement. The second hump then is engaged as the trigger is pulled through these stages until remaining engagement is released.

The sear pivots instead of dropping straight down, camming the cocking piece rearward to barely compress the mainspring. This direct-pull system acts to prevent the trigger from releasing if the cocking piece is jolted. The slight spring tension on the mainspring also aids to push the trigger forward into full engagement once again if the shooter does not wish to fire the rifle. Pressure from the mainspring over the sear pivot aids to push the sear up into engagement. Direct-pull military triggers may vary somewhat, but are similar in principle and design.

Modifying double-pull military triggers to a single-stage type is not difficult if you know what you are doing beforehand. Certain types are easier than others, the Springfield '03 being the simplest. However, modification does require a number of individual operations. All metal parts must be polished or stoned to reduce friction or drag. Pins also must be checked for rough spots, burrs and shape; they must not be bent or out-of-round. Sear engaging surfaces should be smooth and square with all edges being sharp. Stoning a sear's bearing edge is easier said than done. It is critical that the stone is not rocked during use or the angle will be changed and corners rounded. It is extremely precise work requiring expertise. However, bolt-action rifle sears and cocking pieces are easier to work than smaller pistol sears such as that of the .45 auto.

To achieve a crisp trigger pull with a sharp let-off in two-stage triggers it is necessary to reduce sear engagement between the bottom of the cocking piece or the top of the sear. This procedure is not recommended for the amateur. I would suggest replacing the two-stage trigger, but many riflesmiths do alter double-pull triggers for fine results. The key to accomplishing modification, by working on either the bottom of the cocking piece or the top of the sear, lies in the fittings between the bolt, bolt sleeve, and firing pin assembly in the receiver.

If there is a loose fit, alteration of the trigger should not be done as the rifle will be made unsafe. By tightening the cocking piece and sleeve, any movement will be reduced until the rifle is cocked and the trigger pulled. Any play or wobble could cause the cocking piece to override the sear, accidentally firing the gun.

Modifying Mauser military triggers presents an additional problem. Since the mainspring compresses and the cocking piece is moved rearward slightly during trigger pull, the angle of either the cocking piece or the face of the sear must be retained during the stoning operation to maintain the same position while the sear disengages. It is best accomplished a little at a time, the trigger unit being replaced in the action and continually tested.

With the trigger pull smoothed and adjusted, the trigger may now be changed from a two-stage trigger to a single-stage. There are several ways to eliminate the first stage or take-up.

The trigger has a small lip on its front edge which engages the bottom of the sear preventing forward movement. It can be built up with hi-temp silver solder or lengthened by building up a weld. The weld is shaped, then drilled and tapped for a set screw. A 6x48 screw works well. The screw enables the trigger to be held back to the second stage just before let-off, camming down the sear.

There are a number of ways to reduce overtravel or backlash in the military trigger. One of the easiest is to install a small screw through the rear of the trigger guard and adjusting it to stop trigger pull immediately after let-off has been completed. The same results can be achieved by installing the screw in the trigger and having it contact the back of the guard.

To insure that wobble or excess play has been eliminated when modifying military triggers, the cocking piece must be held tightly by the bolt sleeve. It is possible to peen the edges of the sleeve to achieve tighter alignment. It may be necessary to lay a bead of silver solder around the inner rear edge of the sleeve and reshape the bearing edges to better hold the cocking piece.

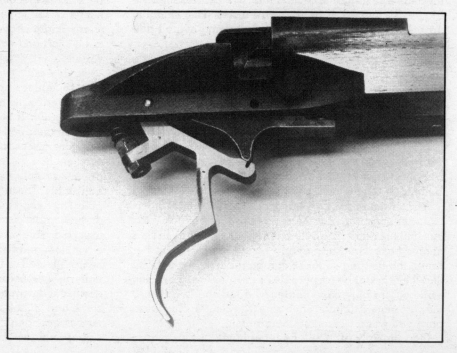

Override trigger design introduced in 1936 on Winchester Model 70 rifle was first successful single-stage trigger on a commercial bolt-action rifle. It proved highly efficient and it is still one of the best in use.

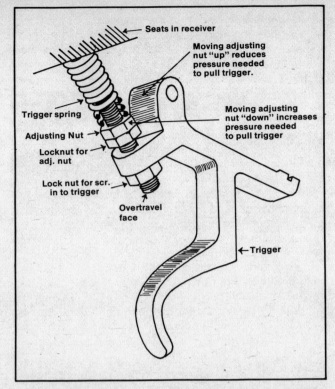

Seats in receiver

Moving adjusting nut "up" reduces pressure needed to pull trigger.

Moving adjusting nut "down" increases pressure needed to pull trigger

Trigger spring

Adjusting Nut

Locknut for adj. nut

Lock nut for scr. in to trigger

Overtravel face

Trigger

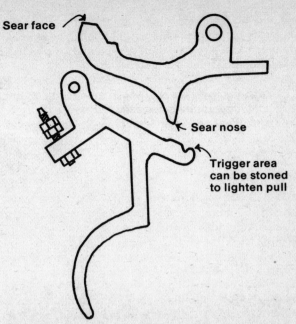

Sear face

Sear nose

Trigger area can be stoned to lighten pull

Left and above, trigger pull on Model 70 is adjusted by increasing or decreasing spring tension on trigger spring with adjustment nut. Face of screw determines overtravel. Arrow points to area on trigger that can be stoned to lighten trigger pull. Both sear nose and face may be polished smooth but great care must be exercised not to alter the critical angles.

If trigger pull is too light after alteration, this may be remedied by removing metal from the top of the trigger allowing the sear to ride higher in the receiver. The humps will have to be stoned or filed down about an equal amount. However, the rear hump controls final let-off and removing metal also reduces sear engagement. By the same token, removing metal from the front hump or camming surface will increase trigger pull and decrease take-up. But let me say again that I recommend replacement with either a Timney or Canjar single-stage trigger to military trigger modification.

Today's commercially manufactured rifles offer good to oustanding adjustable triggers. The Winchester Model 70, the first of its type, was introduced in 1936 and still is considered one of the best available. It features a "break-away or override" design. This principle was used first in the 1860s, but Winchester developed it for use in the bolt-action rifle providing the shooter with a trigger that could be counted on for crisp let-off, adjustment and smooth pull.

Stuart Otteson, in *The Bolt Action,* best describes the Model 70 trigger saying, "While it has a single or continuous take-up, in contrast to the double or interrupted take-up of the classic military direct-pull trigger, the essential difference involves the actual mechanics of sear release. In the override trigger the sear is separate and is spring-urged upward to block the cocking piece. The firing pin assembly can easily overpower the sear, which thus must depend on support from the trigger. Displacement of the trigger piece allows the striker to instantly snap it down. This "breakaway or override" action distinguishes it from the direct-pull type, where the sear is not overridden, but is cammed down by the trigger.

"The override trigger can function with a minimum of trigger pull, much less than practical in a direct-pull type. Because of the inherent play in the cocking-piece/bolt-sleeve assembly, either type requires a substantial engagement between the sear and the cocking piece to hold safely when the bolt is closed hard. In a direct-pull trigger this engagement controls trigger movement. In an override type it represents only the automatic secondary release. Instead, engagement between the sear and the trigger piece controls trigger movement. This can safely be made much smaller, thus affording a finer action, because the sear can be located in a much more certain and precise manner relative to the trigger piece than to the cocking piece."

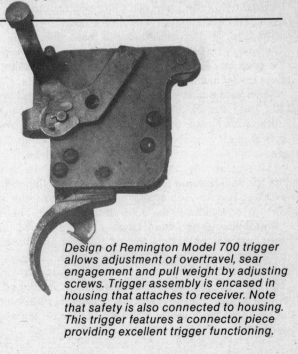

Design of Remington Model 700 trigger allows adjustment of overtravel, sear engagement and pull weight by adjusting screws. Trigger assembly is encased in housing that attaches to receiver. Note that safety is also connected to housing. This trigger features a connector piece providing excellent trigger functioning.

Sako single-stage override trigger is one of the best designs on the market, with an efficient safety.

Most Model 70 rifles have an excellent trigger pull straight from the factory. Adjusting the trigger pull is done by removing the action from the stock. In the rear of the trigger is the poundage adjustment made up of a spring and two adjustment nuts. The nut and projection running through the nut hole on the bottom side are for overtravel adjustment. The trigger pull can be adjusted by separating the adjustment nut and locknut and revolving them in opposite directions. Adjusting them away from the spring will reduce spring tension. If trigger pull is still too heavy with the nuts backed off as far as possible, it may be necessary to cut a half-coil or more off the spring. However, Model 70 triggers should be adjustable down to 2½ pounds simply by adjustment of these poundage nuts. The front of the trigger nose just in front of where it engages the sear may be stoned to lighten the pull. Both the sear nose and sear face may be polished, but no metal should be removed nor angles changed. The Winchester Model 70 trigger has proved to be one of the best for more than forty years. Newer commercial triggers may be easier to adjust in some respects by the amateur, but this trigger design needn't take a back seat to any of them.

Most of the newer override commercial trigger designs are inside a housing. This housing then is fastened to the receiver bottom. Adjustment on many can be made without having to remove the action from the stock. There are several easy-to-reach adjustment screws for overtravel, sear engagement (or creep) and pull weight. One of the best of the newer breed is the Remington 700 trigger. It features a unique connector piece mounted to the trigger. This is a small piece of hardened steel positioned between trigger and sear to enable precise trigger functioning without the need of perfect surfaces on the trigger ledge.

Timney triggers are excellent replacement triggers for military two-stage triggers. Simply by adjusting the convenient adjustment screws outstanding results can be achieved. They are reliable, consistent, smooth and crisp.

Semiautomatic rifles such as the M1 Garand or the commercially manufactured Ruger Mini-14 employ a disconnector type trigger system. The disconnector is necessary to prevent the gun from going fully automatic or not firing at all. As the trigger is pulled and the gun is fired it will not fire again until the trigger finger is relaxed allowing the trigger to move forward and set itself until pulled again. The disconnector serves to disconnect the sear and spring after firing, enabling the sear to once again engage the hammer or firing pin and recock. Browning has used this system since the early 1900s. This type of trigger does not lend itself well to fine adjustment due to design and safety.

To accurately measure trigger pull either a trigger pull gauge or trigger pull weights are necessary. One problem with using the gauge is as the tension is increased until the let-off is complete it is difficult to ascertain the reading at time of let-off on the gauge. There is one "recording" type featuring a pointer that remains in place to accurately indicate pull weight. The recording trigger-pull gauge is available in three models. One measures trigger pull from one ounce to six pounds, a second from six to twelve pounds and another from twelve to twenty-five pounds.

Trigger-pull weights are extremely accurate and are the NRA-approved method of determining trigger pull weight. When using the weights it is critical that the gauge hook be positioned in the middle of the trigger and the action pulled straight up. The weights will give a more accurate reading if they are first positioned on something soft like a pillow. The action then is lifted vertically quite gradually until let-off is complete. Both systems are available through Brownell's.

I do not intend to completely analyze set triggers. They are primarily used for target rifles and, in this writer's opinion, do not lend themselves well to use in sporting rifles. There are different types of set triggers, identified as single-set and double-set triggers. They will permit extremely light trigger pulls, but are not as fast to use in the field on a fast-moving target. It only takes a fraction of a second to set the trigger, but that is generally all the time a deer needs to get to cover. If the trigger is set beforehand the hunter is an accident going somewhere to happen.

Double-set triggers work by pulling a rear trigger until it sets. A simple touch of the front trigger will fire the rifle. They can be set down to just a few ounces. The double-set triggers are not connected to the sears. The rear trigger requires quite a long pull which moves into a notch in the front trigger. A spring is compressed holding the rear trigger under tension. When the front trigger is touched, it disengages the rear trigger permitting it to move upwards kicking the sear out of engagement. The trigger arm of the rear trigger during this movement engages a small attachment fitted to the sear called the kicker. These triggers do have an adjustment screw.

The single-set trigger works quite similarly to the double set and some models like the Canjar are quite outstanding. They have the advantage of being used as a set trigger by exerting slight pressure behind the trigger to set it or it can be used in the conventional manner.

I have found that one of the simplest ways to improve trigger pull that could especially benefit the amateur because it requires no machining or stoning is to simply cock the empty rifle, hold the muzzle down and place the palm of the hand against the cocking piece exerting a goodly amount of pressure. Pull the trigger, recock the gun and repeat the pressure at the back of the cocking piece about twenty times. This trick also works well on exposed hammer rifles, pistols or shotguns.

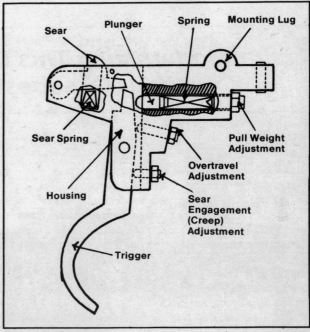

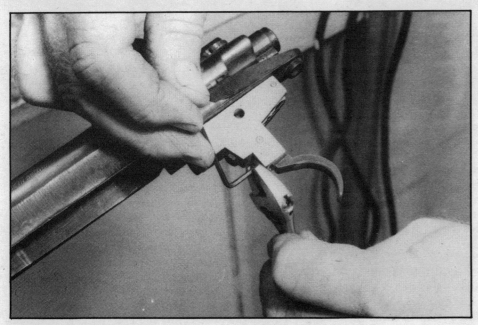

Timney single-stage triggers make excellent replacement for double-pull military triggers when converting rifles to sporter status. Several types are offered. Left, a new Timney trigger being installed in a Mauser action, here undergoing adjustment with hex wrench.

Chapter 14

CUSTOM SAFETY INSTALLATION

Modernizing This Mechanism Could Be Your Cheapest Life Insurance!

At left is the three-position military Mauser safety in the intermediate position. This position permits the gun to be in safe condition, while the action is worked, feeding the cartridges through. (Right) Winchester Model 70-type custom safety by Pete Grisel was installed to permit use of low-mount scopes; it has graceful lines usually admired.

POPULAR MILITARY actions such as the Mauser and Springfield often are converted to custom sporter rifles. As most custom sporters are fitted with low-mount scopes, the original safeties must be replaced. Only the safety design of the Enfield lends itself well to sporter status. The safety thumb pieces on both the Mauser and Springfield rotate through their safety positions, causing interference with a scope. Replacing them with custom safeties is not a difficult task, if directions are followed.

Custom safeties also are used quite often on commercial rifle actions. However, most commercially manufactured rifles incorporate well designed safety mechanisms. The change usually is more cosmetic than essential.

Most bolt-action rifles employ three-position safeties.

Let's examine the military Mauser safety to better understand how and why they work. In his book, *The Bolt Action,* Stuart Otteson describes the system best when he says, "The Mauser safety is of one-piece construction. Its spindle occupies the top of the bolt sleeve, with the thumb piece straddling a flange on the left and top circumference. It clears the flange on the right side, but is retained by the cocking piece. Detents in each position are formed by notches in the safety hub. Thus retention and detenting of the safety are again neatly built into the design, requiring no extra parts.

"The thumb piece swings a full half-turn. Turned upright, the safety hub engages the front rim of the cocking piece, camming the firing pin back .05 inch. At the same time, the spindle nose clears the bolt rim, allowing bolt

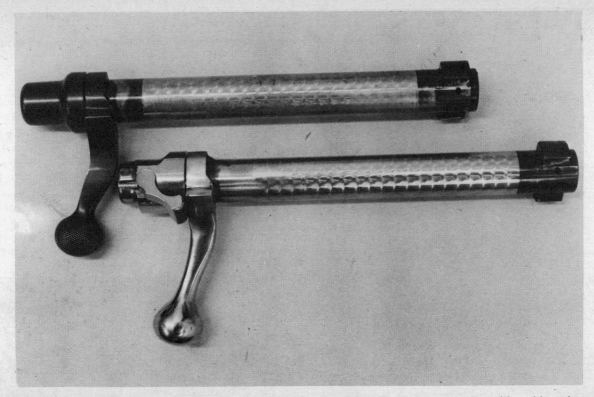

Remington Model 700 bolt at top is standard factory type. One beneath has Jantz custom 3-position side swing safety.

lift. The advantages of this intermediate position, justifying the inclusion of the special bolt-sleeve lock which it made necessary, are that it permits working cartridges through the action with the firing pin locked, and it simplifies bolt disassembly.

"Turned right to *Safe,* both the firing pin and bolt are locked. The safety hub continues in contact with the cocking piece, while the spindle nose now locks into the bolt-rim notch.

"Finally, with the thumb piece turned left to the *Fire* position, the firing pin assembly is eased back onto the sear. A cutout in the safety hub lines up ahead of the cocking piece and the spindle turns clear once again of the bolt rim, freeing both the firing pin and bolt."

This type of safety blocks the motion of the firing pin or striker and is considered much safer than those that only block trigger motion. If a rifle using the latter system is dropped, the sear may be disengaged from the trigger, causing the gun to fire. Of course, no safety should ever be considered foolproof. Every firearm safety should be checked before going into the field and after any modification or replacement by the riflesmith. It may be tested by cocking the firing mechanism — be sure the chamber and magazine are empty. The safety should cam

Disassembly of bolts for Ruger Model 77 or Remington 700 is facilitated by using special tool made by Harry Lawson.

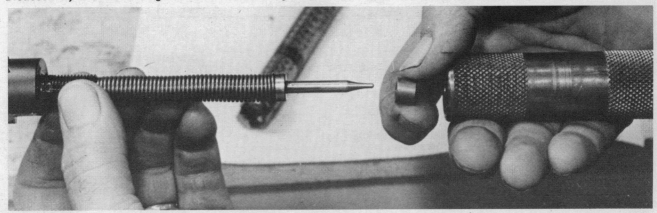

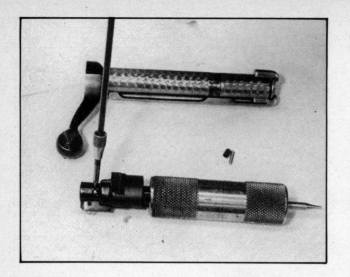

The Lawson-made bolt disassembly tool is used to compress spring, allowing removal of pin in cocking piece body.

the cocking piece rearward and out of contact with the sear when the safety is switched to the *Safe* position. The trigger is now pulled and the safety immediately switched back to the *Off* postition. If modification or replacement was done improperly the rifle may fire as the safety is released. Stoning the bottom engagement of the cocking piece will permit the safety to cam the cocking piece out of engagement with the sear, correcting this problem.

I prefer three-position safeties, although many commercially manufactured rifles use the two-position type. With the latter, when the safety is turned to the *On* posi-

After notching cocking piece to 30-degree angle, it is polished smooth on polishing wheel. (Below) Diagram shows angles, dimensions of cuts for fitting Jantz safety to Remington and Ruger bolts.

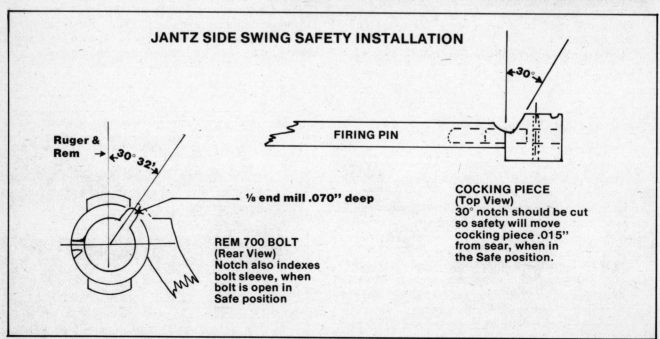

JANTZ SIDE SWING SAFETY INSTALLATION

Ruger & Rem → ←30° 32'

FIRING PIN

⅛ end mill .070" deep

REM 700 BOLT
(Rear View)
Notch also indexes bolt sleeve, when bolt is open in Safe position

←30°

COCKING PIECE
(Top View)
30° notch should be cut so safety will move cocking piece .015" from sear, when in the Safe position.

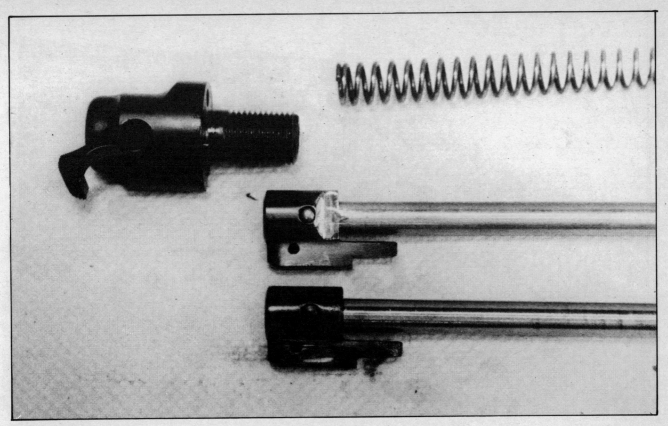

The unaltered cocking piece is located on bottom in the photo. Altered cocking piece, showing angle, is above it.

tion, both the firing pin and bolt are locked. When switched to *Off* the rifle is ready to fire. These two-position safeties are quite reliable.

The custom riflesmith must consider a safety's function and appearance to best suit each rifle. One of the best in each department is the Winchester Model 70 safety. This type of safety is offered to gunsmiths and shooters by Pete Grisel of Bend, Oregon, and Ken Jantz of Sulphur, Oklahoma. A third manufacturer, Maynard Buehler of Orinda, California, also produces an excellent safety that is both reliable and streamlined in appearance. All are simple to install, reliable, smooth and quiet in the field.

I observed as Sterling Davenport installed a Jantz Side Swing safety (Model 70 type) on a Ruger Model 77 rifle. Actually, the Ruger safety is one of the best and conveniently positioned on the action's tang. However, the customer has several rifles with the Model 70-type safety and prefers it out of habit. Davenport uses a bolt disassembly tool designed by Harry Lawson of Tucson, Arizona, to compress the firing pin spring enough to remove the pin holding the cocking piece. Disassembly of the Model 77 bolt is rather difficult without such a tool They are also manufactured by Brownell.

With the bolt completely disassembled the Jantz safety is fitted by first grinding a thirty-degree relief cut into the cocking piece where it cams against the safety. The Ruger 77 and the Remington 700 both require cutting approximately a one-eighth-inch notch about .070 inch deep at the rear of the bolt at an angle thirty degrees,

thirty-two minutes from the top centerline of the bolt. This notch indexes the bolt sleeve when the bolt is open in the safe position. Ideally, the notch should be cut on a milling machine with a one-eighth-inch end mill cutter, but a Dremel Moto-Tool and carbide deburring bit will work quite well. The pin protruding from the bolt sleeve locks the bolt closed.

After the cuts are made the bolt is reassembled and the safety is checked for proper functioning. If the job has

Arrow on the photograph indicates the position of the notch in bolt which is necessary to fit Jantz safety.

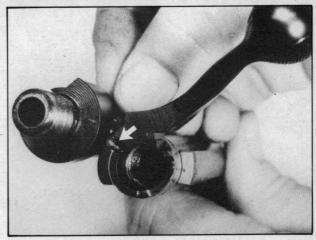

The conventional rear tang thumb safety on Ruger 77 is positive, convenient and low profile. (Below) Ruger rifle has been equipped with the recently introduced three-position side swing custom safety marketed by Ken Jantz.

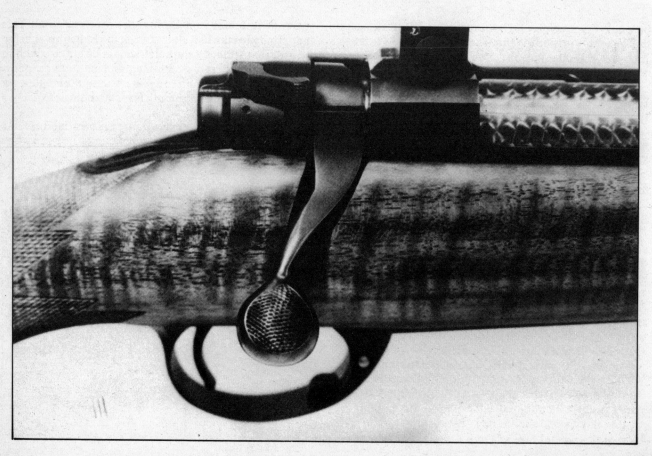

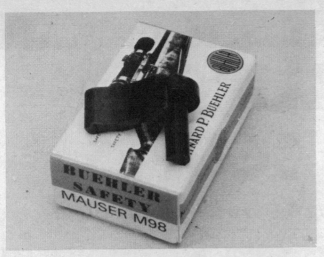

This particular custom safety from Maynard Buehler is an outstanding touch when installed on Mauser 98.

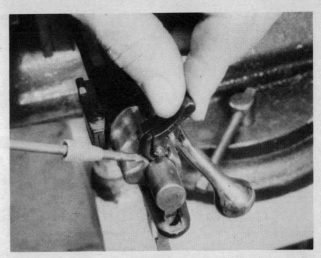

Scribe is used to indicate area on leading edge of the cocking piece; it requires bevel for proper engagement.

been done improperly by cutting the relief cut too deep on the cocking piece, the rifle may fire when the safety is switched to the *Off* position, as the cocking piece will slip past the safety sear and rest on the trigger. The safety must withdraw the cocking piece far enough to allow the sear to retract about .015 to .020 inch and out of engagement. If this does occur, removing a bit of metal off the cocking piece should correct the situation.

The Buehler safety is quite simple to install. The bolt is disassembled and the old safety removed. The bolt then is reassembled. The new safety is disassembled and the new safety spring compressed and placed in the pin hole. The new safety is slipped into position and screwed in place. If this safety does not work initially, a forty-five-degree bevel 1/32 inch back on the leading or left edge of the cocking piece engaging surface should be made with a hard Arkansas stone. Stoning or grinding, as the case may be, is done after disassembling the safety. It is

polished smooth and reassembled, all the fitting required for a good functioning safety.

However, if too much metal has been ground or honed away, while in the cocked position the striker may move too far forward for the safety to operate properly. To correct this, remove the safety and, with the gun in the cocked position, measure the space between the bolt head and the firing pin engaging surface. It must measure 3/64 inch on Springfields, 3/32 on Mausers, 7/64 on Winchester Model 54 and .2 inch for the Krag. It may be necessary to grind back the cocking piece shoulder until arriving at these dimensions, then rebevel.

It does not take a great deal of machining to install today's new custom safeties. However, proper engagement is critical to the overall safety of the firearm. A qualified gunsmith charges little to install a new safety and this could be the best and cheapest life insurance policy you can buy.

Below (left): The cocking piece has been marked for proper engagement. The cocking piece (right) had been beveled for engagement with the new Buehler safety. Author feels such safeties offer proper custom touches to any rifle.

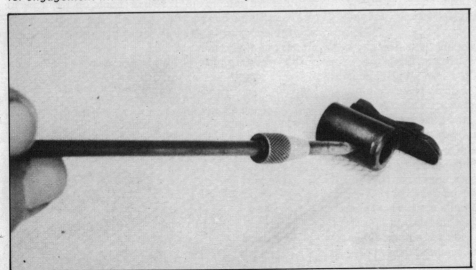

Chapter 15

INSTALLING SIGHTS & SCOPES

Iron Sights Still Serve Many A Purpose In The Field

Typical stamped metal rear sight with elevator adjustment. Most utilize standard ⅜-inch dovetail base.

Known as a ladder sight, this one on a Mauser 98 is typically seen on many older military rifles.

Browning .22 rimfire rifle features folding leaf, screw adjustment sight.

METALLIC SIGHTS serve an important function. They enable the shooter to aim the rifle for accurate shot placement. They are often maligned for missed shots when it is the shooter's inability to use them properly. The trend today is toward scopes for hunting and competitive shooting. Actually, this is in the best interests of both the average hunter and the game he stalks. Scopes do provide greater accuracy and require less marksmanship ability, which leads to fewer wounded game animals and overall safety to other hunters in the field. However, metallic sights of good quality, properly installed and correctly sighted in, can produce remarkable accuracy for the skilled rifleman.

Most factory rifles are fitted with open sights. The peep or aperture sight has a hole in the rear sight. Open, peep and aperture sights also are called iron sights. Front sights are generally bead, blade, or globe type and may or may not be positioned in a front ramp. They range in diameters from thin to thick and may have small ivory, plastic, gold or copper inserts to provide a more distinctive aim point for light or dark weather conditions.

Metallic sights range from abominable to excellent quality and from almost useless to ingenious design. There are a few that are incredible mixtures of each. Two types readily come to mind. The so-called buckhorn open sights can be quite well made, but the design hardly lends itself to a hunting rifle. It has wide, tall ears on either side of the aiming slot that effectively block out the shooter's vision everywhere except straight ahead. Trying to hit

a rapidly moving deer with such an arrangement is quite challenging to say the least.

The tang aperture or peep sight is another design that would have been better left on the drawing board when considered for high-power rifles. Although the aperture sight is excellent in military, hunting, and target work, it can be downright dangerous when placed on the tang of a high-powered rifle. This is particularly true on uphill shots. I know of more than one hunter snatching the rifle to his shoulder to fire at a fleeing deer or goat only to have the aperture sight severely damage the eye when the rifle recoiled. No pointed metal device should be that close to a shooter's face or eye. Unfortunately, the aperture sight is designed to have the eye as close as possible to achieve proper sight alignment.

The great majority of firearms writers seem to lean

Number 25 Lyman sight base, left below, may be used to mount #16 Lyman folding leaf rear sight, at right. Base is installed with screws atop barrel or receiver where dovetail slot is undesirable.

Simple peep arrangement on Ruger Mini-14 has proven fast, accurate in the field.

Patented in 1911, Lyman #48 aperture sight, left, became popular for use on sporterized '03 Springfields after WWI. Somewhat more advanced model peep is Williams' windage and elevation adjustable model.

heavily toward the use of scopes over metallic sights, often suggesting that open sights are almost worthless. I totally disagree. Well designed open sights have effectively killed game on this and other continents for the past two hundred or so years. There are even occasions when open sights are superior to telescopic sights. This includes both hunting and military use. Few will argue that the wide V sights of British origin and used on their Nitro Express rifles are still much in use today for dangerous game; these are efficient and fast. Open sights are better in thick brush and heavy woods. Most shots are within 150 yards; well within effective range of open sights. They give the shooter a better field of vision to find and lead his quarry, are lighter and have less tendency to catch on vines or branches leading to hunter fatigue. Neither will they fog up or be knocked out of adjustment as fast as a scope if the rifle is dropped or jolted. Open or iron sights do have their place and have proved their worth when used by a skilled rifleman.

Open rear sights are quite simple in design. Lyman Corporation, Marble Sights and Williams Gunsight Company have long been the leaders in the United States and can supply just about any need. Open sights usually are placed about 4½ inches forward of the front receiver ring. This may vary slightly with each rifle.

The sights most often are attached by fitting a dovetailed base into a corresponding dovetail slot in the barrel. They generally have either a U or V notch cut into the blade which lines up with the front sight for aiming purposes. The open sights are either leaf, folding leaf or ladder style and may or may not have adjustments for windage or elevation.

The leaf sight most often will have a small notched piece called an elevator. This is held in place under spring tension and may be moved forward or back to adjust for elevation. The folding leaf variety allows the sight to be cammed forward and down against the barrel when not in use. Most of these sights, regardless of manufacture, have a standard three-eighths-inch dovetail. The No. 16 Lyman folding leaf sight can be fitted to rifles without a dovetail slot by using their No. 25 base. This base fits to the barrel which is an easier task than cutting a

dovetail. The Lyman No. 16 is adjustable for elevation only. Williams makes a sight that is also attached by two screws that is adjustable for both elevation and windage called the Williams Guide.

Open sights are adequate on small-caliber rifles such as the .22 rimfire. However, as we move up into the heavier-caliber center-fires, greater vibration in the barrel can lead to the sight moving or turning in the barrel's dovetail slot. If the sight is held in place with screws, these screws may tend to back out and cause the sight to fall off the barrel.

A problem for the riflesmith is in encountering rifles that have dovetails already cut too deep, too shallow, undersize, oversize or even at the wrong angle. The inner sides of the slot may not have been cut straight, preventing the male dovetail in the sight from fitting securely. Before we get into ways to improve the fitting of sights remember that sights are driven out from left to right; they are inserted from right to left. Use a brass, nylon or plastic drift punch to prevent damaging the sight and destroying the bluing.

One of the surest ways of tightening a loose rear or front sight is by peening down the edges of the female dovetail slot in the barrel with either a brass hammer or a brass drift punch and hammer. It helps to have an old sight inserted into the barrel slot to prevent the edges from being peened over too much. Another way to get a tighter fit is to use a hammer and centerpunch in the barrel slot. The centerpunch should be angled slightly from right to left as each depression is made. It will cause the metal to have high spots. Hitting the punch at an angle will make installation and removal of the dovetail much easier.

Aperture or peep sights have been used for many decades for both hunting and target work. Lyman intro-

At left, Williams' Shorty ramp with brilliant bead mounts on barrel of Remington Nylon 66 .22. Many rimfire and center-fire rifles use simple bead.

duced their No. 48 aperture sight in 1911. It featured elevation and windage adjustments to minutes-of-angle and was refined to quarter-minutes of angle in later years. A No. 49 Lyman aperture sight was available for hunting purposes with neither elevation nor windage adjustments. The sights were quite accurate, but a large reason for their initial sales success was due to the fact that they fit such surplus military rifles as the 1903 Springfield.

Aperture sights are more accurate than open rear sights. The sight itself is nothing more than a small hole, but it works on the principle of the eye's ability to center objects. This type of sight must be located farther back on the rifle than open sights to be close to the shooter's eye. It does allow a rifleman to concentrate almost exclusively on the front sight. These sights are used today on the Ruger Mini-14 and on the military M-14 and M-16 rifles.

The sights usually have small discs that can be installed or removed with a simple screw arrangement. However, the small disc is found more often on target rifles than hunting or military types. This sight offers a rather unimpeded view of the target to aid in fast alignment. However, once elevation and windage adjustments have been made, it takes a bit of time to readjust them, hardly conducive to getting off accurate shots at a variety of ranges for the hunter in the field.

Installing aperture or peep sights is not a difficult job, but does take a bit of know-how and careful calculation. Installation requires drilling and tapping the receiver. A good machinist's level and some parallel-jaw toolmaker's clamps are essential. The sight is positioned against the area of the receiver and adjusted until the final permanent location is determined. The toolmaker's clamp is used to hold the sight securely to the receiver while the level is placed on the bottom of the receiver and top of the sight to make certain all alignment is correct.

Use a scribe to mark one of the screw holes. With the sight being held in place by the clamp, also check to make certain that the sight will not interfere with any of the functioning parts of the rifle.

Problems of installing sights generally result from the receiver being too hard. It may be impossible to get the scribe to mark the metal preparatory to drilling. If this happens, apply a thin coat of Dykem fluid to the area before installing the sight. Rather than scribe the spot a sharp punch can be used to center the screwhole. Be certain when making the hole mark that it is made dead center of the screw hole located in the sight base.

If the steel in the receiver is quite hard, it may have to be annealed before attempting to drill and tap the screw holes. If annealing is the way you wish to go, make sure to polish the area first, wrap the surrounding area in wet cloth to prevent damaging hardened bearing surfaces, then heat the spot with a small welding tip until it turns a dull red and allow to cool slowly.

Drilling screw holes for any sight should be done with the work securely positioned in a drill press vise or sight jig. All drilling should be done with a drill press. The slower the drill turns in hard metal the better it will cut. The drill bit should be sharp and the cutting edge angled properly.

If the metal refuses to accept the drill, place a few drops of turpentine on it. This will allow the drill bit to grab and begin its cutting action. It is critical that the holes be drilled cleanly and absolutely parallel to the bottom of the receiver and at a ninety-degree longitudinal axis to the receiver. If the holes are drilled at an angle or are oversize due to drill bit wobble, the screws may tend to work loose during firing of the rifle.

Sight screws usually are either 3x56, 6x48, or 8x40, the 6x48 probably the most common. A No. 31 drill works well for tapping screw holes of this dimension. However, the hole should be drilled first with a smaller drill.

After drilling through the receiver with the smaller drill change to the No. 33 bit. By using the smaller drill first the larger one will have less metal to remove, thus reducing the chance of bit wobble making the hole oversize.

After tapping the first hole, place the sight onto the receiver and screw it in place. After checking for exact placement use the smaller drill again to begin the second hole. Be careful that it does not contact the edges of the sight-base hole. Next, remove the sight, drill the second hole to the correct diameter and tap.

Before assembling the peep sight to the receiver, clean up the edges of the holes with a file to remove any high spots or burrs caused by the drilling. Put some Loc-Tite or medicinal iodine on the screw threads and tighten the sight to the receiver. That's all there is to it other than cleaning up the metal chips inside the receiver and shortening the protruding screws in the receiver that might contact the bolt. A Dremel Moto-Tool with a grinding point and small round files work nicely.

Many rifles are fitted with dovetail-slot front sights. The sight itself is either of bead, blade or globe shape. The front edge of the front sight sits approximately three-quarters-inch back from the edge of the muzzle. The sights have a male dovetail base with the standard length on most of three-eighths-inch. Although depths may vary they are usually .090-inch. Flat blade top sights are well suited for target work. The beads may have plastic, ivory or copper inserts at the rear edge of the sight to aid sighting in light or dark shooting conditions.

One way to cut the dovetail slot in a rifle barrel is with a special dovetail sight base cutter on the milling machine. The cutter makes a precise sixty-degree shoulder cut by .359-inch in length to accommodate the standard three-eighths-inch sight base. The operation involves nothing more than setting the barrel up perfectly level in a horizontal position. The depth of the cut will match the particular sight base, but that is generally .090-inch! It is important that the machine be running at a slow speed — about 700 rpm — to prevent damaging or breaking the cutter. These cutters are available through Brownell's.

The other method of cutting the dovetail in the barrel is by hand. The tools required are a hacksaw, mill file, pillar file, sight-base file (a three-square file featuring two "safe" sides with only one side cutting) and a straightedge. The slot is laid out using Dykem fluid, the straightedge and a scribe.

Before doing any cutting or filing, make certain the barrel is in a secure horizontal position. Either a hacksaw or the edge of a mill file can be used to cut to almost full depth through the narrow top edge of the slot. Two or three cuts can be made with the hacksaw in parallel lines. This is a fast way to remove as much metal as possible before

Band front sight mounts are common on Mausers and Ruger Mini-14s. Williams Gunsight front sight pusher tool prevents marring blued surface, right.

REGULAR RAMPS

3. Measure outside diameter of barrel at muzzle. Divide this figure by 2.

4. Subtract this figure from your answer in Step 2 above.

MARBLE Chart To Determine Overall Sight/Ramp Heights												
Sight No.	Ramp	Total Height	Sight No.	Ramp	Total Height	Sight No.	Ramp	Total Height	Sight No.	Ramp	Total Height
26NR	3/16"	.3545	29NR	3/8"	.572	34NR	7/16"	.6875	34NR	9/16"	.8125
29NR	3/16"	.3845	31NR	3/8"	.594	41NR	3/8"	.692	53NR	3/8"	.820
31NR	3/16"	.4065	50NR	5/16"	.5945	50NR	5/16"	.7195	50NR	7/16"	.8445
34NR	3/16"	.4375	37NR	5/16"	.5945	37NR	7/16"	.7195	37NR	9/16"	.8445
37NR	3/16"	.4695	26NR	7/16"	.6045	26NR	9/16"	.7295	41NR	9/16"	.8795
26NR	5/16"	.4795	34NR	3/8"	.625	45NR	3/8"	.732	53NR	7/16"	.8825
41NR	5/16"	.5045	41NR	5/16"	.6295	41NR	7/16"	.7545	45NR	9/16"	.9195
29NR	5/16"	.5095	53NR	3/16"	.6325	53NR	5/16"	.7575	50NR	9/16"	.9695
31NR	5/16"	.5315	29NR	7/16"	.6345	29NR	9/16"	.7595	53NR	9/16"	1.0075
26NR	3/8"	.542	31NR	7/16"	.6565	31NR	9/16"	.7815			
45NR	5/16"	.5445	37NR	3/8"	.657	50NR	3/8"	.782			
34NR	5/16"	.5625	45NR	5/16"	.6695	45NR	7/16"	.7945			

WILLIAMS Chart To Determine Overall Sight/Ramp Heights														
Sight Height & No.*	Ramp Height	Total Sight Height	Sight Height & No.*	Ramp Height	Total Sight Height	Sight Height & No.*	Ramp Height	Total Sight Height	Sight Height & No.*	Ramp Height	Total Sight Height	Sight Height & No.*	Ramp Height	Total Sight Height
260	1/8"	.292	281	3/16"	.375	345	9/32"	.469	345	5/16"	.5645	.406	3/8"	.688
281	1/8"	.313	375	3/16"	.4695	406	9/32"	.594	406	5/16"	.594	345	3/8"	.719
312	1/8"	.344	260	5/16"	.500	312	5/16"	.594	375	5/16"	.5945	375	7/16"	.7195
260	3/16"	.3545	312	9/32"	.5005	375	5/16"	.5945	260	7/16"	.6045	260	7/16"	.7295
345	1/8"	.377	281	5/16"	.5005	260	7/16"	.6045	437	9/32"	.625	406	7/16"	.7305
281	3/16"	.3755	437	3/16"	.5315	437	5/16"	.6255	406	7/16"	.6255	281	7/16"	.7503
312	3/16"	.4065	312	5/16"	.5315	406	5/16"	.6255	281	7/16"	.6255	437	7/16"	.7815
375	1/8"	.407	345	9/32"	.533	345	5/16"	.627	312	7/16"	.6255	312	7/16"	.7815
406	1/8"	.438	345	9/32"	.542	437	5/16"	.627	345	7/16"	.6565	345	9/16"	.8145
345	3/16"	.4395	260	3/8"	.563	312	3/8"	.6565	375	9/16"	.8755			
260	9/32"	.4695	375	9/32"	.563	437	3/8"	.657	406	9/16"	.9065			
437	1/8"	.469	281	3/8"	.563									

This gives you the overall height needed for ramp and sight.

5. Look in the columns above headed Total Height or Total Sight Height for the measurement closest to your final figures. This will give you sight and ramp heights.

LYMAN SLIP-ON RAMPS

Follow Steps 1 and 2 above.

3. Divide inside diameter of Lyman ramp band being used by 2.

4. Subtract this figure from .668-inch. (This gives you height from barrel top to bottom of dovetail.)

5. Subtract this figure from your answer in Step 2 above. This gives you sight height needed for the sight/ramp combination.

Suggestions on ordering sights for Lyman Ramps: Look in the Marble sight specifications chart for nearest height. If exact height is not listed, use next highest. Rear sight adjustment when sighting in will bring point of impact up to where you want."

Ramp sights come in a standard size and shortened editions appropriately called shorty ramps. The standard size heights range from 3/16, 5/16, 3/8, 7/16 to 9/16 inch in height. Short ramps are either 1/8, 3/16, 9/32 or 3/8 inch high.

If the front ramp sight is to be attached by a combination of sweating and screw or one or the other, it is best to

---

filing. The depth should be within five to seven thousandths of the .090-inch maximum depth. The pillar file then is used to remove metal to at least the width of the top edge of the slot.

After enlarging the sides of the cut with the pillar file, Brownell's three-square dovetail sight-base file is employed to set the proper depth and angles of the slot. When the slot has been cut almost completely, each side may be tapered minutely to accept the sight base as it is driven into the slot from right to left. This job is not difficult if done carefully to prevent canting or slanting the bottom of the slot or the inner sides.

Band front sights have been used for many years and are still a good arrangement. The Ruger Mini-14 employs a band-type front sight. The diameter of the barrel will determine which size band sight must be ordered. It has a slight taper and is installed using a mallet to seat it so the front edge of the band is located approximately three-eighths-inch from the edge of the muzzle. After checking that the sight is perfectly upright and the proper distance from the muzzle, it is soldered, brazed or screwed into place. Many will be both soldered and screw tightened for permanency.

The ramp front sight is extremely popular with both open and aperture sights. It may be soldered and/or screwed into position on the barrel. The simplest way of determining the proper ramp/sight combination is explained in Bob Brownell's *Gunsmith Kinks* with the accompanying chart:

1. Measure outside diameter of barrel at location of rear sight. Divide the figure by 2.

2. Determine minimum height of rear sight to be used. Add this figure to your answer above. (Both Marble and Williams show this information.) If a peep sight is to be used, add one-eighth-inch (.125) to your answer.

FRONT SIGHT ELEVATION CORRECTION CHART (FOR IRON SIGHTS)

Chart Courtesy Marble Arms Co., Gladstone, Michigan

Distance Between Front & Rear Sights	14"	15"	16"	17"	18"	19"	20"	21"	22"	23"	24"	25"	26"	27"	28"	29"	30"	31"	32"	33"	34"
AMOUNT OF ADJUSTMENT NECESSARY TO CORRECT ERROR																					
Amount 1"	.0038	.0041	.0044	.0047	.0050	.0053	.0055	.0058	.0061	.0064	.0066	.0069	.0072	.0074	.0077	.0080	.0082	.0085	.0088	.0091	.0093
of Error 2"	.0078	.0083	.0089	.0094	.0100	.0105	.0111	.0116	.0122	.0127	.0133	.0138	.0144	.0149	.0155	.0160	.0166	.0171	.0177	.0182	.0188
at 3"	.0117	.0125	.0133	.0142	.0150	.0159	.0167	.0175	.0184	.0192	.0201	.0209	.0217	.0226	.0234	.0243	.0251	.0259	.0268	.0276	.0285
100 Yards 4"	.0155	.0167	.0178	.0189	.0200	.0211	.0222	.0234	.0244	.0255	.0266	.0278	.0289	.0300	.0311	.0322	.0333	.0344	.0355	.0366	.0377
Given in 5"	.0194	.0208	.0222	.0236	.0250	.0264	.0278	.0292	.0306	.0319	.0333	.0347	.0361	.0375	.0389	.0403	.0417	.0431	.0445	.0458	.0472
Inches 6"	.0233	.0250	.0267	.0283	.0300	.0317	.0333	.0350	.0367	.0384	.0400	.0417	.0434	.0450	.0467	.0484	.0500	.0517	.0534	.0551	.0567

use a Forster sight jig for alignment of holes to be drilled.

When drilling a hole for a front sight, one must be extremely careful not to drill completely through and into the muzzle. However, it is quite safe to drill within one-thirty-second-inch of the bore for a standard size 6x48 screw. Although high-power rifles do have chamber pressures upwards of 50,000 pounds per square inch (psi), the pressures have subsided to around 12,000 pounds when the bullet exits the muzzle of the barrel. The exact distance for depth is calculated on the drill press stop.

There are a number of front sight jigs available to hold the sight in position while silver soldering it in place on the barrel. It is a good idea to spread soldering talc around the edge of the sight to prevent the solder from sticking and making cleanup more difficult.

When setting the screws into position to hold the sight in place, Loc-Tite should be used to prevent the screws from backing out of the holes. Installing sights need not be difficult if all work is carefully performed and thought out beforehand.

Proper Installation Of A Scope's Concoction Of Metal And Glass Is A Must For Good Shooting!

TODAY'S RIFLE scopes are a direct result of Space Age technology in a highly competitive field. The modern telescopic sight is the most accurate method of aiming a rifle. Most are rugged, reliable and are reasonably priced. The shooter has a wide variety of types, price ranges, and different manufacturers from which to choose. Continuous research and development by such companies as Redfield, Weaver, Leupold, Burris, Zeiss, Tasco, Lyman, Williams, Bushnell, Swift and Unertl have prouced scopes to fit any need.

As good as scopes are today, if the stock is not properly bedded to the action, the scope bases will not position correctly; if the whole arrangement is not securely tightened and the scope not properly sighted in, the unit becomes nothing more than pieces of steel and glass incapable of hitting the paper and certainly not the target.

Fortunately, the manufacturers of scope bases and rings, as well as the folks who make installation jigs, have kept pace with the scope manufacturers. Types of scopes could easily fill a book. The choice of crosshair, post, dot, diamond, rangefinder, circle, or combination of any reticle is best left to individual taste. The novice shooter would do well to check with his local shooting club or gunsmith to match his rifle and type of shooting to the particular variable or fixed-power scopes available. It is more important to figure out how to combine the rifle, bases, rings, and rifle, then assemble all into one accurate, reliable shooting system.

Scope rings and bases should be made of good-quality steel. A high-power center-fire rifle exerts great vibration and stress on each as the rifle recoils; aluminum and other alloys will not stand up to abuse as well as steel. One-piece ring bases are easier to install, provide more

The Forster Universal Sight Mounting Fixture provides precise alignment for drilling and tapping screw holes for rifle scope and sight installations.

strength and rigidity and are more likely to be installed correctly than two-piece bases. However, they are heavier than the two-piece bases and if put on incorrectly tend to torque, which can adversely affect accuracy and lead to breakage in the field or on the firing line.

The Ruger Model 77 features integral scope ring bases built into the receiver. This is an excellent system generally found only on expensive European rifles. The unit provides strength and stability to the scope, while eliminating the possibility of someone drilling and tapping for the bases incorrectly, a common problem in the trade.

The most difficult part of installing a scope is drilling and tapping the screw holes accurately in precisely the correct spots. The hole on the receiver ring closest to the barrel must be drilled to exactly the right depth. This is a blind hole directly over an area of the chamber that is subjected to the rifle's greatest pressures.

Before any drilling is attempted, the receiver should be tested for hardness. If it is too hard to accept the drill it may have to be spot annealed. This involves determining the exact screw hole placements, then heating the area with a torch. It is necessary to polish the area first to be able to watch the colors change in the metal as the heat is applied. A small welding tip is used and the spot is heated with the neutral flame until it turns a deep blue.

It may be easier to try a few other methods before going to this trouble. Dremel Company manufactures a number of grinding tips. One is cone-shaped with a sharp point. It may be chucked into a drill press and used to grind the hardened surface carefully. The drill press should be running at a slow speed, as drill bits cut hardened steel much more effectively when turned slowly in the metal. At times they may be hand-turned.

If the drill bit won't grab, adding a few drops of turpentine will help the bit cut into the metal. The drill bit should

B-Square sight-mounting jig, left, is mounted atop Mauser action before drilling. Grinding tip chucked in Dremel Moto-Tool, right, penetrates case-hardened metal.

Buehler sight bases, left, and Redfield rings are high-quality steel for strength, durability.

be quite sharp with the cutting edge set at the proper angle. Once the drill does beign to cut, continuous cutting is necessary or immediately pull the bit out of the steel. If the tip just rides in the steel the metal in the receiver will work harden, dulling the drill bit.

Two sight-base jigs or fixtures currently manufactured allow accurate drilling and tapping for scope bases. The first is the Universal Sight Mounting Fixture manufactured by Forster Brothers of Lanark, Illinois. I first encountered this tool at gunsmithing school in Colorado several years ago. The instructors raved about its versatility and quality construction. I have used it several times since my student days and it does aid in precise drilling for scope bases on a large number of rifles. It will handle any single-barrel gun — bolt-action, lever-action, or pump-action —as long as the barrel can be laid into the V blocks of the fixture. The fixture locates the holes to a standard spacing predetermined by the standard spacing built into the over-arm, or any other spacing by sliding the over-arm, or any other spacing built in to the over-arm in either direction. Run out of the drill is impossible as it is guided in a hardened and ground drilling bushing.

When ready to tap the hole, another slip bushing of correct size is substituted for the drill bushing to guide the tap straight and true. This prevents breakage of taps due to cocking, the major cause of tap breakage. The sliding over-arm has three holes with standard spacing of .500 and .860 inch between centers into which the interchangeable drill bushing and tap guide bushing fit. The over-arm is keyed and slides in a T-slot. The arrangement provides true alignment with the exact center of the gun barrel. It has two V blocks of hardened steel that are adjustable for height.

This fixture can be set up to drill and tap rifle actions and barrels for top mounts and target scope blocks, receiver sights, ramp sights, beads on single barrel shotguns as well as side mounts whenever the mounting holes are in line with the centerline of the barrel.

To use this fixture the barreled action is laid in the V blocks, the action over the end of the fixture's clearance slot. The barrel to be drilled should be positioned so that the action is close to the rear V block, with the cylindrical or straight portion of the barrel supported by the front V block.

The over-arm then is slid into place over the portion of the action to be drilled and the rear V block is raised up to bring the action into contact with the correct-size drill bushing. The diameter of the barrel is measured with a micrometer at the points of contact at the front and rear V blocks. Since most barrels are tapered, it may be necessary to raise the front V block. To arrive at the exact difference in height, subtract the small diameter from the

larger diameter, multiply this value by .707 and raise the front V block that much higher than the rear V block. Measurements should be taken with a feeler gauge between the top of the machined boss and the bottom of the V block. Clamp the barrel lightly, using aluminum pads under the clamp screws to avoid marring the barrel.

On bolt-actions, raise the flat top support pad into firm contact with the flat bottom of the action to square it. The clamp on top of the leveling block is used to hold the action when the clamp is removed to move the over-arm over the action. A level should be used to double-check alignment.

To locate the base holes, place them on the action or barrel in the desired position and mark the forward hole with a scribe. Now use the locator pin through the front hole of the over-arm and slide it over the gun so that the point lines up with the mark, then lock it in place. The hole now may be drilled and tapped.

Screw the base to the gun using the one screw hole. Loosen the over-arm and locate the next hole and again lock the over-arm in place. Now lock the spacer block against the over-arm. The over-arm now can be moved out of the way, the base removed and the over-arm reset against the spacer block.

The second hole then is drilled and tapped. Other holes are located and drilled in the same manner. Do not drill holes in the action when the base is in place as it may cause them to be off-center.

When drilling holes in the receiver all but the forward hole over the chamber may be drilled completely through. The formula to determine the screw hole depth over the chamber is: barrel diameter minus the barrel groove diameter, divided by two, minus .125 inch. For example, using the calipers measure the barrel diameter. Let's say it measures 1.003. The caliber of the rifle is .338 which is also the groove diameter. 1.003 minus .338 equals .665. This figure is divided by 2 equaling .332. By subtracting .125, we get a safe maximum depth of .207 inch. The stop-mark on the drill press can be set up easily to drill this exact distance.

After all holes are drilled and tapped, the surrounding surfaces should be filed level and any protruding screws through the receiver must be cut back flush with the bottom sides of the receiver. It is important that the base screw holes be tightened securely. A drop of Loc-Tite will prevent them from backing out. To keep the scope from moving or turning in the rings, sprinkle a bit of powdered rosin on the inner ring surfaces.

Above, one-piece sight bases may be machined down to reduce overall weight. Al Lind built custom Sako L579 in 7x57mm, stocked with New Zealand Circassian walnut, mounting Redfield rings, Leupold 4X scope, below.

Chapter 16

THE INS & OUTS OF EXTRACTION, EJECTION

Often Confused, Each Is An Individual Operation Requiring Individual Attention

EXTRACTION AND ejection sound similar as words, but are two totally separate functions. Extraction is the method of getting the cartridge out of the chamber. Ejection throws, flips or kicks the cartridge or empty case out and away from the firearm.

There are different types of extraction and ejection systems. Some are excellent, many are adequate and a few are poor. However, even the best system may fail due to a variety of causes. The working riflesmith not only must understand the functional design of each type, but must be able to diagnose and eliminate potential problems before the shooter carries the gun to the field.

Several factors can influence the extraction cycle. Dirt, corrosion or foreign matter are major causes in faulty extraction. This is especially apparent in .22 rimfire rifles. When a .22 caliber rifle is taken out for a bit of plinking it is not uncommon to shoot several boxes of ammunition; it's still relatively inexpensive and fun. Unfortunately, powder fouling builds up rapidly in the breech area. It clogs the extractor cuts in the barrel and extractor slots in the bolt to prevent the extractor hook or claw from engaging the case rim. If corrosion gets into the bolt extractor spring recess, the extractor will be held out of position, unable to reach the case rim. Disassembling the rifle and cleaning it thoroughly in solvent will remedy the problem.

There is another common problem with rifles chambered for the .22 long rifle cartridge. Repeated firing of .22 shorts burns a ring in the chamber at the mouth of the short case. The result is escaping gas that is forced around the

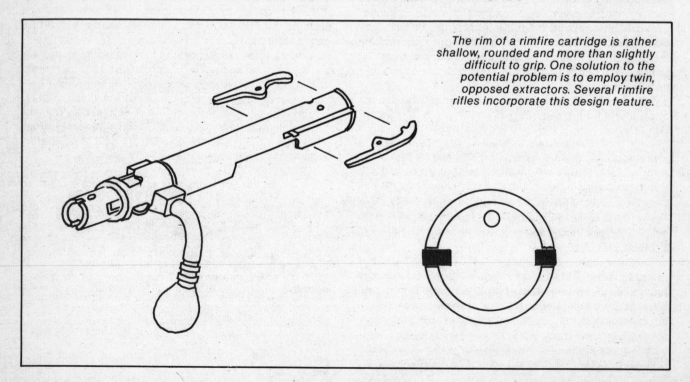

The rim of a rimfire cartridge is rather shallow, rounded and more than slightly difficult to grip. One solution to the potential problem is to employ twin, opposed extractors. Several rimfire rifles incorporate this design feature.

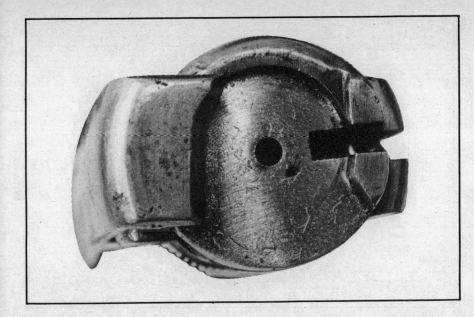

Here is the massive spring-steel claw extractor mounted along the outside of the bolt for a Model 98 Mauser.

bullet before it enters the rifling, this cutting a ring in the steel. The case expands, swelling into this depression to cause serious extraction problems. To cure the problem, the barrel may have to be set back and rechambered, a new barrel added or the barrel may be bored out and a liner used.

Worn extractors in .22 rimfire rifles affect extraction adversely. Sometimes the extractor can be recut with a file for better engagement and a new stronger extractor spring installed.

Extraction problems increase when the rifle is subjected to sustained rapid fire. The steel expands as the barrel becomes hot, increasing friction between case and barrel chamber. The hotter the barrel, the greater the chance of jamming due to faulty extraction.

If .22 rifles — especially older models — are subjected to repeated dry-firing, the chamber mouth will develop a burr. The burr should be peened over if possible and the area cleaned up and polished with a Dremel tool and small Cratex polishing wheel.

Many center-fire bolt-action rifles have coil springs providing tension to the extractor. Oftentimes they will bind in the spring recess in the bolt causing faulty extraction. If bent or ill-fitting, replacement will rectify the situation.

When certain military actions and barrels are modified and rechambered to magnum calibers, it is not uncommon to develop a swelled chamber. This is caused by the steel being too soft or — in some cases — defective. The barrel must be replaced. Not only will extraction be extremely difficult in this instance, but the shooter risks the possibility of the barrel blowing apart.

A rough chamber will cause rough extraction. It is quite important after rebarreling a rifle and chambering that the new chamber be polished using a portable drill with about 400-grit wet-or-dry paper. However, be extremely careful only to polish out any scratches or tool marks and not enlarge the chamber area. If the chamber does have scratches, extraction will be difficult; if the chamber is enlarged, the barrel must be set back and rechambered.

The best way to check is by use of a chamber cast to measure chamber specifications.

Extraction problems will develop due to incorrect cartridge case sizing. It should be standard practice to full-length resize all fired cases if they have been used in another rifle. Also, if the case does not retain its hardness during reloading, the extractor claw may rip off the case rim during the extraction cycle. Firing hot loads can create excessive pressures causing the cases to stick in the chamber adding to further extraction problems.

The wrong type of powder also can lead to extraction problems. Pressures can create dents in the case shoulder causing it to stick in the chamber. The Ball Powder used by the military in the M-16 rifle rather than the IMR (improved military rifle) powder recommended by the

Sako bolt with Mauser-type extractor fits slot above RH locking lug, anchored by dovetail at rear. Small lug under head holds extractor lengthwise. Approach eliminates need for actuating spring, retaining collar.

Remington counterbored bolt head has small extractor claw fitted into internal groove in bolt head which engages cartridge head extractor groove during bolt closure. Tip of the spring-loaded plunger-type ejector can be seen at lower right, protruding from the face of the bolt.

designer of the rifle, Eugene Stoner, burns longer and slower. This powder has a tendency to foul the gas port and gas port tube, causing faulty extraction. Unfortunately, to the best of my knowledge the military is still using Ball Powder for this rifle.

The first phase of extraction is called "primary extraction." Essentially it covers the period in which the fired case is being freed from the walls fo the chamber. Since the case expands tightly into the chamber walls this first step requires a certain amount of force to break it loose.

In bolt-action rifles this force is exerted by lifting the bolt handle. For example, the Mauser has a camming surface on the handle that engages another camming surface located on the top back edge of the receiver bridge. Early military tests proved this system boasted an eight-to-one leverage ratio. This strong leverage ratio and the massive extractor claw are two reasons most hunters of dangerous game have favored the Mauser action over the past eight decades. These important camming surfaces should be inspected for burrs or rough spots when safety checking a rifle. Stoning the burrs or marks takes only a few minutes and will aid in smooth extraction. Lapping in the camming surfaces with 500-grit silicone carbide may be substituted for stoning if preferred, but make sure all lapping compound is removed with a solvent after smoothing.

By the time primary extraction has taken place in a bolt-action rifle, the high chamber pressures have subsided enough to continue complete extraction of the cartridge case from the chamber. Even though pressures may exceed 50,000 psi (pounds per square inch) it has been reduced below 12,000 psi by the time the bullet has left the muzzle. Thus, there is virtually no danger of cycling the action too quickly between shots as long as the bolt is in the closed position each time the rifle is fired. I use the term psi because most shooters and gunsmiths deal in this terminology. Actually, pressure is measured in copper units of pressure (CUP), in chamber testing today.

After breaking the cartridge loose to complete the primary extraction stage, the extractor claw mating with the extractor groove of the cartridge is pulled from the chamber with the rearward travel of the bolt until ejected from the rifle.

There are a variety of extraction systems used in rifles. Double extractors are found most often in .22 caliber rifles. The right-hand extractor handles the extraction function while the left-hand extractor serves primarily as a guide to apply enough pressure on the cartridge for better holding power of the right extractor.

Top extraction systems are used occasionally. The best example of this is the Winchester Model 94. This system eliminates use of a top-mounting scope however. The position of the extractor now can be seen as quite impor-

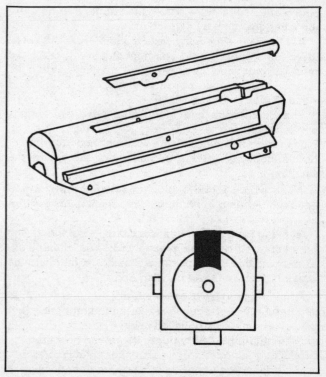

Diagram shows top extraction system, as found in the Winchester Model 94 lever-action carbines.

tant since it plays an active role in which way the spent cartridge case is thrown from the gun during ejection.

The extraction system is a bit different in rifles using the recessed bolt-head system. The bolt face is recessed allowing the cartridge head to fit inside (.12 inch in the Remington 700, .15 inch in the Weatherby Mark V). A small spring-steel indented ring fits into an undercut in the recess. This extractor hook rides over the case rim as the bolt is locked in the closed position. This system is less expensive to manufacture and makes for a stronger breech lock system.

I doubt that this extractor is as strong as the massive Mauser claw, but it has proved extremely reliable since its introduction. The modern Ruger 77 uses a partially enclosed recessed bolt head, but retains the Mauser-type extractor.

EJECTION

To throw, flip or kick the spent case or cartridge from the firearm, the rifle must have an ejector. Most ejection problems develop from broken or worn ejectors. It is possible that the ejector may be blocked before contacting the cartridge, causing ejection failure. Ejector springs, especially in the 1917 Enfield, are quite weak and break easily.

Generally speaking, ejection works best when the lever, bolt or slide is cycled quickly. Slow movement may not allow the ejector to clear the cartridge or spent case, causing a jam.

Rifle ejectors are generally either movable or a plunger type. Fixed plungers are found on automatic pistols such as the 1911 Colt .45 ACP and on many .22 caliber rifles. The spring-loaded Mauser ejector is an example of the movable ejector. It rides along the bolt body as the bolt is pulled back during extraction and is pushed by the ejector spring through the ejector slot on the left locking lug, striking and ejecting the cartridge. There are several variations of this system accomplishing the same purpose.

Spring-loaded plunger ejectors positioned into the bolt face are also quite common. This type of ejector is found in the Winchester Model 94 for example. It is compressed against the cartridge head when the action is closed. as the action is opened and the bolt moves away from the chamber the ejector pushes against the cartridge kicking it out as the edge of the cartridge nose or empty cartridge leading edge clears the chamber.

There are other ejection systems, but these are the main types most encountered by the working gunsmith. Ejectors may have to be shortened or lengthened if the cartridges are being thrown out at an improper angle, but the majority of extraction and ejection problems are caused by a dirty rifle. Examining the spent cartridges will identify many problems. Simply polishing any burrs off extractor claw edges also will solve a multitude of extraction problems.

As the Mauser claw extractor pulls the cartridge out of the chamber, the ejector — under spring tension — is forced through the left locking lug slot in the bolt, making contact with the cartridge head and flipping it away from the firearm and out through the ejection port, handling spent cases or loaded rounds the same.

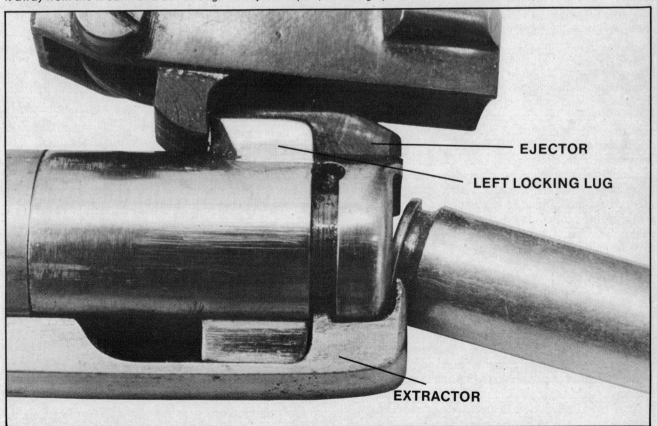

EJECTOR

LEFT LOCKING LUG

EXTRACTOR

Chapter 17

STOCK WOODS

Knowing The Qualities Of The Various Species Can Simplify Your Proper Choice

SINCE THE beginning of mankind wood has played a key role in the development of weaponry and its accessories. Man has a natural affinity with wood. It surrounds him as forests, houses him, sacrifices itself to the fire that warms him. Wood can be worked and shaped to perform innumerable functions. Boasting beauty, strength and adaptability, it is one of the few natural renewable products on the face of this planet. Nowhere is it brought to a higher state of the art than in custom stockmaking.

Woods chosen for gunstocks are based on certain criteria: weight, elasticity, strength, density, stability, beauty. There are numerous woods that meet many of these requirements, but walnut meets them all and is ideally suited for gunstocks and especially custom gunstocks.

A gunstock must be light enough to allow the rifle to be carried easily in the field. It must be elastic enough to withstand continuous firing without compressing. It must have the strength to survive rough use. It requires density to allow shaping, machining, checkering and finishing. Stability is necessary to reduce shrinkage and warpage

American black walnut trees usually range from thirty to seventy years, when harvested. Some European walnut species, however, are harvested when only fifteen years old. The older wood usually makes a better rifle stock.

This tree is being cut at Calico Hardwoods, Windsor, Calif. Note the concentration of spectacular figure in the stump portion of the log. Only five to ten percent of a harvested tree will produce highly figured stock blanks.

due to climatic conditions. For custom gunstocks, the wood must be beautiful, while possessing strength through the pistol grip, toe and recoil bearing surfaces.

The ideal weight of the wood for a gunstock is considered to be between thirty-five to forty pounds per cubic foot. According to the American Walnut Association, "American black walnut runs thirty-eight pounds per cubic foot. The differences in weight can be critical to a competitive shooter who is both mentally and physically fatigued."

However, within the species of any given tree, including walnut, the weight may vary considerably because of different types of soil, moisture conditions and the amount of nutrients available. Areas having moist clay soils initiate rapid growth, but result in low-density and porous wood. Trees that grow under hilly clay conditions grow more slowly to create a denser wood. Wood cut from either the juncture of a large limb or the stump will be heavier than the wood from the main log.

The elasticity of wood is greatly affected by the type and duration of the drying operations after cutting the log. Usually lower grades of wood are kiln dried which adversely affects the wood's resiliency. Air drying of wood for stocks requires from two to five years, but is the pre-

ferred method. The paraffin, shellac or tar painted on the end grain aids to prevent loss of moisture that could result in the wood cracking.

The strength of a stock is not only dependent upon the wood's innate properties, but by the way it is cut at the factory as well. Slab or flat-sawn blanks will have greater strength than those that are quarter sawn. When the wood is cut for a certain pattern, such as a standard sporter, the grain must be straight through critical areas such as the pistol grip. According to the American Hardwood Association, strength and shock resistance are measured in terms of pounds per square inch (psi) as it applies to the modulus of rupture and crushing strength. Modulus of rupture is that unit of measurement that gives the internal resistance for strength of a piece of wood before it disintegrates in any direction. Part of a stock's strength is its ability to resist crushing. The crush strength deals with the law of physics that says for every action there must be an opposite and equal reaction. The higher the crushing strength, the more recoil the stock (rather than your shoulder) will absorb and the less the stock is apt to deform over the years. Black walnut, for example, has a crush strength related to 10,660 psi as opposed to French walnut at 7320.

Each section of sawn lumber is examined carefully before it's cut to stock blank size, retaining strength, beauty.

After the log has been cut, stock blanks are air-dried from two to five years. End grain is coated with tar or shellac to prevent any cracking during shrinkage.

Worker uses stock template to determine how to cut the walnut to proper size for stock blanks.

After choosing the shape for the stock blank, worker cuts log to proper shape with a band saw.

The stockmaker is particularly concerned with the density of wood. It determines a great deal as to how the wood will hold up when chiseled, machined, checkered and finished. Dense woods with close pores have less tendency to crack, splinter or chip. The checkering diamonds will be cleaner and sharper with less tendency for the wood to "fuzz" as the cutter makes each pass. Finish will build up faster rather than be absorbed. Both French and English walnut are excellent in regard to density.

A stock's stability is critical to both strength and accuracy. Some woods tend to shrink or swell more than others due to moisture. American black walnut, French and English walnut show remarkable traits in this area after proper seasoning. However, highly figured blanks, especially crotch cuts (point of limb intersection with trunk) are not as stable as other sections of the blank. Any wood displaying a large amount of figure should have the figure portion in the butt stock region with the straight grain running through the pistol grip.

A large number of different woods are quite attractive, yet it is walnut that not only meets all the specific requirements of a gunstock, but also displays the greatest range of color and grain. For example, grading of American black walnut gunstocks — as well as all other stockwoods — is determined by grain variation and generally is divided into two categories: field grade and fancy grade. Grading is both difficult and subjective, since the inherent grain variation in stock wood makes each gunstock as individual as fingerprints.

According to the American Walnut Association, "field-grade walnut has no fancy figure on either side of the stock. These straight-grained blanks are widely available and are actually preferable to fancy wood for certain guns. For example, in high-powered rifles a straight-

GOOD STOCK CHARACTERISTICS

POOR STOCK CHARACTERISTICS

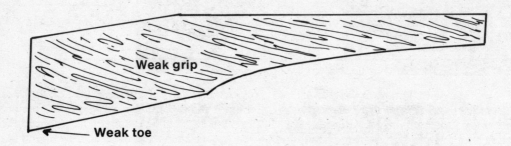

Weak grip

Weak toe

Examples of strong and weak stock blanks are illustrated in artist's concept. Grain should run parallel or slightly upward for maximum strength. Grain that tends to run from high to low through toe area will crack, break easily.

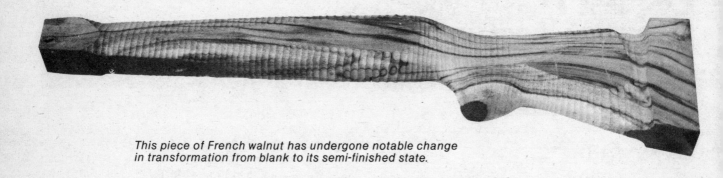

This piece of French walnut has undergone notable change in transformation from blank to its semi-finished state.

grained stock is more suitable. Although the top grades of English walnut cost approximately three times that of American black walnut, the plain grades of both species are pretty close in cost and American black walnut is far more colorful.

"Although all walnut has some grain variation which makes each stock, whether field or fancy, unique, only five to ten percent of the total production of walnut gunstock blanks are highly figured. If the wood is figured on both sides of the stock and both sides match, the piece is considered No. 1 fancy grade. Feather figure always comes from the crotch of the tree, the area where the wood

wrinkles as the limbs undergo a change in direction. About one percent of the total walnut blank production falls into this category and this wood is primarily used for commemoratives or custom stock work.

"About twenty-five percent of the fancy grain walnut is fiddleback figure. Fiddleback is cut from the grain which runs throughout the body of the tree; it is exceptionally strong and considered a straight-grained wood with curly figure. Fiddleback walnut has been traditionally used on the backs of violins or fiddles since it can be cut out to various thicknesses needed for acoustical variation (acting as an amplifier) without splitting.

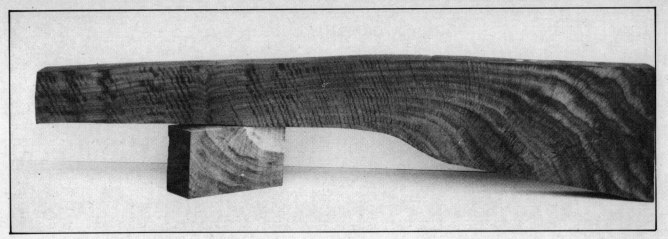

This beautiful stock blank fashioned from California claro walnut is from Calico Hardwoods, a California company.

"If the feather is perfectly matched on both sides of the stock it is considered full-fancy. This type of walnut is exceedingly rare since the stock must be cut from the exact center of the crotch to achieve the balanced feather pattern."

Although the association naturally is more interested in the homegrown woods, they do make a point of which stockmakers should be aware: *"Juglans nigra* (black walnut) should not be confused with its cousin, *Juglans regia,* which is indigenous to France, Spain, Italy, Greece, Turkey and Iran and goes by different names such as French walnut, Turkish walnut, Circassian walnut, English walnut, Himalayan walnut and Hindsi. A fast-growing tree that peaks in fifteen years, *Juglans regia* is grown primarily as a nut crop and compared to American black walnut has a much higher percentage of soft, white wood and less dense black wood. It should be pointed out that American black walnut gunstock blanks are processed by American manufacturers who have total responsibility for the tree from the woods to the actual gun manufacturer. This responsibility ensures a consistent quality product. On the other hand, English walnut passes through many hands on its way to becoming a finished product, i.e., timber cutters in Europe and Asia, lumber processors, numerous brokers, forwarders, handlers and importers."

There are other woods quite acceptable for gunstocks beside the various walnuts; some have been used on rifles for hundreds of years quite successfully. Each wood has strengths and weaknesses that lends itself better to one type of firearm than another. Let's take a brief look at a few of the stock woods available to the riflesmith:

ENGLISH WALNUT is quite rare, but excellent for gunstocks. It has rich brown tones with good markings. It works well with hand tools, although not quite as strong and hard as the American black walnut. Average weight is thirty-five to thirty-eight pounds. It checkers quite well and requires no staining prior to finishing. English walnut trees have been successfully transplanted in our Western states improving availability at reasonable prices over the past few years.

These photos show both sides of an exhibition-grade stock blank from Calico Hardwoods. Although the butt shows an excellent figure, this particular blank will be cut in such manner that the straight grain runs through pistol grip.

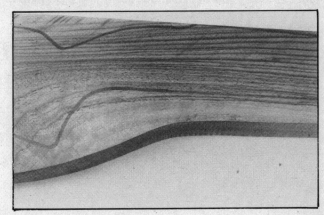

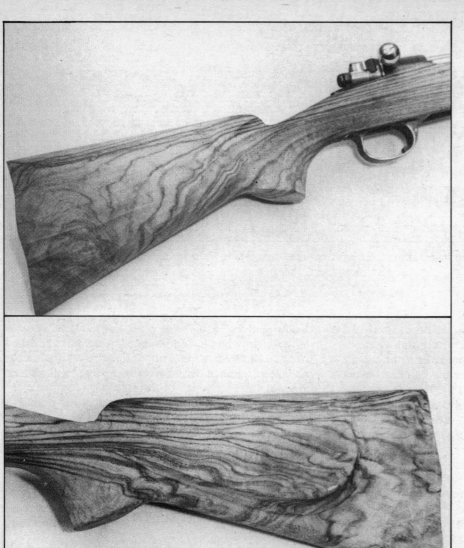

After shaping the blank, the pistol grip has figure that is in straight line to axis of the bore. This piece of French walnut has burl figure at toe.

EUROPEAN WALNUT is referred to generally as European walnut or by its country of origin, but this *Juglans regia* species is actually a native of western and central Asia, extending from China to northern India. Grown commercially in Turkey, France, Italy and Yugoslavia, it is variable in color with grayish-brown background marked with irregular dark-colored streaks. The figure is due to the infiltration of coloring matter and sometimes accentuated by a naturally wavy grain. Highly figured pieces are the result of cuts from the stump, burl and crotches of the trees. The wood is a bit heavier weighing about forty pounds per cubic foot after being air-dried. The wood may vary greatly in color, figure and texture.

French walnut is generally paler and grayer than English, while the Italian variation is characterized by elaborate figure and dark, streaky coloration.

European walnut is excellent for rifle stocks, being strong with dense characteristics that lend themselves to checkering and finishing extremely well.

AMERICAN BLACK WALNUT *(Juglans nigra)* grows from Vermont to the Great Plains and southward into Louisiana and Texas. The heartwood varies from light to dark brown, while sapwood is nearly white and up to three inches wide in some trees. It works extremely well and has the strength, elasticity, density and beauty neces-

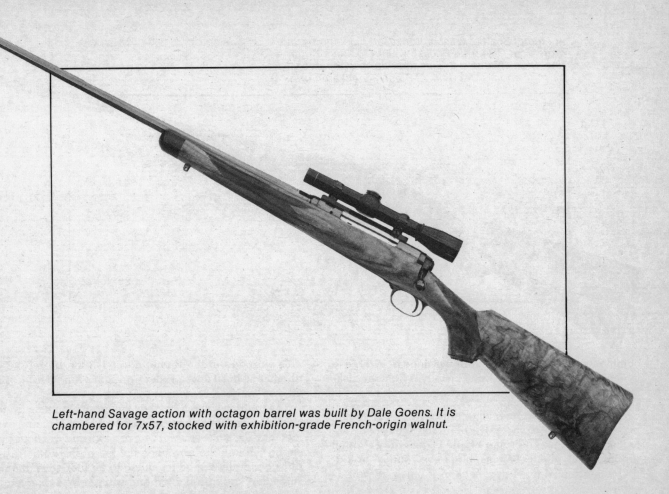

Left-hand Savage action with octagon barrel was built by Dale Goens. It is chambered for 7x57, stocked with exhibition-grade French-origin walnut.

sary for gunstocks. Highly figured pieces lend themselves well to custom stocks. The wood checkers nicely.

CIRCASSIAN WALNUT was obtained originally from the Circassian region on the Black Sea in Russia. Transplanted to the United States, it is available in sufficient quantities. Distinguished by its rich brown color and fine figure, it has all the desirable traits of the other walnuts. It checkers and finishes quite well.

CHERRY, known as *Prunus serotina* or black cherry, wild black cherry, wild cherry or chokecherry grows throughout southeastern Canada, the eastern and central half of the United States. The heartwood varies from light to dark reddish-brown with distinctive luster. Sapwood is narrow in the older trees and almost white in color. The wood machines well and has good strength, elasticity and stability. It is not quite as hard as walnut and slightly lighter in weight. It checkers well and is quite acceptable for gunstocks.

BASTOGNE WALNUT is a cross between the English and California Claro walnut. It is exceptionally strong and stable. The figure is predominantly fiddleback similar to Claro, but has a color more like that of English walnut. It is an excellent wood for gunstocks and checkers almost as well as the French species.

CLARO WALNUT is native to California and similar to American walnut, although not quite as hard. It has contrasting grain color and generally is darker than American black walnut.

MYRTLEWOOD is more dense than walnut, while quite strong and stable. It accepts finish and checkers quite well. It generally is distinguished by its light blonde color interrupted with rich brown streaks.

MAPLE has been used on gunstocks for hundreds of years. Different types include sugar maple, black maple, silver maple, red maple, box elder and bigleaf maple. Sugar maple is also called hard maple, rock maple and sugar tree. Black maple is called river maple, swamp maple and water maple. The sugar maple and black maple are known as hard maple. Silver maple, red maple and box maple are called soft maple. The sapwood is

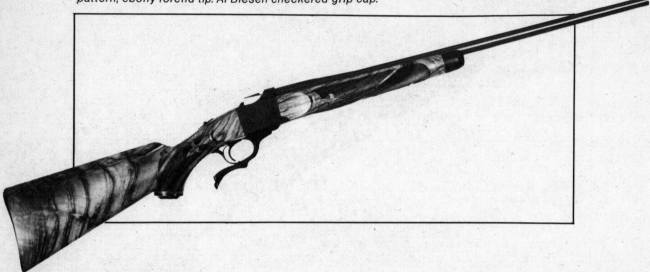

Al Lind of Seattle, Washington, used exhibition-grade crotch-cut California English walnut to stock Ruger #1 rifle. Stock features 24-line fleur de lis with ribbon pattern, ebony forend tip. Al Biesen checkered grip cap.

commonly white with a reddish-brown tinge from three to five inches thick. The heartwood usually is light reddish-brown, but often is considerably darker in color.

Hard maple has a fine, uniform texture being strong, hard and resistant to shock. It is also a bit heavy and subject to shrinkage. The sugar maple is generally straight grained, but often contains birds-eye, curley or fiddleback grain. It does not checker or finish as well as walnut.

Blanks may come either plain or quarter-sawn. The first will result in a stock having the grain lines running in a vertical direction. This type of cut will produce the more beautiful stocks, revealing their figure. The warping tendencies of the plain-sawn blank will be from side-to-side.

This warpage in the forend can push the barrel out of alignment, but it does produce greater strength in the pistol grip and butt regions.

The quarter-sawn blank has the grain running side-to-side and will not show the figure like the plain-sawn method. The stock will warp up or down and will not be as strong through the grip or in the toe of the butt. Target rifles generally are better suited to quarter-sawn blanks since they are free-floated and will not be subjected to vertical warping and there is not as large a role played in the beauty of the stock.

If a finished stock made of walnut should warp through the pistol grip region or if a shooter requires a bit more cast-off, all that is required is to apply a wet cloth on the stock at the bend. Place a low heat source such as a 100-

This 7x57 rifle was stocked by the late Lenard Brownell with European walnut in the popular Mannlicher style.

Sako .375 H&H has been stocked in American black walnut by Sterling Davenport. It features Conetrol base, rings. Lower rifle is customized 1909 Argentino Mauser .30/06 stocked in French walnut by Davenport. It has Interarms KM X trigger guard, Pachmayr Olde English recoil pad, Biesen grip cap, 24-line fleur-de-lis, ribbon checkering.

watt light bulb within a few feet. After a few days, it will be possible to bend the stock in the desired direction, holding the bend in place with a weight. After the stock dries it will retain its new angle.

POISONOUS WOODS

ARCWOOD (*Tabebuia guayacan*)
Yellow dust produces mild dermatitis; breathing may cause severe irritation of upper respiratory tract.

COCOBOLO (*Dalbergia spp.*)
Has same effects as Arcwood, but may cause poison-ivy-like rash.

MANCHINEEL TREE (*Hippomane mancinella*)
Milky sap is powerful irritant, causing blistering of skin. Smoke from burning wood has produced inflammation of eyes.

OSAGE ORANGE (*maclurapomifera*)
Milky sap produces contact dermititis.

WEST INDIAN BOXWOOD (*gossypiospermum praecox*)
Milling operations (dust) causes severe facial swelling. Victim may require hospitalization.

In certain instances individuals may be super sensitive, and may exhibit allergic symptoms, such as itching of skin areas, severe sneezing, watering eyes, or coughing from the following wood dust:

ROSEWOOD
PURPLE HEART (*Amaranth*)
BUBINGA
IMBUI
JACARANDI
SUCAPIRA

These are usually used for inlays, grip caps, forend tips, pistol, and revolver grips.

**The Duplicator
Is The Easy
Route To
Stock Shaping**

180

THE GUN DIGEST BOOK OF RIFLESMITHING

Sterling Davenport draws needed guidelines on the stock blank in preparation for drilling holes that will be used for positioning.

MOST FULL-TIME stockmakers agree that the use of a duplicator is a much faster alternative than cutting a rifle stock by hand with mallet and chisel. Unfortunately, a duplicating machine is an expensive piece of equipment, a commercial model starts at $3000, escalating in price if the machine is set up to cut multiple blanks at the same time. Since the single-model duplicating machine can serve the custom stockmaker quite well, we will concentrate on this type for the one-man custom gunsmithing shop.

I have heard some riflesmiths complain that the duplicating machine will not provide the precise inletting or desired overall shape that a completely handmade stock will produce. Most complaints are generally aimed at gaps in the magazine box region or the barrel channel. These problems are the direct result of the pattern stock

and not the machine. It is wise to check out the pattern or master stock before shipping off your favorite blank for shaping. This problem does not exist if you wish to duplicate one of your own stocks which may be sent along with the blank for duplication.

It may be helpful to any full-time stockmaker interested in purchasing a duplicator to accept work from other gunshops; offering this service can help pay for the machinery.

Using a duplicating machine is not difficult. In less than ninety minutes a stock blank can be rough shaped completely, the guard screw holes drilled, the barrel channel and the magazine box inletted in preparation for final hand shaping and inletting. Anyone who has done the same work by hand knows it can take more than a week to accomplish the same results.

Riflesmith Sterling Davenport built his duplicator with

the aid of well-known gunsmith Harry Lawson of Tucson, Arizona. The former begins shaping a stock blank by making an outline of the stock — in this case a classic Mauser sporting rifle — by using a plastic template and a marking pen. By moving the template around the side of the blank he can better choose the best spot to cut it to maximize the blank's grain structure and strength.

After the outline has been drawn on the blank, Davenport cuts it on a bandsaw to match the pattern design that will be used on the duplicator. The next step is to draw layout lines to drill the supporting holes in the stock blank to match the holes in the pattern stock. Sterling uses a fixture of his own to drill the holes in the blank in precisely the correct spots. The holes are drilled in the area of the buttstock and match the supporting pins on the duplicating machine.

The next step is to place the stock blank and pattern stock in the duplicator holding it in place with the staples at the buttstock end and a center at the other. With

Davenport uses a small jig of his own design for use in drilling the positioning holes in the rifle stock blank.

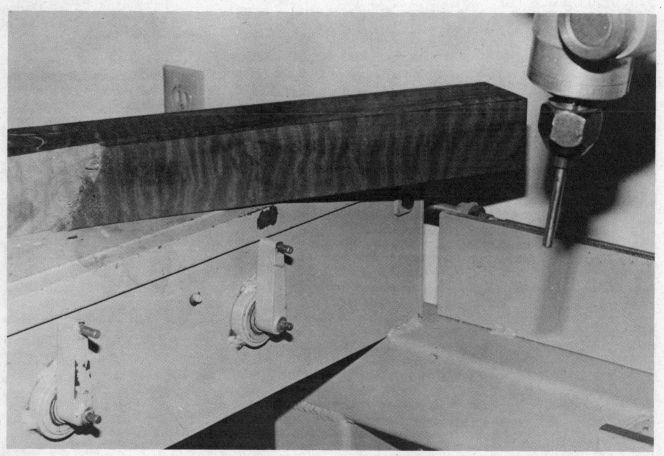

The pattern stock and the uncut blank both are held in place on the duplicating machine by means of the holes that have been drilled for the holders. By this means, it is possible to duplicate the exact shape of pattern.

Davenport utilizes a small hand level to determine that the pattern stock and blank are level with cutter and stylus.

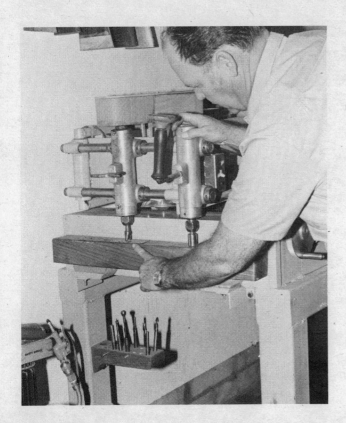

the work place, Davenport uses a small level to perfectly level the work in the machine. The level is placed on top of the pattern stock's barrel channel. This step allows perfect perpendicular cuts through the magazine box which is the basis for achieving a symmetrically rough-shaped stock.

On the outside of the duplicator is a perfectly flat and level block of wood. After placing the stylus to trace the outline of the pattern stock and the cutter to cut and shape the stock blank on the level board, Davenport now employs a plastic shim between cutter and level board. By using this shim, the cutter will cut to precise depth minus the diameter of the shim, allowing the blank to be rough shaped but slightly oversize in this initial cutting phase. The riflesmith begins cutting the blank by running the stylus over the pattern stock.

After the initial rough-cut has been completed to shape the stock Davenport repositions the cutter by placing it and the stylus back on the level board, but does not use the shim at this point. The next cut brings the blank down to perfect tolerances with that of the pattern stock.

The riflesmith places a plastic shim of about .020-inch in thickness under the cutter to allow for oversize in the initial rough cutting of the blank he will use.

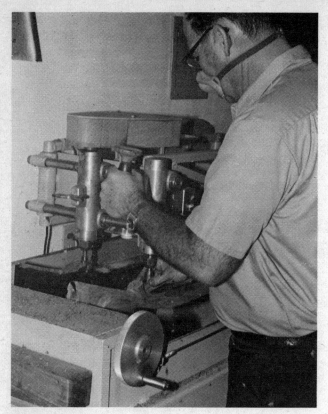

A smaller cutter is used to drill magazine box, rear tang, barrel channel recesses. It is critical that the work be perpendicular to cutter. Small level is used to check that both blank and pattern stock are level.

After cutting the blank to tolerance, the rough cutter is replaced with a smaller finish cutter to cut the magazine box, rear tang, and barrel channel. Before any cutting is attempted the work is again checked with a level to insure perfect perpendicular cuts. This small cutter also will cut the stock screw holes.

As the stock blank came closer to completion Davenport continually checked the blank's dimensions against those of the pattern stock with a vernier caliper. The entire

Using the duplicating stylus, Sterling Davenport runs over the outline of the pattern stock to match it to the walnut stock blank that he is about to rough shape.

After the oversize cut has been made on the blank, the cutter is lowered to the depth of the stylus. This results in the stock blank being cut to the exact dimensions of the pattern stock, wood being removed in circular cuts.

THE GUN DIGEST BOOK OF RIFLESMITHING

The handle in foreground is used to adjust both pattern stock and the blank so that they are perpendicular to both the cutter and stylus, assuring exact duplication.

operation took slightly less than an hour and a half and could probably have been done more quickly.

If one cannot afford to purchase a duplicator it might be wise to find a stockmaker who has one. His charge to shape a blank for you would be worth the price in the amount of time and effort of attempting to shape a stock from a blank. Final shaping and inletting will still be necessary to fit all metal parts to the stock insuring a perfect fit with no gaps.

There is one manufacturer of duplicating equipment that I do know sells to the gunsmithing trade. For more information write to Don Allen, Inc., RR 4, Northfield, MN 55057.

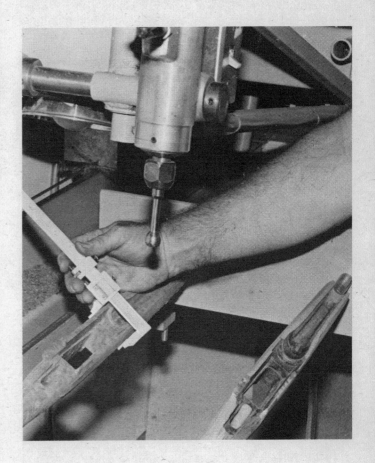

Chapter 18

INLETTING, SHAPING SEMI-INLETTED STOCKS

They're Faster To Work Than Blanks To Produce The Same Results

SEMI-FINISHED STOCKS have been produced commercially for the gunsmithing trade since the mid-1930s. Today they are available in a multitude of styles for almost all rimfire and center-fire rifles past and presently manufactured. They may be ordered in several grades ranging from standard, through several choices of fancy, to presentation and exhibition grades. Most manufacturers have large inventories of popular hardwoods such as American, Bastogne, claro, and French walnut, maple, cherry, myrtlewood and even laminated varieties from which to choose.

The cost of semi-inletted stocks is barely more than an unfinished blank, the small additional charge is more than offset by the time and effort saved in having to lay out and rough-shape the blank by hand. One of the few problems rarely encountered when ordering semi-finished stocks is finding that the action recesses are a bit oversize

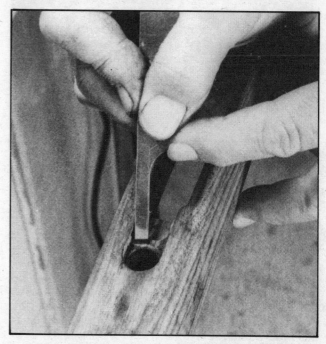

Left: Semi-finished stocks have much of the inletting done. In this one, the magazine box mortise is cut and recess for trigger guard is 90 percent finished. (Above) After the trigger guard is inletted, scrapers are used to eliminate high spots in it and other recessed areas.

The magazine box should not fit too tightly into inletted area, as it could lead to cracking of the wood in the web area during the recoil.

resulting in gaps between metal and wood. Established manufacturers such as Fajen, Pachmayr, Bishop, Sile, Western Gunstocks and Royal Arms take great pains to produce an error-free product, but it is a good idea to measure certain diameters like the width of the tang before any inletting is begun. If there is a problem, most companies will immediately replace the stock or refund your money.

Inletting a semi-finished stock properly is not difficult provided one pays close attention to detail, has patience, the correct tools for the job and performs each step in the necessary sequence. The tools can be purchased, but the patience comes from within. A good rule of thumb is "the closer you get to completion the slower you go." It is the final bit of fitting that determines the perfect marriage betwen wood and metal.

Good inletting is neither too tight nor too loose. An action that is fitted so tightly that it must be driven into the stock with a mallet may result in so much pressure from the inner stock walls that the action binds and does not bottom properly in the right spots. Accuracy will be affected adversely, and when the guard screws are tightened down the loss in accuracy will be increased.

Also, if moisture gets into the stock the pores will swell resulting in a chance it may crack. There is also a strong possibility that when the action or trigger guard are removed the mating surfaces of the wood will splinter. A loose fitting job results in unsightly gaps between wood and metal, the mark of shoddy workmanship. Loose inletting in the necessary contact points also will cause the barreled action to shift and twist during recoil resulting in twelve-inch groups at one hundred yards; hardly acceptable. Good inletting should have no gaps between wood and metal; the trigger guard and action should be removed easily from the stock, but bottom securely at the necessary bearing points.

Inletting requires minimum tools. A vise with soft jaws, wood chisels, scrapers, inletting black, mallet, files and inletting pins will suffice. A Dremel Moto-Tool with wood-cutting bit and sanding discs are handy, but not used for final inletting.

There is a definite sequence to be followed when inletting a rifle. Actions that have a one-piece trigger guard such as Mausers, Springfields and Enfields are inletted trigger guard first. Others with two-piece trigger guards like the Winchester Model 70 have the action inletted

INLETTING PIN SIZES

Mauser	¼"x22
Enfield	¼"x30
Springfield	¼"x25
U.S. Krag	¼"x25
Norwegian Krag	¼"x20
Jap 6.5	.238"x28
Jap 7.7	.223"x34
Carcano	¼"x25
Sako	.233"x26
Win Model 52	.220"x36
Win Model 52 (B & C Models)	¼"x32
Win Model 70	¼"x32
Win Model 54	¼"x36
Weatherby MK V	¼"x28
Ruger Model 77 (rear)	10x32
front	¼"x28
Remington 700	¼"x28
Savage 110	¼"x28

first. Inletting the trigger guard first allows us to use the screw holes in the guard as guides for the inletting pins placed in the action. That enables us to seat the action in precisely the same spot each time as we attempt to bottom it in the stock.

Before inletting the trigger guard the stock must be securely positioned in a vise with soft jaws to prevent damaging the wood. I prefer to have the stock held in the vise at its receiver ring area to prevent possible cracking. I also place a block of wood under the comb near the edge of the stock heel. This technique offers a stable, horizontal work surface.

For demonstration purposes we will be inletting a Mauser action into a semi-finished blank made by Sterling Davenport on his duplicating machine. The wood is French walnut purchased in blank form from Calico Hardwoods of Windsor, California. The trigger guard is integral with the magazine box. If you should have to inlet an action with a trigger guard that is separate from the magazine box, inlet the trigger guard first, then the box.

Inletting the trigger guard and magazine box does not require a great deal of effort as the duplicating machine already has removed most of the wood. With the magazine box mortise already cut, it is a simple matter to establish proper position for assembly. Begin by placing

Sterling Davenport has inserted inletting pins in the Mauser action to ensure precise alignment. The bottom of the rifle action has been smeared with inletting black. This leaves outline of wood to be removed, when receiver ring has been given a good rap with a rawhide mallet to indicate where the high spots in the wood still protrude.

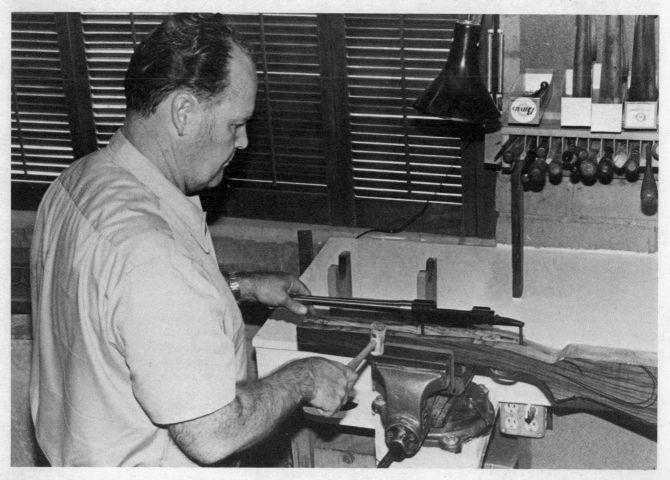

THE GUN DIGEST BOOK OF RIFLESMITHING

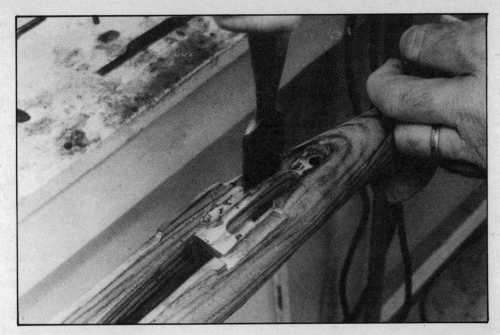

A straight-edge chisel is necessary to cut inside receiver lines and thus assure it will bottom in the stock without gaps.

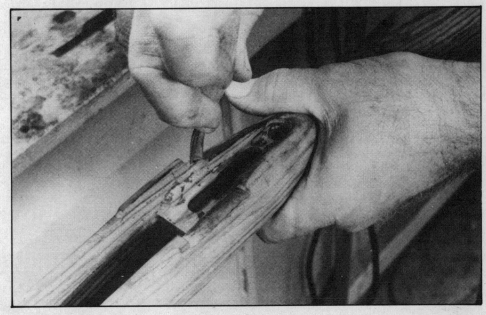

Small curved chisels are used by the riflesmith to get into the tinier recesses in the stock.

guard and box into the mortise to check alignment between guard holes and stock holes and how far the box will go before seating. The box is tapered and will go quite a ways before wedging into the stock. Don't force it, as you could crack the stock. If the alignment appears to be perfect, the whole unit may be inletted straight down. However, a bit of shifting forward or back may be necessary to get the holes to line up. This is no problem, as there is extra wood in this area specifically for this purpose.

Apply inletting black to the sides and front of the box and place it into the stock motrise until it seats. Remove and use a file or rasp to remove the wood that has been spotted by the inletting black. This process is appropriately called "spotting." Continue spotting until the undersides of front and rear trigger guard extensions touch the wood. Scribe an outline to indicate the area of wood that must be removed to allow the guard to bottom in the precut recess. Use small straight and curved chisels to remove the wood, making certain all cuts are straight down into the wood. When the guard is inletted completely into the stock, do not be alarmed that the edges of the guard assembly are deeper than flush with the stock's outside surface. This excess wood is left purposely by the manufacturers to accommodate the many variations between different style and size Mauser guards. It will be removed later during the stock shaping. Check to see that the guard bottoms with the stock uniformly. If not, the guard can be bent about one-sixteenth-inch for better fit. This often happens with Enfields and Springfields. They may have to be bent as much as one-eighth-inch. The angled rear guard screw will still align with the action, although the guard screw hole in the stock may have to be slightly enlarged.

With the magazine box and trigger guard inletted turn

the stock upright in the vise to begin inletting of the action. If the guard has been inletted too loosely stick a small piece of wood between guard and gap to act as a wedge. The gap will be repaired later. To inlet the action precisely, inletting pins are necessary. The pins align with the guard screw holes in the trigger guard insuring proper positioning each time the action is removed and replaced into the stock. The pins may be purchased through Brownell's.

You will note that the action recess in the stock has been almost completely inletted while the barrel channel is considerably undercut. This is critical since the manufacturers do not know whether the action has been barreled for a small featherweight or large bull barrel. With the inletting pins in the receiver insert the barreled action into the precut inletted stock and gently push down as far as it will go. Use a scribe or pencil and outline where the receiver bottom rests against the wood. Now use a straight chisel to cut straight down inside the lines. Continue this method until the bottom of the receiver enters the stock going approximately one-eighth-inch below the stock's top line. At this point we must allow for proper positioning of the action's recoil lug. Coat the bottom of the lug with inletting black. Place the action into the stock. You will note that the semi-finished stock already has a precut oversize recoil lug cut into it. With the inletting completed to the point that the bottom of the recoil lug on the action bottoms on the lug flat of the stock, take a mallet and give it a good whack on top of the receiver ring. Remove the action and note the impression the lug has made on the flat. Use a straight-edged chisel to cut straight down into the stock at the rear edge of the impression flush with the precut bottom flat. We can now expect an exact fit between recoil lug and stock lug recess, a key to the rifle's accuracy and strength.

There are a few tips that will make inletting the barrel channel faster and easier. When the action is inletted into the

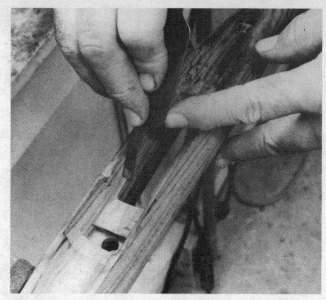

During the final spotting for excess wood that could cause problems, inletting black and scrapers are used to remove those minute high spots in the inlet areas.

stock, the barrel will bottom on the upper inner surfaces of the barrel channel. Use a pencil or scribe alongside the barrel from receiver to the front edge of the forend tip. Remove the action and check the pencil lines to see if the barrel is aligned correctly with the center-line of the stock's barrel channel. If so, use a straight-edged chisel and cut straight down about three-thirty-seconds-inch just inside the scribe lines the entire length of each side of the channel. Do not use the edges of the channel as a fulcrum to hog out the wood as it may crack. Use inletting rasps, bedding tools and scrapers to round and smooth out the area. After cutting this preliminary channel the

Scrapers, kept razor-sharp, are fashioned to contour with surfaces of stock where removal of wood is required.

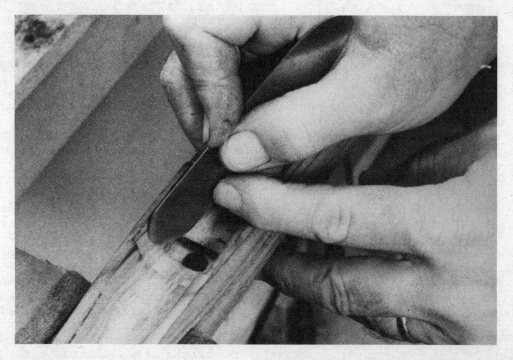

Bearing surface between back of the recoil lug, stock lug recess must be smooth, sans high spots.

During final seating of barrel into the stock channel, don't remove additional wood from top side of the channel or gaps may develop that will be unsightly.

receiver and barrel are coated with inletting black for final fitting using the spotting method.

We are now entering the final phase of inletting. Continue to use inletting black to mark high spots in wood to be removed. Use only scrapers to shave away the black spots. As the bottom of the action begins to rest in the action check to make certain we have good contact for approximately 1½ inches in front of the recoil lug recess, the flat just behind the lug recess, the surface bearing against the recoil lug, around the rear guard screw in the tang region, and for about one to two inches from the forend.

To prevent gaps between barrel and channel walls do not remove the blackened areas at the uppermost edges of the walls during the final inletting. If you continue to scrape these edges approximately one-eighth-inch from the top of the walls, gaps will result. The barrel should be inletted to half-depth in the stock. A good way to check this measurement after inletting and during the shaping of the stock is with a square placed into the center of the channel with the square's edge. The edge should bottom in the channel, but each side of the square should touch the top inner edges of the walls.

Although one should strive for a perfect job, all is not lost if a mistake is made. For example, if the rear tang should be inletted too deeply it can be corrected by glu-

To achieve utmost in accuracy, there should be good contact between the barrel and barrel channel from the end of the forend tip, extending rearward 1½ inch.

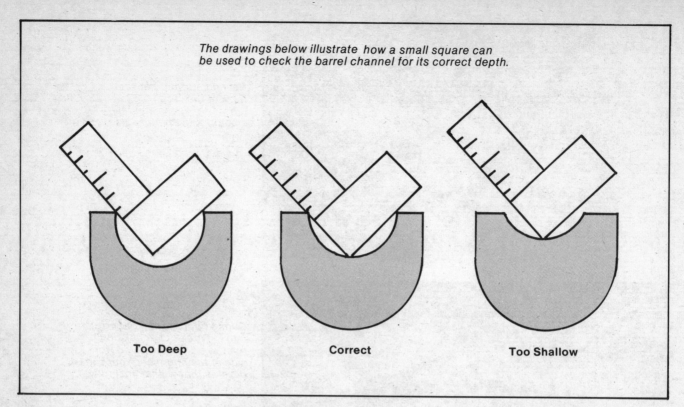

The drawings below illustrate how a small square can be used to check the barrel channel for its correct depth.

Too Deep   **Correct**   **Too Shallow**

ing a small piece of hardwood into the tang screw region acting as a shim. The action is then re-fitted to the stock. After inletting the receiver bottom should be within one-sixty-fourth-inch of the top of the magazine box. If we've inletted a bit too deeply just file the top of the box off evenly until the proper distance is obtained. If the magazine box seats to full depth with no gap on sides, or at front or back, remove it from the stock and relieve all sides with a file. We do not want the magazine box to flush fit with the stock as it could crack the web during recoil.

Another check is to place trigger guard, floorplate and barreled action into the stock. Tighten down the front guard screw, then tighten the rear guard screw and check for any movement of the rear tang. If there is movement, either the tang area of the stock must be shimmed or more inletting is necessary on the bottom of the recoil shoulder, the receiver ring area and/or the barrel channel. There must be no movement for optimum strength and accuracy of the rifle. The final check involves the tension of the barrel against the forend tip. This is accomplished by

The Mauser receiver has been inletted fully into stock. Note lack of gaps between wood, metal.

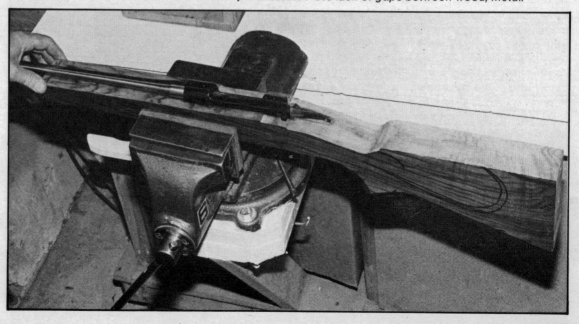

AVERAGE RIFLE STOCK DIMENSIONS

Length of pull — center of trigger to center of buttplate	13½"
Drop at comb from line of sight	1-11/16"
Drop at heel from line of sight	2⅞"
Length from heel to point of comb	9¾"
Length from center of trigger to point of comb	4½" to 4⅝"
Length from center of trigger to nearest point of pistol grip cap	3½"
Drop of front edge of pistol grip cap below center of trigger	1⅝" to 1¾"
Length of butt plate	5⅛"
Width of butt plate at widest point	1-11/16"
Pitch (down)	2½"
Circumference of grip	4⅞"
Cast off at butt	0
Cast off if desired, Heel	3/16"
Cast off if desired, Toe	5/16"

grabbing the barrel and pulling upwards away from the forend tip. If there is too much tension further inletting at this point is necessary. If there is no tension or a gap, the action must be deepened or the forend built up using Acraglas or similar product.

Some riflesmiths prefer glass bedding over simple wood to metal fit saying it gives added strength and superior bedding to the action. It is certainly easier. Oftentimes heavy magnum rifles are glass bedded and/ or have a recoil plate inserted for additional strength. However, on small and standard caliber rifles, inletting a stock correctly will yield excellent accuracy and provide sufficient strength. The feeling with most custom riflesmiths is that the challenge to mate metal and wood to a perfect marriage without epoxy and glass aids can be

accomplished and is a reflection of their dedication to perfection.

The final shape of any stock is up to the individual, but there are certain guidelines offered here for consideration when building a stock in the "classic" tradition and a definite sequence followed to arrive at all necessary dimensions.

The first important measurement must be made even before the stock is inletted. Unless stocking a rifle in the Mannlicher-style, the forend tip stops half-way up the barrel. To determine this measurement, measure from the tip of the barrel to the edge of the receiver ring. If you have a twenty-two-inch barrel, measure back eleven inches from the muzzle and mark the stock accordingly. Semi-finished stock manufacturers leave the forends long specifically for this purpose. If a forend tip is to be added, subtract an additional two inches. All that is left to do now is cut off the excess. Another dimension pertaining to the forend tip is its depth from the barrel. It is measured after the inletting is completed and the bottom of the stock is flushed to the trigger guard. Using a straight edge held parallel and flush with the guard extend a pencil line to the forend tip. Sport stocks generally have a 1⅛-inch depth while varmint and target rifles will have a 1½-inch depth.

If an amateur is building a rifle from a semi-finished stock for his personal use, or the custom riflesmith for a customer, measurements such as length of pull, drop in comb, pitch, cast off, circumference of grip and so on will all vary. I have included in this chapter a chart of average rifle stock dimensions as a guide. It is possible to arrive at all the right dimensions in building a rifle from a semi-finished stock perfectly and still achieve a custom look and good overall weight balance.

Begin shaping by removing the wood from the underside of the stock until the edges of the wood surrounding the trigger guard are flush. The line from the trigger

Inletting is continued until all necessary bearing points are achieved in the stock and barrel is at half-depth.

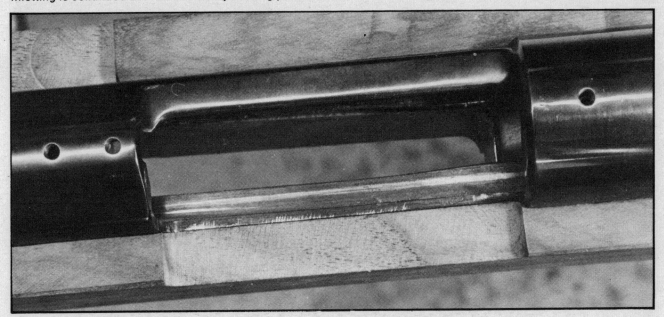

Shape of a stock is a matter of personal preference, but certain master lines should be established. The purpose of this is to create a balanced stock that is not only functional, but pleasing to the eye as well.

guard to the forend tip with its 1⅛-inch depth should also be a straight line. One will notice immediately that with the bottom of the stock at its proper depth in relation to the barrel line that the sides must be contoured and rounded for a balanced look. As we shape each side to match the bottom other areas will become noticeably oversize and require shaping such as the sides of the stock at the magazine box. A good way to judge the symmetry of the lines is to step away from the work and view it from all sides.

The amount of pitch is the angle formed by the intersection of the line of bore and line connecting heel and toe of the butt. It is determined by placing the butt of the rifle on a horizontal surface such as a floor with the receiver resting against a wall. The distance between the muzzle and the wall is the amount of pitch. Sporter rifles are generally 2½ inches. The pitch governs certain other angles such as the comb drop. After determining the length of pull desired use a tape measure and mark a spot from the center of the trigger to the center of the butt. The butt is then cut

Stock shaping is accomplished with files, rasps and a variety of sandpapers. Sterling Davenport is using a round file to work specific areas in final shaping.

off perpendicular to the line of pitch. If a recoil pad is to be added, its width must be taken into account.

The Monte Carlo cheekpiece may be shaped, but no wood removed from its side at this point. It will be one of the last tasks completed since it should be carefully measured by having the customer hold the rifle in a shooting position and checked for fit. We can remove wood to fit, but can't replace it.

The pistol grip should be shaped to the length and

After establishing top and bottom lines, sides of the stock are contoured. File is used here to deepen a shadow line in Monte Carlo.

curve that suits the customer although circumference is generally 4⅞ inches for strength. More on that as we inlet the grip cap later.

One other important design line in the rifle stock when shaping to the so-called classic style is the lower stock line. It is usually angled so that the line running from the bottom or toe of the stock through the pistol grip intersects at the edge of the back trigger guard loop. With these master lines established additional shaping results in a truly balanced appearance.

Contouring areas under the bolt release, making shadow lines around the Monte Carlo and the flutes at the front sides of the comb are performed after shaping the stock in conformity with the important master lines. Final balancing of the rifle is accomplished during sanding of the stock in preparation for finishing.

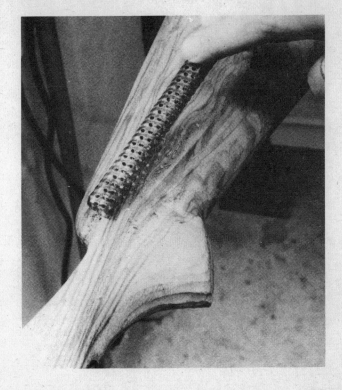

The flutes are roughed into the stock wood with a rasp. There will be further shaping with files and a final sanding before Sterling Davenport is satisfied with it.

Pistol Grip Caps Enhance A Custom Rifle And Installation Is Not That Difficult

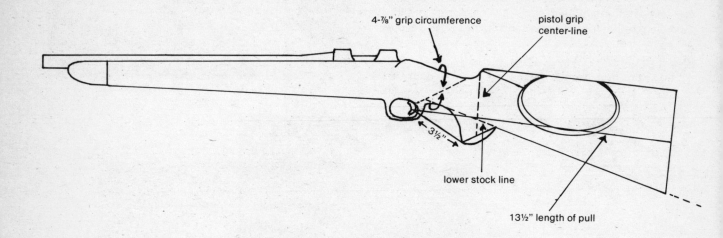

4-⅞" grip circumference

pistol grip center-line

3½"

lower stock line

13½" length of pull

AVERAGE PISTOL GRIP DIMENSIONS

MOST SEMI-INLETTED stocks for sporting rifles are designed with pistol grips unless a straight stock is requested specifically by the customer. The pistol grip is purposely left oversize to accommodate pistol grip caps in varying sizes as well as allowing the amateur or professional riflesmith to shape it to fit the customer's hand and position the cap farther to the rear if the rifle is to have a longer than average length of pull. This additional allowance results in a better balanced firearm.

The pistol grip should be shaped to blend perfectly into the lines of the stock's intended design. Proper shaping can add greatly to the rifle's overall appearance or just as easily destroy that particular aim. The pistol grip is an important aid to a steady grip if shaped and positioned to the particular shooter's physical makeup.

Length of the pistol grip is measured from the center of the trigger to the edge of the grip cap. For a rifle with a standard length of pull of 13½ inches, a distance of about 3½ inches will do nicely. For each one-half-inch additional length of pull the grip cap edge is set back an additional one-eighth-inch. Average circumference of the grip is generally between 4½ and 4⅞ inches. On heavy caliber rifles, the grip tends to be made larger for additional strength to the stock. I have noticed that a good many top riflesmiths position the center of the pistol grip in a perpendicular line to the front edge of the comb.

Although the most important consideration in shaping the pistol grip is that it fit the shooter's hand, its shape should blend with the top and bottom lines of the stock as well as the forearm and butt stock. The diameter of the grip — running from the bottom of the grip to the top —

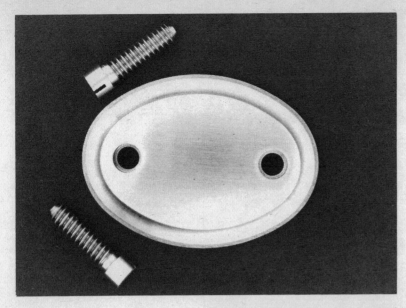

All of the grip caps pictured here are manufactured by Pete Grisel of Bend, Oregon. At left is his solid steel grip cap of two-screw design. The solid center allows engraving.

This steel skeleton grip cap features a two-degree draft to serve as an aid in inletting. The two screws prevent the cap from turning after it has been installed on the grip.

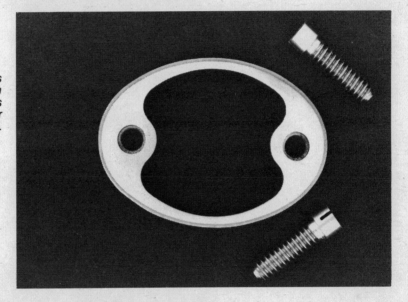

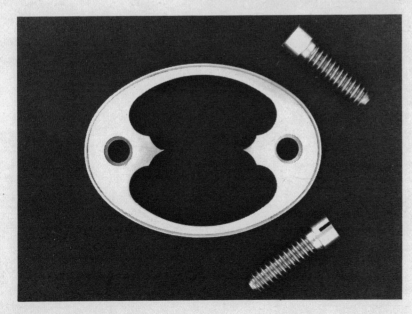

This scalloped design by Grisel is slightly more ornate but still a practical design. It also has the two-degree draft for inletting it.

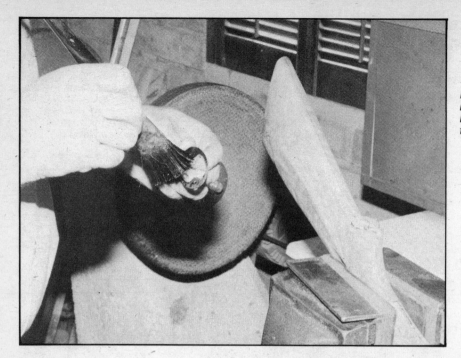

Bottom of grip cap is coated with inletting black, positioned on the bottom of pistol grip to establish the area that must be inletted.

Small chisels and files are used to spot in the area. In this instance, Sterling Davenport is using one of his knife-edge files for fine work.

THE GUN DIGEST BOOK OF RIFLESMITHING

There should be full contact with the inner edges of the cap to the inner surfaces of grip to prevent gaps after final seating. Note care used in making cuts.

Grisel caps come with long screw heads that are filed flush with cap after all inletting is completed. The screw head on left is filed down, one on right isn't.

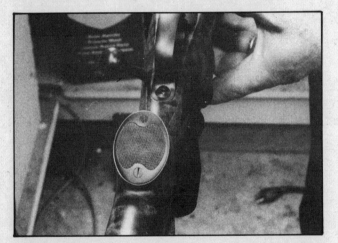

A custom Grisel skeleton cap has been fully inletted, blued. Note that bottom of the grip is checkered. This was done by Davenport as an added custom feature.

Solid steel pistol grip cap has been installed, blued. Note that screw slots are in perfect alignment and are flush with the grip as outlined in accompanying text.

should measure approximately 1¼ inches while the width between is 1¾ to 1⅞ inches. Do not make the grip perfectly round as it will not blend with pistol grip caps and tend to look amateurish.

After taking all measurements, and the initial shaping of the pistol grip has been completed, the bottom of the pistol grip is faced off. It must be absolutely flat if a conventionally shaped grip cap is to be used or gaps will show after it has been installed and final shaping is completed.

After squaring off the area, establish the exact center. If the cap has a screw in the center it is a simple matter to mark the spot, drill a hole slightly under the minor diameter of the screw and attach the cap. It may be moved forward or rearward of dead center to align at the correct distance from the center of the trigger and/or under the front leading edge of the comb. It then is simply a matter of final shaping and sanding down to the edges of the grip.

Inletting skeleton grip caps takes a bit more time than standard solid types. After establishing the cap's position inletting black is applied to the underside and pressed

into the desired spot, leaving a perfect outline. A small chisel then is used to cut stright down at the inner rear edges of the marks about one-eighth-inch. The chisel then is held at a ninety-degree angle and wood removed up to the cut lines. The cap is placed back on the grip and the spotting technique is continued until the cap is positioned lower than flush with the surface of the grip. Of course, the height of the cap is added to the length of the grip before inletting is begun to allow seating at exactly the right distance and height after the work is completed.

One type of skeleton grip cap is made by Pete Grisel of Bend, Oregon. He makes the cap screws with long heads so that, after all inletting is finished, the screw heads may be flushed with the cap and inner surface of the bottom of the grip. Sterling Davenport prefers to checker the bottom of the grip after inletting is finished as an added custom option.

Small chisels, files, some inletting black and a bit of patience and attention to detail are all that are needed to install grip caps to a rifle. The effort greatly enhances the appearance of any custom rifle.

Installed Correctly, It Is A Joy To Behold; Incorrectly, It Becomes A Pain In The Butt!

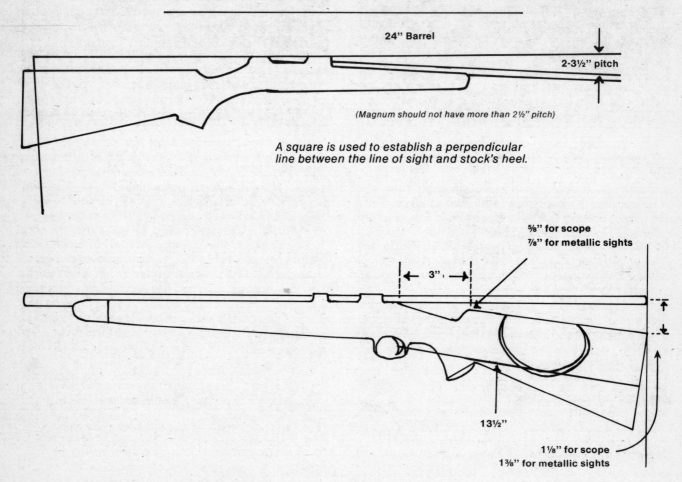

24" Barrel

2-3½" pitch

(Magnum should not have more than 2½" pitch)

A square is used to establish a perpendicular line between the line of sight and stock's heel.

⅝" for scope
⅞" for metallic sights

3"

13½"

1⅛" for scope
1⅜" for metallic sights

STOCK BUTT

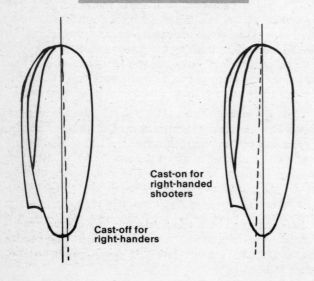

Cast-on for right-handed shooters

Cast-off for right-handers

MANUFACTURERS OF semi-finished stocks purposely leave excess wood in the butt region of the stock. Before adding the butt plate, the stock shaper must be aware of three important considerations necessary to fit the new stock perfectly to the shooter. All three are critical to the overall appearance, accuracy and comfort of the finished rifle.

Length of pull, degree of pitch and amount of cast-off or cast-on determine the placement of the butt plate. Physical size and makeup of the customer for whom the rifle is being built determines these three critical dimensions.

One way to determine length of pull is to have the customer hold the finished rifle in the crook of his elbow, which is flexed to a ninety-degree angle. Determine whether he can reach the trigger with the index finger, between its

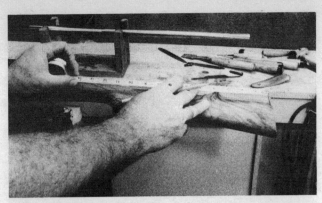

Length of pull is determined by measuring from center of the trigger to the center of the butt. Davenport has determined position of trigger, marked it with a pencil.

end and the first joint. About one-quarter-inch less is right for sporting rifles.

Brownell's makes a pull and drop gauge that also works quite accurately for measuring stock pull and amount of drop at the heel. The average length of pull measured from the center of the trigger to the center of the butt for most rifle shooters of average size is 13½ inches. Other considerations such as the customer's arm length and peculiar physical build also must be taken into consideration.

The degree of pitch also determines the placement and angle of the butt plate. Pitch is simply the distance of the front sight from the perpendicular when both the heel and toe of the butt plate are flush on a horizontal plane such as the floor. Although pitch is more important in shotguns than rifles, it still must be calculated in building the semi-finished stock. If the stock has no pitch, there will be a tendency for the shooter to shoot high due to the excessive amount of pressure by the toe of the stock against the shoulder. This principle will be most noticeable in short-armed, heavy-chested individuals and women with full busts. Improperly pitched rifles also cause more discomfort from recoil than does a properly fitted rifle. The normal pitch on sporting rifles for average size shooters is 2½ inches.

Cast-off is the amount a rifle is moved left or right from the exact center of the rifle at the butt. By drawing a line from the front sight through the rear sight over the top of the comb to the edge of the butt will determine the exact center of the butt stock. A line is made on the back of the butt perpendicular to heel and toe of the stock. Moving this center line to the right for a right-handed shooter is called cast-off. If the line is moved to the left of the center line it is known as cast-on. The average amount of cast-off placed on a standard sporting rifle for the "average" right-handed shooter is approximately three-sixteenths-inch at the heel and five-sixteenths-inch at the toe.

Before attempting to position the butt plate, one set of final dimensions must be considered. They are the drop of the comb and at the heel. The front leading edge of the comb usually is placed about three inches back from the rear edge of the receiver. However, the shooter's hand and his overall size will be the final determination as to where it is located. The height of the comb also is dependent upon whether the rifle is to be set up for metallic sights or a scope. By placing a wooden dowel approximately

With the edges of the barrel channel trued during the inletting of the action, a square is positioned along the edge to pencil mark indicating the length of pull. A perpendicular line is drawn as a guide with pencil.

After determining the amount of pitch that is required, Sterling Davenport measures from the top of the stock's heel to a pitch mark that already has been established.

the size of the bolt through the receiver bridge with a length of the wood extending to the rear of the stock it is simple to compute the desired height of comb and heel.

After making a mark three inches or so back from the rear edge of the receiver (assuming the stock is to be fitted to an average-size individual) make a mark on the semi-finished stock's comb. Using the dowel inserted into the receiver use a ruler and measure down five-eighths-inch from the middle of the dowel to the comb and mark a spot. If the rifle will have only metallic sights measure down seven-eighths-inch and mark. By intersecting the marks where the front edge of the comb will be, and its height using the dowel, we have the location and height of the front edge of the comb. To determine the drop at the heel again use the middle of the dowel and measure down to a distance of $1\frac{1}{8}$ inches and mark for a rifle with a scope or $1\frac{3}{8}$ inches if it is for metallic sights. Use a straight-edge to draw a straight line from the comb to the heel. The semi-finished stock must have all wood above this line removed and contoured.

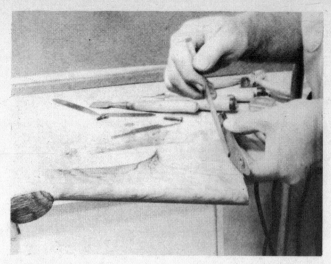

The edge of the steel butt plate is laid flush with the length-of-pull line. Plate then is outlined with pencil.

Using a band saw, the rifle stock is cut to match the curvature of the plate. This is accomplished with proper match to correct length of pull and amount of pitch.

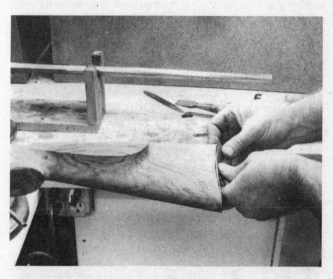

After butt is cut, plate is aligned with cast-off or new center-line, using screw holes as guides. Outline is drawn with scribe or pencil. (Below) Butt plate must be coated with inletting black, spotted for inletting.

For final fitting and installation of the butt plate, begin by measuring from the center of the trigger to the center of the butt to get our desired length of pull and make a mark with a pencil. Use a file or rasp to remove wood from the top of the stock to establish the drop from comb to heel. Make certain that you finish with a straight line. We will contour the sides later.

Use a stright-edge to draw a perpendicular line at the length of pull mark by running a straight-edge along the front receiver ring and bridge back to the butt.

Next use a straight-edge placed at the top edge of the heel exactly on the perpendicular line already made and angle another line down toward the toe to establish the amount of down pitch desired. This line will end up any-

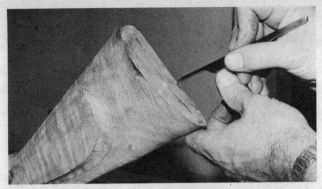

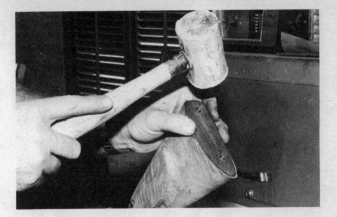

Small scrapers must be used to shave away tiny high spots until one attains perfect mating of plate, butt. (Right) A rawhide mallet is used to settle plate on the butt in effort to determine possible high spots.

where from 2½ to 3¼ inches in from the perpendicular line at the toe.

Since we will be installing a skeleton butt plate it is not necessary to adjust the length of pull to compensate for the diameter of the plate. With the stock placed on its side lay the edge of the plate at the cutoff line and outline the curve of the plate on the stock.

The stock now is ready to be cut off at the butt along the butt plate outline. Place the stock receiver-side-up in a vise and draw a center line down the back of the butt from heel to toe. From the center line measure to the right one-quarter-inch or whatever cast-off is to be built into the stock. Run a parallel line alongside the center line. The manufacturers have left the stock wide enough to accommodate for cast-off or cast-on.

Use the screw holes in the butt plate to line it up on the cast-off line and outline the plate. Use a sharp chisel to remove the wood at the outer edge, leaving the center high. Coat the inner surfaces of the butt plate with inletting black and carefully remove all high spots until there is a perfect bearing surface on all sides and the plate is set slightly deeper than flush with the wood.

By using the spotting technique when the plate is inletted completely there should be no gaps between wood and metal at the outer or inner sides of the plate.

With all inletting completed, screw holes are now drilled using a bit equal to or slightly under the minor diameter of the screw. When tightening the screws attempt to have

them bottom so that the slots face straight up and down. With the plate positioned correctly the sides are contoured to match the curve of the comb and the bottom of the stock from pistol grip to toe. By using a straight-edge to keep the sides flat from the pistol grip to the butt plate, the butt stock will take on the classic lines expected of a custom rifle.

Remember one more additional trick: When running the bottom line of the stock from the toe back to the pistol grip attempt to have the line extend through the grip at an angle to intersect with the back loop of the trigger guard.

The semi-finished stock manufacturer supplies a product that will accommodate shaping a stock to fit just about any size individual. Any additional requirements such as fitting a stock for someone of unusual proportions can be made by contacting the manufacturer and explaining your needs. If the amateur goes slowly and accomplishes each step carefully and in the necessary sequence, there is no reason he can't do a credible job.

Note that all slots in the screw heads run in the same direction, in line with plate; another professional touch by gunsmith.

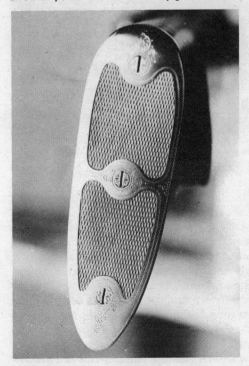

After fitting the plate, the sides of the stock must be brought in line with plate's edges in final fit.

Chapter 19

BEDDING THE ACTION

The Most Simple Approach Also May Be The Best

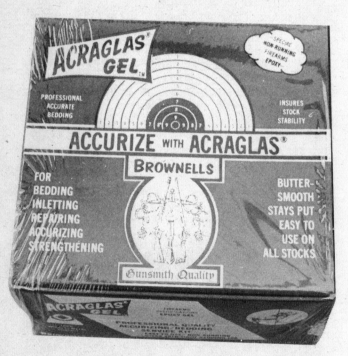

Acraglas Gel is new from Brownell. The author found it to have all the strength characteristics of the standard Acraglas, but easier to use, simpler in clean-up phase.

resorting to glass bedding. Others argue that it does result in a better fit and adds strength to the firearm. Few will argue that glass bedding is not simpler or easier.

Glass bedding can be accomplished without leaving telltale signs. When relieving the wood in the barrel channel, the top edges on each side of channel are not touched. Bedding is begun after all inletting is completed. It is up to the individual whether he wants to bed the action and barrel completely to the forend tip or just around the action contact points and first few inches into the barrel channel to free-float the barrel. I prefer to free-float a rifle when glassing since I would prefer no contact rather than possibly creating a bind on the barrel at one or more contact points as the barrel expands due to heat during repeated firing.

After all inletting is completed and the barreled action, trigger guard and floor plate are seated to proper depth they are removed from the stock. The wood must be relieved to accept the bedding compound. If the entire barrel channel is to be bedded, the channel must be widened and deepened. Do not remove additional wood

The Acragel comes as a kit. The 1:1 ratio between resin and hardener makes measuring easy. Powdered aluminum or steel may be added to mix for added strength.

BEDDING AN action simply means fitting the lower half of the rifle barrel into the barrel channel and the receiver — especially bearing points such as the recoil lug and tang — to the mating surfaces in the stock. Proper bedding requires a perfect fit between wood and metal; fit should not be too loose, showing revealing gaps, but if too tight, this may create uneven stress points that destroy accuracy. Some custom riflesmiths frown on using glass or epoxy to aid in fitting, insisting that a perfect fit can be achieved without

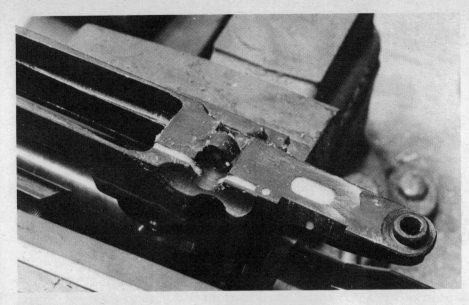

All bearing surfaces of barreled action, guard screws, trigger guard and floor plate must be liberally coated with release agent provided with the kit. All openings including screw holes and slots usually are filled with modeling clay. Author substituted Trewax as plugs, which worked out well.

Mixing instructions should be followed closely for best results. Resin and hardener are stirred for exactly four minutes. If powdered aluminum or steel are added, two minutes of stirring produce consistency of peanut butter.

points in the stock around the recoil lug recess, the channel surrounding the front receiver ring and the tang is quite important. I usually cut two channels with a one-quarter-inch flat chisel about three-sixteenths-inch deep, running parallel up to and through the stock recoil shoulder. I then continue to cut straight down into the lug recess. This will permit a large amount of bedding compound to fill this important bearing surface adding strength to the region. I also use a small veining tool and make relief cuts where the stock recoil shoulder meets each side of the stock wall. The compound is stronger than the

Adding the Acragel mixture to the recoil lug areas, the first 1½ inches of the barrel channel and around the rear tang screw hole affords strength, ultimate accuracy.

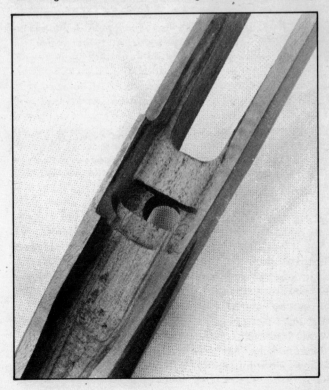

from the channel edges or there will be a line of glass left between wood and metal after the bedding is completed. A bedding tool and/or chisel is used to deepen and widen the barrel channel. Approximately one-sixteenth-inch should be removed from sides and bottom. A veining tool or even a checkering tool can be used to scratch tiny channels from the forend tip back to the recoil lug recess in the stock to assist adhesion of glass to wood. Also, make certain the inside of the channel is roughened up with a round file which makes a better bond as well. Do leave a few high spots in the channel, however. After all bedding is complete, they may be removed by sanding. These high spots ensure that the whole action and barrel will not be sunk too deeply or possibly at an improper angle.

Relieving the proper amount of wood from the bearing

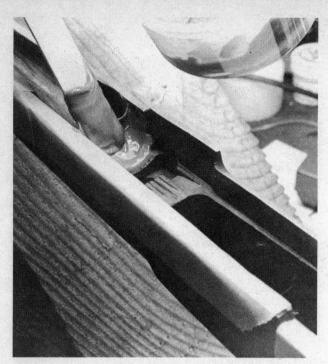

The author has cut channels and grooves into areas of the stock to be bedded. The Acragel will fill these depressions, providing better bonding and strength.

Acragel is easier to apply than old-style compound, as it doesn't run through openings such as guard screw hole. All bearing surfaces of the stock are liberally coated with the compound to ensure full bedding contact.

wood and when these two recesses are filled with compound chances of the stock cracking through this region are minimized.

Relief cuts also should be made at the contact points where the receiver sits in the stock just behind the magazine mortise and around the tang screw hole.

Before any bedding can be done the action, barrel, screws and trigger guard must be coated with a release agent. Trewax may be substituted in a pinch if there is no available release agent. Liberally coat the barrel, all obvious contact points on the action, guard and screws if you don't want to play hell getting the whole thing apart after the bedding compound has set up. All holes such as sear access, sear pivot pin hole and the safety slot hole on certain rifles must be filled with either modeling clay or wax to prevent compound from seeping in to cause all sorts of problems.

I have used most of the bedding compounds with great success. For the past several years I've used Brownell's Acraglas with excellent results. However, this company recently developed a new product called Acragel. After using it, I now prefer it to anything else I've tried to date. Being in a gel form, it doesn't run or drip; this makes the whole bedding job a neater operation and eliminates a lot of cleanup operations afterward. It has the consistency of peanut butter and is a snap to use.

The hardener is mixed on a 1:1 ratio with the resin and stirred for a total of four minutes. Included with the unit is an amount of powdered aluminum, purpose of which is added strength. I mixed in slightly less than the 1:1 ratio of aluminum for that additional strength. This compound allows more than sufficient time to apply before setting up and its rather thick consistency gave me plenty of time to

apply it to all areas without it running all over the stock or workbench.

Before placing the barreled action in the stock, I carefully taped off all top edges of the stock as a precaution. Sometimes when the action is seated into it, the compound will be squeezed up between the sides of the barreled action and the wood creating quite a mess, as well as the need to sand and refinish the stock. Since I had no wish to refinish the Harrington & Richardson Model 340 on which I was working, the few seconds required to mask off the area was well worth the effort.

There are several opinions as to the best way to achieve perfect bedding. Some gunsmiths simply lay the action and barrel into the stock with hand pressure. The theory is that, if the guard is inserted and the screws are used to tighten it down, the compound will be squashed out of the important bearing contact points. Others say this won't happen if high spots have been left to hold the action in proper placement until the bedding hardens. While a

After the compound hardens and barreled action has been removed, excess Acragel may be removed with chisels, files, garnet paper. The recoil lug recess in the stock forward of, below the barrel recoil lug must be relieved.

Masking tape at top edges of stock channel, sides of stock makes clean-up simple if compound has squeezed out of channel.

Bearing surface around the rear guard screw also should be bedded. (Left) Acragel allows all surfaces to be coated before hardening.

gunsmithing student I asked four different instructors the same question on this theory only to get four different answers. I decided then to gather as many different opinions as possible, then to use whatever made sense to me.

After applying plenty of Acragel into the stock around the contact areas, I prefer to place the trigger guard into position and use the guard screws. However, I don't tighten them down, I just turn the screws to the point that another three-quarter revolution would tighten the action in place. My feeling is that after the Acragel has hardened, the guard screws should be tightened completely. This creates a tendency for the action to be pulled down into the stock with added tension creating an extremely stable relationship between the important bearing points between wood and metal resulting in greater accuracy.

After removing the action from the stock it is important to remove any bedding compound that bears directly onto the front and bottom of the action recoil lug. The bearing surface should be against the back of the lug. Cutting away some of the compound to leave clearance in front and underneath the lug will assist in greater accuracy.

While bedding any action the stock should be held horizontally in a vise. I also use a block of wood positioned under the forend. It is easier to apply the bedding compound and do any relieving of wood with chisels with the stock in this position. If a product such as Acraglas or Acragel is used, make certain it is mixed for the full amount of time prescribed. Also, it will work better and dry faster between seventy-two and seventy-five degrees Fahrenheit.

If any excess bedding compound should be squeezed up when the action is put in place, use a cloth or stick to remove it before it hardens making cleanup much easier. It also may be removed by using an X-acto knife, but be careful not to scratch any blued metal surfaces.

If you've never bedded an action to a stock before, don't panic when it comes time to separate the two after hardening. Because of the tight fit, getting them apart can often take a bit of muscle. The Acragel directions suggest a plastic mallet to give the barrel just forward of the forend tip a few good whacks.

I usually hold the rifle with one hand around the pistol grip, the other around the forend and give the barrel a whack on the wooden surface such as a wooden table top. That usually will free it. If you still can't separate the barreled action from the stock, you could have a major problem. You may have neglected to apply release agent to the metal and the bedding compound doesn't want to let loose. Trying to bang it out could crack the stock, but that does show you the importance of coating all metal parts with the release agent. If this problem does occur, place the entire unit into a freezer. When the metal contracts due to the freezing temperature, it should break itself loose. I've never tried this method, but it sounds feasible.

Properly glass bedding a stock will increase its accuracy and forgives a multitude of poor inletting sins. It also protects the barrel channel from warping in the field during adverse weather conditions. It greatly strengthens the stock against cracking during recoil and can be used successfully by any amateur who follows directions.

Chapter 20

A TIP ON FORENDS

This Simple Addition Can Dress Up Any Rifle Stock

FOREND TIPS constitute a popular addition to all types of sporting rifles. Many manufacturers such as Winchester, Weatherby and Remington offer them on many of their current models. The tip offers a bit of style, especially when the material contrasts with the stock wood, and can dress up a stock that may be on the plain side.

Of the exotic woods available for forend tips, rosewood, ebony, cocobolo and zebrawood are a few of the popular choices. In choosing a particular type of exotic wood keep in mind that contrast with the stock wood is an important consideration. However, two types of wood may not accept a finish equally as well. Rosewood and ebony both excrete their own unique oils which can cause problems in applying certain oil finishes to the stock. One way to seal these particular woods is to apply a light coat

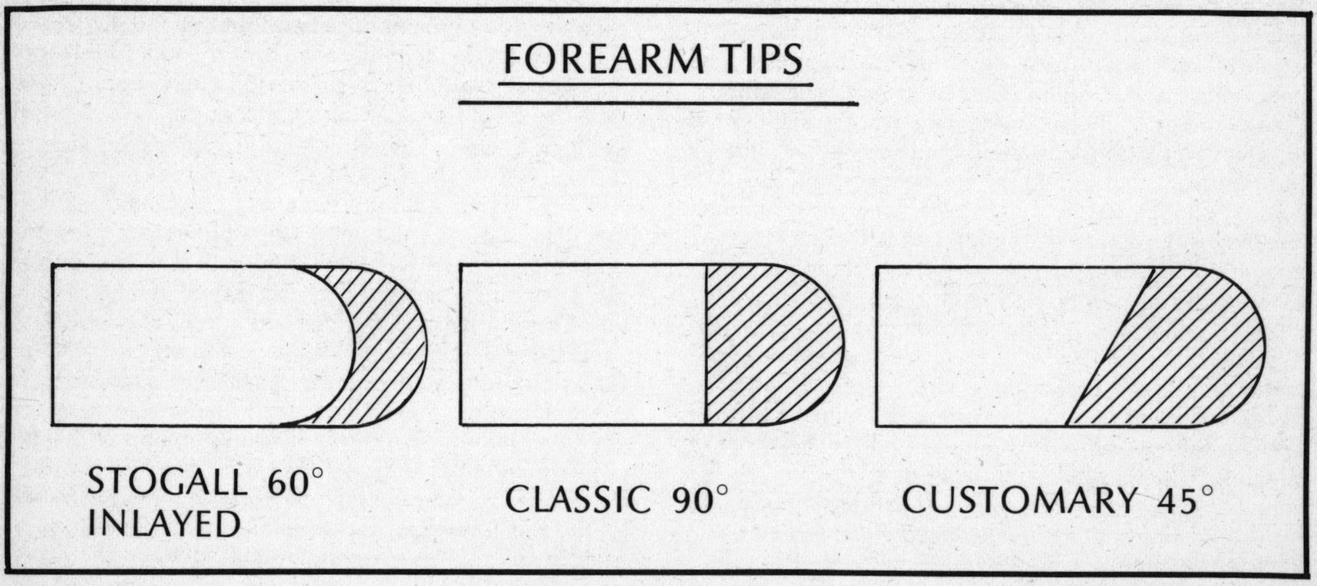

FOREARM TIPS

STOGALL 60°
INLAYED

CLASSIC 90°

CUSTOMARY 45°

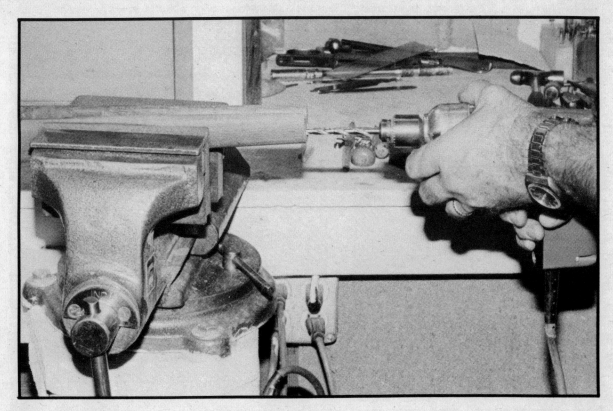

Drill the holes for the support dowels slightly oversize and at an angle of ninety degrees to the stock line. The depth of the holes need not be more than 1½ inches, as the recommended angle will do much to supply strength.

To determine the location of dowel holes in the forend tip, place it against the dowels, ensuring that top and bottom of the tip align with the stock. Be certain that the grain of the tip runs parallel to the barrel.

The dowels used to attach the forend tip should be in close alignment and protrude about an inch. This allows them to mate with the holes drilled in the forend tip.

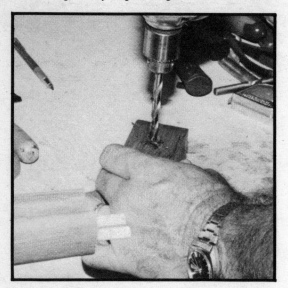

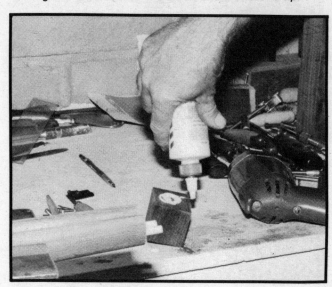

of Brownell's Acraglas if the stock is to have a plastic type finish. If you choose an oil finish, these exotic woods should be cured properly to prevent problems later in finishing.

Fitting a forend tip to a rifle is not a difficult task, but it is important that there be no gap between the stock and the tip. The grain of the tip should run parallel to the rifle barrel and the tip must be fitted securely to the stock as it does play a bearing role in accuracy. Fortunately there are some excellent bonding agents available that are stronger than the wood they will hold in place. The aforementioned Acraglas is excellent and Brownell's new Acragel is just as permanent and doesn't run. Wilhold's industrial-grade aliphatic resin glue, used in the furniture industry for years, is outstanding for bonding forend tips to stocks.

There are several styles of forend tips. Popular today are the sixty-degree Stogall, the forty-five-degree angle tip, and the classic ninety-degree style. Many factory-installed forend tips feature a thin plastic spacer between the stock and the tip itself for additional contrast. However, many custom riflesmiths believe such plastic spacers do not belong on a custom rifle and I tend to agree.

To fit a classic ninety-degree forend tip to a custom sporting rifle, Sterling Davenport installs two dowel joints for optimum strength. Although this addition may not be required on light calibers it is the method used by most riflesmiths. It should always be used on big bore rifles.

With the stock secured in a soft-jawed vise, Davenport drills two holes into the stock for the dowels of three-eighths-inch hard maple. The depth of each hole is not critical as the glue will fill any dead spots. Be careful to drill at precisely ninety degrees to prevent the possibility of the drill exiting through the stock. It's also easier to fit the dowels into the holes of the forend tip when perfect

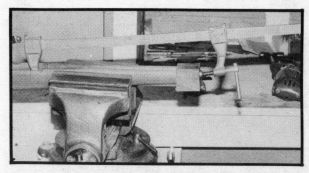

A bench clamp is necessary to provide pressure to tip and stock during drying period. A bicycle tube can be stretched from the tip to the butt as a substitute.

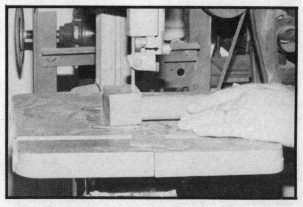

An easy method for removal of excess wood from forend tip is to do it with a bandsaw. This is quick, efficient.

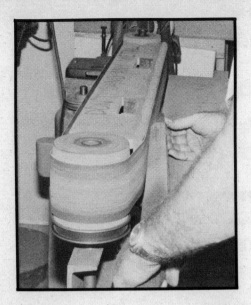

Left: Davenport uses a homemade belt sander of his own design to contour the forend tip before final handwork.

After exterior contouring of the tip, excess wood in the barrel channel is removed. Final bedding is done as described elsewhere, using barreled action, screws.

ninety-degree holes are drilled in both pieces. A drill bit that is a bit oversize can make alignment simpler. Place the two dowel lengths into the stock so that they protrude about one inch from the wood.

Place the forend tip against the tips of the dowel and scribe around them onto the flat surface of the tip. Be certain that the top of the tip is higher than the top of the stock line and check that the grain of the tip is running parallel with the rifle barrel. Using the same bit, drill the two holes in the forend tip at ninety degrees.

Ready for the gluing phase, begin by placing a liberal amount of glue in all the holes. Insert the dowels into the stock and check for alignment. Then spread a thick coat of glue over the mating surfaces of both stock and tip.

The two surfaces ready to be joined, it is imperative that both pieces are held together under pressure until the glue dries. For this Davenport uses a large bench clamp.

If you don't have one available an old bicycle tire will suffice. It acts like a large rubber band, and if stretched tightly from forend tip to rifle butt, will accomplish the same end.

After the glue has dried the final step is to shape the tip material to the rest of the stock. Davenport uses a band saw to first remove excess wood, then contours the tip on a large belt sander. This arrangement is much faster than shaping and contouring entirely by hand.

After exterior contouring and sanding has been completed the barrel channel is cut into the tip. It may be rough cut initially, but must be final fitted during stock inletting for perfect barrel bedding.

A forend tip does add class to a rifle. The Stogall type requires a bit more work, but all types of tips are made and installed in essentially the same manner. It is not a difficult operation and usually can be completed in about an hour.

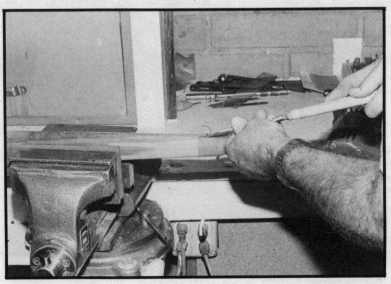

Newly fitted forend tip is ready for its final sanding and application of the desired finish.

Chapter 21

DON'T GO BAD ON A PAD

This Is A Simple Procedure For Avoiding Recoil Pain

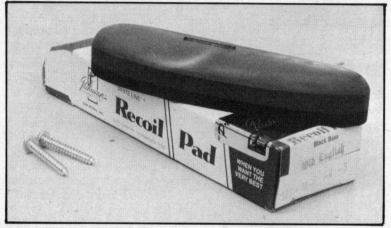

Pachmayr's Old English style recoil pad is a fine choice for custom rifles since the smooth sides won't accumulate dust and dirt as screen-sided pads are apt to do in routine use.

INSTALLING A RECOIL pad on a rifle is a near daily occurrence for the practicing gunsmith. Such installation is virtually the same for rifles and shotguns and is probably the most common long gun modification ordered by customers. It is not a difficult job for either professional or amateur if he takes his time and follows instructions.

There are definite guidelines that determine the degree of resulting professionalism. After installation the recoil pad should be a perfect extension of the stock lines. That includes from the heel and toe of the stock as well as the sides. The length of pull from the back of the pad to the trigger must fit the gun's owner. That means a certain amount of wood must be removed from the back of the stock to allow for the depth of the pad. The fit between stock butt and pad should be flush with absolutely no gaps. If wood must be removed from the butt it must be done at a ninety-degree angle to the stock centerline so the recoil pad will be square to the centerline.

In cutting wood from the stock butt, using either a table saw or a band saw, precautions must be taken to prevent the saw blade from splintering the wood. However, the single most difficult phase of attaching a pad is sanding it down flush with the stock without gouging the stock finish.

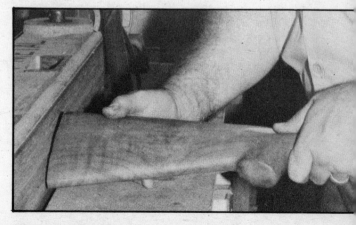

After cutting to length, butt end of stock is sanded true to stock centerline for a smooth, pleasing fit to pad.

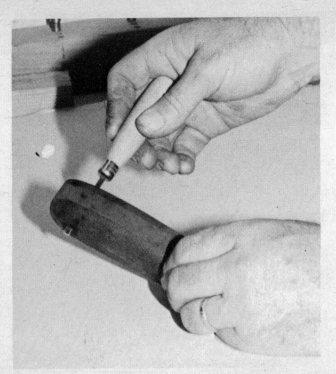

After careful layout, holes for mounting the Pachmayr pad are cut with a sharp chisel, perpendicular to front of pad.

Attempting to repair the gouge or scratches can take much longer than the entire recoil pad installation process. This is particularly true with certain plastic-base finishes on Brownings and Remingtons. It pays to work carefully in removing those last few thousandths of an inch.

Of first importance in attaching a recoil pad is selection of the right type of pad for the particular rifle in the correct size. Most recoil pads have two five-eighths-inch washers imbedded behind the closest layer of rubber to the stock butt located about 3⅛ inches apart. Attempting to fit a large pad to a small stock butt results in sanding away too much pad exposing the washers.

Determining how much wood must be removed from the stock is based on thickness of the recoil pad we intend to attach. If a customer brings in a rifle with a 13½-inch length of pull and requests a one-inch recoil pad, we must remove exactly one inch of wood from the butt.

Before cutting the stock we must establish the centerline on the top, or comb, of the stock. Since the sides of the stock are tapered, we cannot lay the stock down on the band saw table. The resulting cut would be off-center, preventing the pad from being square to the centerline. We also must take stock pitch into account. To insure a

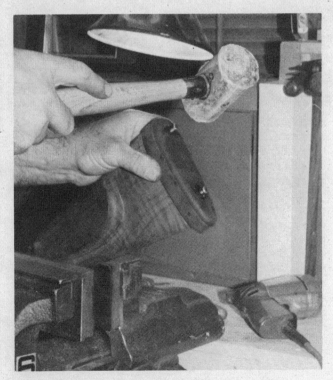

After checking for excess pad stock, screws are coated with wax to prevent tearing the rubber and located on stock centerline, mallet taps to mark.

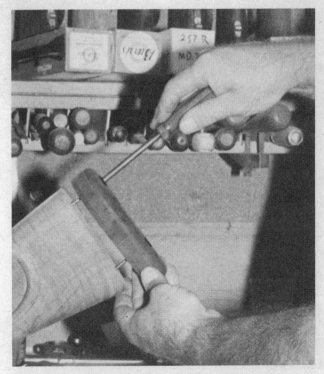

Round-shank screwdriver, coated with silicone or wax, seats recoil pad screws in stock. Appropriate sized holes are drilled at 90° angle for precise fit.

Here, the top edge of the pad has been shaped to the contours of the stock, with the lower edge left to be contoured on the wheel.

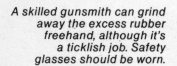

A skilled gunsmith can grind away the excess rubber freehand, although it's a ticklish job. Safety glasses should be worn.

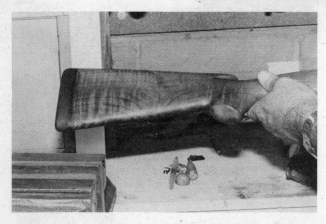

Following the steps outlined previously, the Pachmayr Old English recoil pad has been perfectly fitted to rifle.

perfect cut, first draw a centerline with a grease pencil down the comb to the butt. Next, run a layer of masking tape around the general area to be cut. The tape prevents the saw blade from splintering the wood as we make the cut. Using the centerline as a guide we draw the line around the tape at a ninety-degree angle to the centerline of the comb. Check the line with a ruler to be certain the centerline measures the same distance at the comb and the butt. If the table saw has small sharp teeth, or the band saw as the case may be, the cut should be true enough to make a nearly perfect fit with the recoil pad. If you do not have access to either power saw, a fine-tooth saw used with a carpenter's miter box will accomplish the same results.

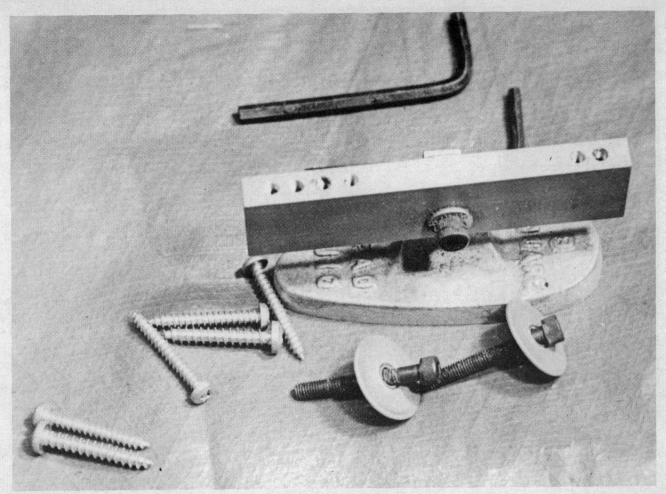

The B-Square Recoil Pad Jig and accessories are simple and easy to use by following the instructions furnished.

After the excess wood from the butt has been removed, allowing for correct pull length and at the proper pitch angle, place the recoil pad against the butt of a power disc sander or use garnet paper and a hard backing.

After cutting excess length from the stock butt the masking tape may be removed or may be left on as a guard against striking the finish with the disc sander. Removing the tape without peeling off the finish can be a problem. To prevent this possibility, soak the tape with either kerosene or turpentine and let sit for a few minutes. Then remove the tape by peeling from the front edge of the tape back toward the butt.

Many riflesmiths then apply transparent tape, only a bit over .001-inch thick, to the surface of the stock butt and take the pad down on the sander right to the tape line. I prefer using fiberglass-reinforced tape. Although a bit

Trewax-lubricated Xacto knife, punch and screwdriver should pass through the rubber without tearing it.

If cut carefully, the vertical screw slots will be invisible after the recoil pad has been installed in the stock.

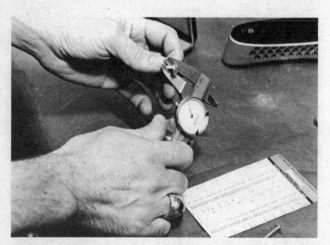

Measure the smaller or minor diameter of the stock screws and drill the holes for them to a diameter slightly smaller to assure optimum holding capability.

thicker, it offers extra protection to the finish should you accidentally get a bit too close.

The standard amount of pitch on a twenty-four-inch-barrel rifle is 2½ inches, pitch being measured from the line of sight. To determine this measurement place the butt of the rifle on the floor with the recoil pad installed, but not sanded down. With the heel and toe both resting on the floor and the gun up against a vertical surface like a wall, measure the distance from the muzzle to the wall. It should be approximately 2½ inches on twenty-four-inch-barrel rifles, more for longer guns and less for shorter.

Assuming the pitch is correct, the surface of the stock butt true and flush with the pad, we are ready for installation. Some gunsmiths relieve the center of the butt with a chisel to get a tight fit around the edges, but if truing of the

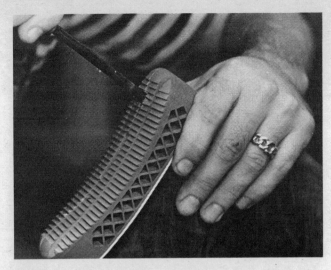

A screwdriver with a round shank, well lubricated with either wax or silicone, should be used for tightening the screws to avoid damage to the pad.

stock has been done correctly I don't feel this step is necessary. The pad may be attached using dowels and glue, screws and glue, or just screws. The first two methods cannot be employed on rifles having stock bolts as you could not disassemble the rifle without destroying the pad. I don't feel glue is necessary in any case if all previous work has been accomplished correctly.

To install the pad using only screws, first take a small, sharp, pointed punch and run it up through one of the screw holes from the bottom of the pad until it makes a slight bulge on the top of the pad. I use an Xacto knife dipped first in Trewax to make a narrow vertical incision at the point of the bulge to the proper diameter of the screw hole. The step is repeated to cut the second hole. Both recoil-pad screws should be lubricated with wax and driven into each hole — taking care not to tear the rubber — until only the screw heads are showing. The

Stock screw holes are drilled at an exact angle of 90° along the laid-out centerline, taking care to space them correctly so as to prevent the rigid base of the pad from being warped when the screws are tightened.

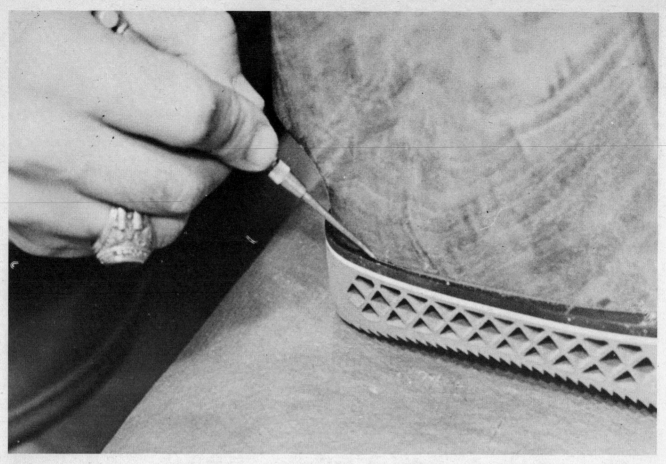

Once the pad has been snugged down onto the butt of the stock, a sharp scribe outlines excess rubber to remove.

After the pad has been removed from the stock, the B-Square Jig, used with a machinist's square, as here, establishes precise angle for toe extension line. With the pivot screw on the jig tightened securely, it becomes a simple matter to finish it.

pad is now placed against the stock butt allowing room for the screws to enter the heel and toe without being too high or low. Eyeball the pad to see that it is centered on the butt's centerline with enough excess on all sides of the butt to allow for contouring. When the work is centered tap each screw lightly with a hammer to determine the two points to be drilled for the screws.

The holes now may be drilled at a ninety-degree angle using a drill bit equal to or slightly less than the minor diameter of the stock screws to insure good holding power. A round-shank screwdriver should be used to screw the pad to the butt. First lubricate it with either wax or a silicone lubricant to prevent tearing the pad.

As an example, Sterling Davenport chose a Pachmayr Old English medium pad with black base for a customer's custom rifle. Solid pads are a favorite for many

A carpenter's square is being used here to adjust the sanding table of the disc sander to a perfect 90° angle for final removal of excess material from pad.

custom rifles; in the field they do not pick up dust and dirt as do screen-sided pads.

When the pad has been screwed to the butt Davenport checks to make certain there are no gaps. The recoil pad now is ready to be contoured on a disc sander so it will blend as an extension to the stock line.

An experienced riflesmith such as Davenport will take the pad down to within a few thousandths of the stock. He then final contours it and removes any scratches in the pad using abrasive grit strips until a perfect mating of stock and pad is achieved.

Attempting to contour a pad freehand on a sanding disc requires experience and steady nerves. After years of practice Sterling Davenport is able to accomplish it without using protective tape around the stock butt. If you're an amateur attempting this task for the first time, with a certain amount of nervous agitation, do not despair. There is an easier and more foolproof method available for pros and amateurs alike.

A few years ago I heard about a marvelous little jig for attaching recoil pads. It is made by the B-Square Company of Fort Worth, Texas. Having dinged a few stocks while attempting to mount pads by the freehand method, I decided to give it a try. I've been using it exclusively ever since — probably more than one hundred times — and it always has given me excellent results. It takes about twenty minutes to get a perfect-fitting pad using the jig and completely eliminates any possibility of damaging the stock.

The B-Square jig is a simple piece of equipment con-

With the pad held in the B-Square Jig, the excess material is sanded down to the exact scribe line. The angle is utterly precise and the final removal is thus accomplished with absolutely no danger of damage to stock.

With pad toe and sides shaped, jig and square are used to establish correct angle at heel of stock.

sisting of the jig, a few screws to hold the pad in place, some Allen wrenches to adjust the pad and angle of the jig fixture, plus a set of easy-to-follow instructions.

Before using the jig the stock butt must be cut to length and trued as described previously. Cut the holes in the pad using a punch and Xacto knife, lubricate the screws and round-shank screwdriver as described for the free-hand method. Draw a centerline down the back of the stock butt and use it as a reference point in lining up the pad and screws.

As for the stock holes, drill them slightly less than the size of the inside or minor diameter of the stock screws. Pachmayr supplies stock screws with an inside diameter of about .121 inch. A 7/64 or .1094 inch drill works well.

Fortunately, Pachmayr pads come with stock screws threaded all the way up to the heads. Every gunsmith I've talked with prefers this type of screw. I don't know why they aren't the standard within the industry.

When drilling the holes, make certain they are drilled square with the work. Holes that do not align at a perfect ninety degrees can warp the pad, causing a poor fit.

Once the oversize pad has been attached to the stock, use a sharp, pointed scribe and carefully mark the stock butt outline on the back of the pad. Making a perfect

Top of recoil pad has been sanded to establish angle, resulting in clean vertical pad/stock line, as seen.

Heel and toe of pad should be perfect extension of the lines of the stock, a simple job as described.

outline is the most important factor in the successful use of the B-Square jig.

Remove the pad from the stock and fasten the pad upside-down on the pad using the special screws furnished. Make sure the included washers are flush on the pad just under the screw heads. The pad toe must match the pad toe of the jig. Snug down the screws, but don't over tighten or you will distort the pad.

Loosen the pad jig clamp screw on the side of the jig with the special wrench and place base of jig on the base of the stock butt. Align the pad jig so that the pad back and stock lower surfaces are square with a carpenter's square. Tighten the pad jig clamp screw to maintain this critical angle. Also use the carpenter's square to make certain the table and the disc sander are perfectly square to each other.

With the B-Square jig base sitting flush on the sanding table sand the toe end of the pad to the scribe line. We are now ready to use the jig to align the heel end of the pad. Loosen the jig clamp screw again with the wrench and place the whole setup back on the butt of the stock. Use a square to align the pad jig and heel of stock. Again, take special care to get a perfectly squared arrangement. Tighten down the screw and sand the pad down to the scribe line.

Remove the recoil pad from the jig and screw it to the stock butt. It should fit perfectly. This method completely eliminates any possibility of damaging the stock, since all sanding is done on the pad with it removed from the stock.

That about covers recoil pad attachment — the standard and B-Square methods. But, what about Murphy's Law? What if you have to attach a standard pad to a curved stock butt? Sorry, Murph, but there is an easy way. Just drop the pad into a pot of boiling water. Allow it set for a minute or two and remove the pad using industrial rubber gloves, which are available through Brownell's. Bend the recoil pad while still hot to a curve just slightly more than the curve of the stock butt and place the pad in cold water to cool. When you screw it to the stock you will find it fits with no gaps.

Installing recoil pads correctly does not take long to do. Since there is a big demand for this service, it pays to do it right.

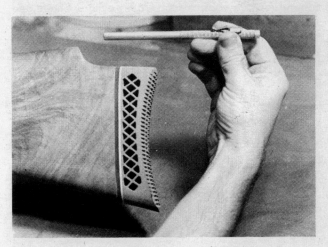

Pad installation with B-Square Jig is fast, accurate and accomplished without danger of damage to stock.

Chapter 22

THE FINISHED LOOK

Going First Class Takes More Time, More Effort But Even The Hunter Benefits In The End!

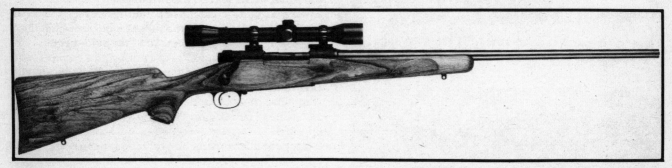

This beautifully stocked pre-1964 Winchester Model 70 was rebuilt by Sterling Davenport, featuring custom oil finish.

I HAVE spent more time attempting to master stock finishing than any other single phase of gunsmithing. I'm still trying.

In the riflesmithing trade the customer generally is offered two categories of finish from which to choose: the "hunter finish" and the "custom finish." The hunter finish is the easy way out for the riflesmith and much cheaper for the customer. It consists of a few coats of finish applied to the stock followed by a quick hand-rubbed coating of Birchwood Casey's Stock Sheen and Conditioner or Lin-Speed.

The custom finish takes much longer and can be a real challenge to the riflesmith. All pores in the stock wood must be filled, there can be no high, low, or orange-peel spots, no dust or sanding scratches left between finish applications, and the stock must be completely scratch and mar-free before finishing is begun. A quality custom finish requires much practice and a great deal of patience.

I've always wondered why the easier and less durable hunter finish has been given that name. I suppose it is because the hunter will be out in the wilds subjecting his firearm to the elements and other harsh treatment that almost assuredly will lead to dings, scratches, swelling when soaked, then drying out in dry, hot conditions. Personally, that type of finish doesn't make sense to me. The

Custom oil finish enhances this Winchester Model 70 that was rebuilt by custom riflesmith Dale Goens of Cedar Crest, New Mexico. The stock is of exhibition grade English walnut and required countless hours for its completion.

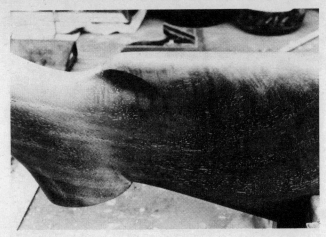

To obtain a custom finish, a requirement is that all of the pores in the stock wood must be completely filled.

hunter more than the competitive shooter or collector needs a finish on his favorite hunting rifle that will stand up to abuse and adverse climatic conditions. The so-called hunter finish, although less expensive, is certainly less durable than the custom finish.

As indicated, a custom finish is extremely difficult for most amateur riflesmiths and is no easy task for many professionals. Today's preferred finishes break down into two types: epoxy or oil. There is no shortage of manufacturers for both. Since the two types are in competition, almost all advertise their own as being simple enough to permit any small child to use. Unfortunately, if applied according to their instructions the results indeed look like a small child tried it. Yet if applied correctly, outstanding results may be achieved with the majority of stock finishes on the market. The key to a custom finish is based on how and when it is applied to the stock.

With today's Space Age technologies the trend in custom riflesmithing has shifted more to the plastic or epoxy finish and away from oil. The former offers a higher gloss and is said to be more durable. It may be more difficult to scratch, but I have seen more of the popular plastic-type finishes crack, chip and peel than I could count. These problems are not encountered with an oil finish. Plastic finishes are supposed to be more water resistant than oil.

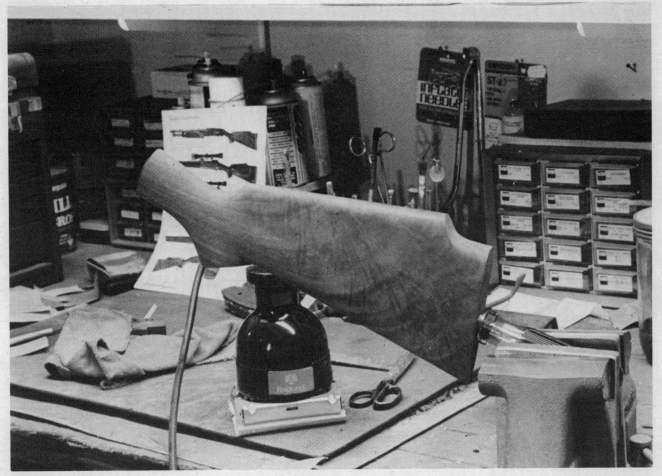

Author has found a Rockwell commercial-duty Speed Bloc to be an invaluable aid in sanding stock for custom finish.

Plastic or epoxy finishes are durable, water repellent and will give wood a high gloss. This particular forend has thirty coats of such finish; each was sanded down before the next coat was applied, then allowed to dry properly.

The real question is in what context do we mean waterproof? If we're talking about leaving a plastic-finished stock and an oil-finished stock submerged for a week at the bottom of a lake, the plastic finish may have an edge — if there are no small cracks in the finish to allow moisture in which will lead to more problems than being audited by the IRS. However, if we're discussing normal field use, the oil finish will shed water equally as well as the plastic.

Two distinct advantages of the oil finish over the plastic should be considered. First, oil finishes are much easier to repair than plastic if scratched or dinged. Second, an

Birchwood Casey's Tru Oil has been one of the popular oil finishes over the years, because it can greatly accentuate the beauty of a stock if properly applied.

Arizona riflesmith Sterling Davenport professes his own preference for Varathane's tung oil finish, which he has found provides excellent custom finish for stocks.

Brownell's acid brush is favored by Davenport to brush the initial liberal coat of tung oil on rifle stock.

oil finish gives a less glaring, richer lustre, thus enhancing the grain and figure in the stock.

The key to successful stock finishing is not necessarily the type of finish you use, but the way it is applied. There are many aerosol plastic finishes on the market. The aerosol can is better left for final finishing coats than beginning. One of the best plastic type finishes for stocks that may be sanded into the wood with each coat is Varathane's Liquid Plastic Clear Gloss. Being able to sand it into the pores of the wood with the initial coats is the important factor. This is not possible with another commercial finish like Deft. Attempting to paint on each coat invariably results in small air bubbles being trapped in the finish. Trying to sand them out between coats only leads to low spots or going completely through the previous coats.

Behr's Super Spar Clear Gloss Varnish is another durable finish that looks good and can be sanded into the stock. This and other spar varnishes make a good custom finish and will not yellow with age, a problem with varnish finishes of years ago.

Tru Oil and tung oil are two of the most popular oil finishes used on custom rifles. Tru Oil requires more coats and requires greater care between coats keeping the stock in a dust-free atmosphere than does tung oil. It is, however, one of the finest finishes ever used to bring out the natural beauty of the wood.

Tung oil has been around since the Thirteenth Century. Originally it was used in China as a weatherproofing and preserving agent for boats, clothing and the walls of houses. An oil processed from the seeds of the tung tree, it was not until the early 1930s, when these trees were planted around Tallahassee, Florida, and allowed to grow, that the American stockmaker could find and purchase the oil for his work. It is extremely water resistant, does not darken with age and protects the wood well against heat or mildew. It is easier to repair scratches with this finish

Supply of 320-, 400-, 600- grit wet/dry paper is required to sand in tung oil for the classic custom rifle finish.

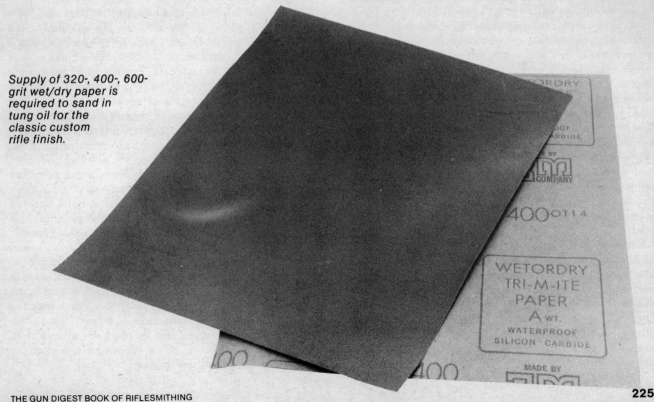

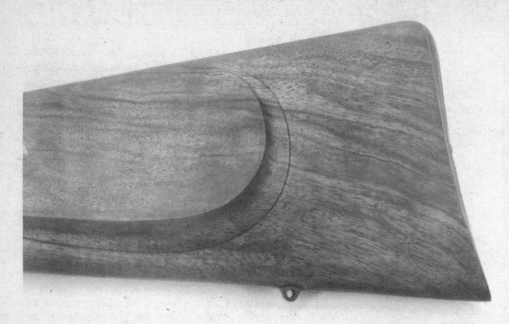

than other oil finishes and it penetrates the wood, giving the grain a classic appearance.

No number of finish coats or the way they are applied will give satisfactory results if the stock has not been prepared properly. All tool marks, scratches, and abrasions must be sanded out or they will stand out as glaring mistakes highlighted by succeeding coats of finish.

To eliminate any scratches, and properly sand out the stock I use a Rockwell Commercial Duty Speed Bloc Sander. It is extremely efficient and a much faster method of sanding than by hand. If hand sanding is your only way, make certain a sanding block is used. Without it, uneven ridges and ripples will occur in the wood. I use 80-grit garnet paper for initial sanding to further shape the stock as well as remove any deep gouges left by the wood chisel. I progress to 120, 180, 220, and finish sand with 280 grit. Be certain to sand small recesses in the wood that are visible such as the area surrounding the bolt stop and the inner recess of the bolt handle.

Many riflesmiths prefer to raise the grain of the wood after all sanding, then final sand once again. I have tried it, but don't feel it is necessary. Raising the grain is done by wetting the stock. It then is air dried or aided by using a torch. If the stock is not completely dry in spots, it will play hell with the finish. If you do wish to experiment with this technique I suggest letting the stock air dry thoroughly before sanding or attempting to apply the first coat of finish.

Rather than divide time and effort between applying the hunter finish as opposed to the custom finish, let's discuss the latter, since it is really a continuation of the former. Understanding how to arrive at a custom finish with all pores filled while expending the least effort is something that has eluded me for several years. I have come quite close on occasion, knowing all the while that there had to be an easier way than applying anywhere from twelve to fifty coats to achieve it.

While visiting with Sterling Davenport I marvelled at the outstanding finishes he accomplished using Varathane tung oil. By following his method of stock finishing exactly, it is possible for the amateur to obtain professional results more effectively than any I have tried over the past twelve years.

Davenport prefers tung oil, because of its durability, ease of repair and ability to penetrate into the wood rather than just sitting on top of it. The manner in which he applies the finish eliminates the problem of dust particles being caught between succeeding coats of finish since it is wiped on and wiped off.

Davenport is no stranger to epoxy finishes and feels they have a place in the industry. He has had much experience with The Fuller Company's FullerPlast which is quite durable and water repellent. This finish also is referred to in the industry as "bowling pin" finish. It is sprayed on in a thick coat, using a spray gun. Next it is leveled, using various grits of garnet paper beginning with 180-grit. It then is sprayed another three or four times, leveled once again with finer grits of paper, finishing with 600 wet-or-dry paper using water as a cutting agent. After final sanding, the stock is rubbed out with DuPont's rubbing compound and given a final gloss sheen by rubbing with Birchwood Casey's Stock Sheen and Conditioner.

Davenport readily admits this finish is quite durable and water repellent, but prefers the tung oil finish. He reasons that the epoxy finish is a built-up finish on the surface of the wood, thus scratches are quite noticeable and require a good deal of work to refinish to acceptable appearance. The epoxy can chip if the stock is dropped in the field or peeling may result if any moisture was in the stock wood prior to spraying. This type of finish requires expensive spray equipment and a dust-free drying cabinet whereas the tung oil can be applied with no more equipment than the oil, some 400 and 600 wet-or-dry paper, and a bit of elbow grease.

The same stock has been sanded out with 320- and 400-grit paper, using tung oil. Note the dark, mudded area on the upper butt stock region between the cheekpiece and butt. This is an aid in filling the pores for final finishing.

After all final sanding is complete, Davenport prefers to "whisker" the stock to raise the grain and make any scratches that may have been missed more noticeable. He takes a small cotton cloth and moistens it with water. It is not soaked. He does not want any more moisture to enter the wood than necessary to raise the grain.

He rubs the moistened cloth over the stock and sets it aside to air dry. He then checks it by carefully rubbing his hand over the entire stock to check that the grain has risen evenly and for any small scratches still remaining in the wood. He now takes 320 wet-or-dry paper and with a small piece of hard rubber backing sands the stock once again until all the raised grain is removed leaving a uniformly smooth sanded stock.

The tung oil finish is now ready to be applied to the stock. Davenport begins by taking a small acid brush (available through Brownell's), dipping it into the can of tung oil and liberally coating the stock. The only area he does not brush the oil over at this time is the barrel channel and magazine recess. It is not necessary at this point to worry about drips or spills. As the oil is brushed over the surface of the wood some areas will absorb the oil faster than others. Davenport will continue brushing these spots until the entire surface is saturated with oil. The stock is now put aside and allowed to dry for one full week. The stock is **not** wiped down before being put aside to allow the oil to harden. Since the stock will be sanded again, dust particles adhering to the finish are not important.

After a week's time the stock is ready for the second coat. Davenport uses 320 wet-or-dry paper without backing at this stage. The paper is dipped into the oil and the stock thoroughly sanded using the oil as a cutting agent. The sanding is continued until he has sanded the first coat of finish down to the surface of the wood. It is important to keep the paper soaked with oil during this sanding process.

In critical areas such as the loading port, trigger guard, floorplate and the rear tang, he employs a small rubber block as a backing to the paper to keep all critical edges sharp and clean. The sanding action of the oil and stock wood dust creates a sort of "mud."

After the stock has been sanded completely there will be a great deal of excess oil and sanded dust or mud remaining on the surface. This mud aids in filling the pores of the wood. The more the sanding, the thicker the mud becomes. When it is thick enough to move it around with the paper and a finger it is spread over all areas evenly and the stock is put aside — without wiping down — for another week to harden once again. This greatly speeds the requirement for filling the pores with the oil and the wood dust.

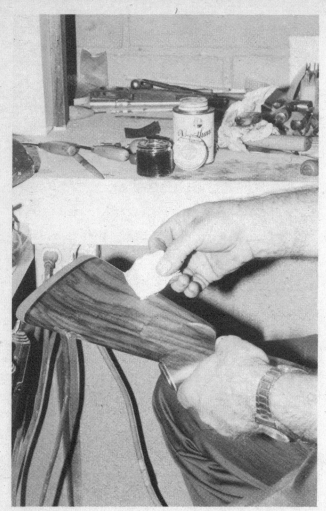

paper, Davenport uses tung oil as a cutting agent, continually wiping with the paper towel as he sands in small areas. The more he now sands the shinier the stock will become. It should take no more than fifteen minutes to work the entire stock. Remember, wipe lightly with the paper towel as we want to leave a light coating of oil on the stock.

The stock is set aside to dry another three or four days, then the process is repeated this time using 600 wet-or-dry paper exactly in the same manner as with the 400. At this time the pores should be completely filled and the stock taking on a shiny appearance.

To check whether all the pores are filled the stock is held up at an angle to a light and the finisher looks down the stock, catching each area of the stock in the light. Any pores not filled will immediately become apparent.

If there is an area or two that still have not been filled, take more 600 wet-or-dry paper dipped in the tung oil and sand this region with the grain until it muds up once again. Sanding with the 600 and oil will result in a light mudding which will fill the pores. After setting aside for another week, sanding one more time with the 600 and wiping gently with the paper towels will leave the finish bright with all pores filled.

After the stock has dried you may wish to leave the

A few drops of Lin-Speed is applied to a small cotton cloth, which is used to rub out the stock after final tung oil coating has been applied to wood by gunsmith.

After the finish has hardened, final finishing is begun. This is done with 320 paper and a supply of paper towels. Davenport sands small areas of the stock with the 320 paper again coated with tung oil as a cutting agent. He usually begins in the buttstock region, working forward. He sands until he goes through the hard mudded area which by now is rather splotchy.

As he sands through the mud he wipes the area with a paper towel — with the grain, never across it — until the dark mud is removed and the grain begins to show through. It is important to sand and wipe until the grain shows through, stopping before going entirely through the finish to expose the pores of the wood once again.

The entire stock is sanded and wiped until the mud is removed. Be careful when wiping to do it gently as we do wish to leave some oil on the surface. Use the small rubber block as backing during this phase around the rear tang, magazine area, loading port and top of the barrel channel to keep the edges clean and sharp. After all sanding has been done a small light film of finish is allowed to remain, only the mud having been removed. The stock is set aside for the finish to harden for a minimum of four days.

With the stock ready to be sanded with 400 wet-or-dry

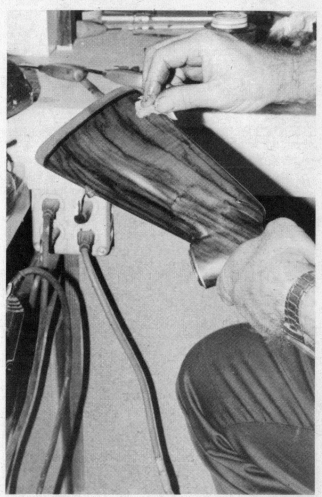

As the highly grained wood is rubbed with the Lin-Speed, the wood begins to take on a rich deep sheen of beauty.

Lin-Speed is an excellent oil finish for use in bringing up the luster of a custom finish on rifle stock.

finish as is. It results in a slightly dull satin finish. If a slightly higher gloss finish is desired, Davenport takes a small one-inch square piece of cotton material saturated in Lin-Speed Oil and lightly rubs the entire stock. The more coats of Lin-Speed, the higher the sheen will become. It is wise to wait a few days between applications of each coating of Lin-Speed. The Lin-Speed not only brings the sheen to the finish, but is quite durable and water repellent as well.

Sterling Davenport is quick to point out, however, that if the stock is later scratched, repairing the scratch with Lin-Speed is more time consuming than if the stock had been left with just the tung oil.

Another advantage to tung oil is that it dries quite satisfactorily on exotic wood forend tips and pistol grip caps. Lacquer finishes present problems on woods such as ebony or rosewood since it excretes its own oil.

If at some time the tung oil finish is scratched it is a simple matter to repair. The scratch is feathered — meaning the area around the scratch is also sanded to prevent a low spot — with 600 paper down to the wood itself and allowed to mud up. After drying it is finish sanded with oil and 600-grit paper and the repair is invisible. Lin-Speed may be applied as before and the job is complete.

If a buildup of tung oil has gotten on the recoil pad while finishing the stock, it may be removed carefully by wiping on lacquer thinner with a cloth.

Davenport prefers to finish his stocks with tung oil before beginning any checkering. The process of checkering through plastic finishes is more difficult and dulls the checkering tools, a problem not encountered with tung oil. After all checkering is completed he brushes in two coats of tung oil to seal the wood. He then brushes in just enough tung oil into the barrel channel and all other inner surfaces of the stock to seal the wood. Enough oil should be applied to seal the wood adequately without allowing any oil buildup which makes fitting the metal a problem. If there is an excess amount of finish inhibiting proper bedding of metal to wood, Davenport uses a scraper to remove the excess finish and lightly coats it again with oil.

This method of stock finishing by mudding to fill the pores works. Davenport's tung oil finishes are accomplished in a minimum of time and give the best possible professional results. After watching him I realized that by following the manufacturer's directions of other finishes and improper advice from other gunsmiths, such as wiping across the grain after applying each coat of finish, had cost me dearly in time and effort for a good many years.

To give a stock a classic professional finish with all pores being filled and no low or high spots does require more than dabbing on a few coats and completing the task in just a few days. However, the difference between a custom finish and the hurried and less durable hunter finish is worth the extra time.

Chapter 23

THE DETACHED LOOK

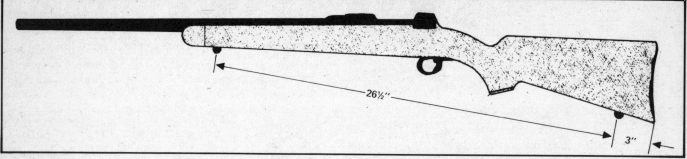

As indicated in this drawing, the rear sling swivel base is located 3 inches from toe of the stock. Front swivel is generally 26½ inches from that point, 27½ inches for a shooter with long arms; never install on the forend tip.

If Sling Swivels Are To Serve Their Ultimate Purpose, Proper Installation Helps

The center-line on the underside of the stock should be established and the rear sling swivel base located 3 inches from the toe of the stock, but it should always be perpendicular to its center line, the author says.

THE MAJORITY of hunters and competitive shooters want their sporting rifles equipped with a sling, which is the most comfortable method of carrying a rifle long distances during hunts and is an essential steadying device for accurate shot placement. Understanding proper sling swivel installation and which types of swivels work best with different rifles is important to the riflesmith.

The most popular swivels for general sporting use today are quick-detachable. Although a bit more expensive than the non-detachable type, they make the chore of sling removal much faster and easier. Michael's of Oregon, a company based in Portland, manufactures a variety of quality swivels for most popular rifles under the name Uncle Mike's. For custom rifles the Pachmayr quick-detachable swivels and Pete Grisel swivel studs offer outstanding design and strength features. The common feature among the three companies is that all of their swivels are screwed into the wood of the stock.

A word of caution: There is a socket-type swivel that, in this gunsmith's opinion, should be avoided. It has a tendency to release if the shooter should accidentally hit the detach button. It also is difficult to prevent chipping or scratching the stock while attempting to seat the socket to the stock.

A strong consideration in choosing a quick-detachable swivel is design; we don't want it detaching at the wrong moment. Both Pachmayr and Uncle Mike's have proved to be reliable in the most critical arena: the field.

A second important factor is that the swivel studs be low profile. A hunter stalking dangerous game in thick brush may have removed his sling to prevent it from catching or snagging, but high studs can catch on vines or twigs to impede progress. It's the riflesmith's job to give him every edge possible.

The last factor, and possibly the most important, concerns strength. The Grisel swivel studs employ two wood screws per stud for additional holding power while the Pachmayr single screw is about twice as wide as any other, effectively doubling the bearing surface between screw thread and stock wood.

The standard sling length (distance between rear and front swivels) on rifles is about 26½ to 27½ inches for

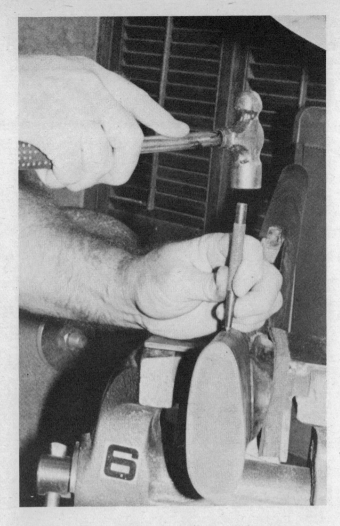

A center punch is utilized to start the swivel base's screw hole before drilling. This move can prevent the drill from "walking" and thus marring stock's finish.

shooters with long arms. The rear swivel base should be positioned approximately three inches in from the toe of the stock. It is always installed perpendicular to the corporal line of the stock.

Front and rear sling swivels from Uncle Mike's are packaged in sets. The rear swivel base generally is a wood screw with an eyebolt arrangement on the end of it. The front swivel base is most often a machine screw with eyebolt that is held in place with a retaining nut having serrated edges countersunk into the stock barrel channel. The nut must be countersunk deeply enough into the channel that it does not contact the barrel or accuracy will be affected. Although the serrated edges will aid in keeping the nut from backing out, it's a good idea to put a drop of Loc-Tite or iodine between the screw and nut to permanently hold them together.

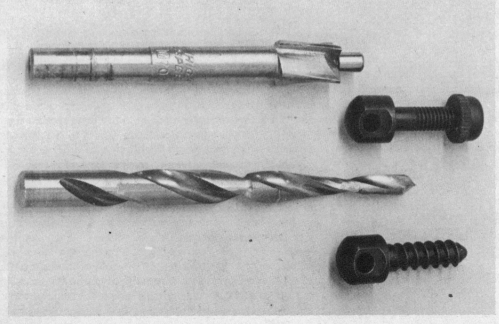

The counter sink is used to recess the forend screw hole in barrel channel. A ¼-inch drill bit can be ground to a taper to use in installation of the swivel base. Resulting hole leaves narrow shaft for good hold, while the larger hole at surface of stock prevents chipping of the wood when swivel eye bolt is inserted.

The area of the stock that holds the rear sling base is quite narrow. Drilling at proper perpendicular angle is essential for optimum strength of the swivel base.

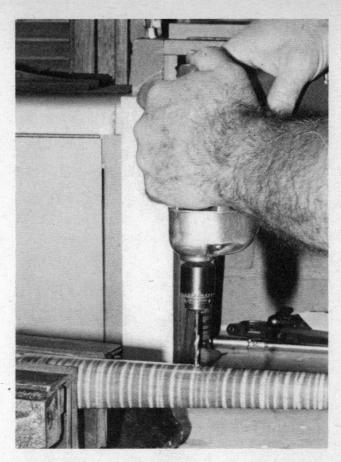

The hole for the front swivel screw should be drilled from outside of the stock toward the barrel channel. Drilling from the other side can cause the stock to splinter as the drill makes its exit through wood.

Following the instructions outlined, the sling swivel of quick-detachable type has been installed properly.

Sterling Davenport uses a tapered one-quarter-inch bit to drill the hole for the Uncle Mike rear swivel base screw. The taper opens up the hole at the stock surface to accommodate the cylindrical mass of the swivel screw base. If this area is not relieved the swivel will protrude too far from the surface of the stock. However, the tip of the drill bit is tapered to a diameter slightly less than the minor diameter of the swivel base screw, thus insuring maximum holding power. The drill bit was ground to this configuration using a bench grinder, then rehardened. Before drilling into the stock, mark the area to be drilled with a center punch. This not only assures accurate placement of the swivel base screw, but prevents the drill from "walking" and destroying or scratching the finish.

It is imperative that the hole be drilled at a right angle to the stock. Since the area that holds the rear swivel is quite narrow any variance in the angle of the hole will affect its holding power adversely. If you do not have a tapered drill bit, first use one the size of the major diameter of the screw and go no deeper than three-eighths-

Hole in the barrel channel must be countersunk to accept serrated retaining nut. The hole must be deep enough to prevent this nut from contacting the barrel; that would adversely affect accuracy.

Right: Countersunk hole for the retaining nut must be centered on the swivel screw hole for proper seating.

inch. Next use a drill bit equal to or slightly under the minor diameter of the screw and drill slightly deeper than the length of the rear swivel base screw. The base screw now can be screwed into the wood using a drift punch inserted into the eyebolt and tightened down.

Installing the Uncle Mike front swivel base is initiated by measuring up from the rear base 26½ to 27½ inches. Make certain to mark the spot to be drilled with a center punch. It must be located in the center of the forearm and drilled perpendicularly to the corporal line. The hole is drilled from the outside of the forearm toward the barrel channel. If it is drilled from the other side the wood can splinter as the drill exits the wood.

The retaining nut should fit tightly into the hole. The serrated edges grip the stock wood to prevent it backing out. A drop of Loctite or ordinary iodine can be used to keep it tight. If the screw should protrude through the retaining nut, file it flush with the nut.

I prefer a drill equal to or just under the major diameter of the machine screw. The hole in the barrel channel must be countersunk to accept the serrated retaining nut. Davenport purchased a commercial reamer with a diameter just under that of the retaining nut. The countersunk hole must be deep enough to prevent the nut from contacting the barrel after it has been installed within the stock. If the front swivel screw protrudes through the nut, shorten it by grinding or filing. A drop of Loc-Tite or iodine will prevent it from backing out.

When installing front swivels never place them in the forend tip.

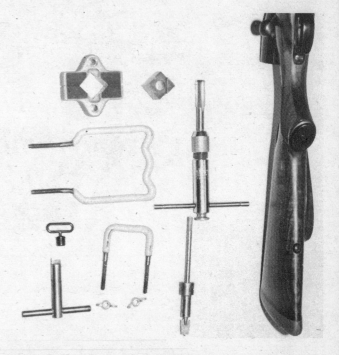

Pachmayr sells a complete sling swivel base installation kit for use with their low-profile swivel base, swivels. Author found installation of the bases simple, efficient.

With the work accomplished in the sequence outlined in the text and photos, the front swivel is now properly placed.

With the Pachmayr base attached to the stock, a special cutter with adjustable stop is inserted through a drill guide to insure perfect placement and depth of the cut.

When Pachmayr's flush-type quick-detachable swivel base is screwed properly into the stock, the design is fast, strong, aesthetically pleasing; reasons for popularity.

A perfectly fitting screwdriver is necessary if one is to prevent the burring of screw heads. This particular tool is included as a convenience with Pachmayr's kit.

Davenport prefers Pachmayr flush-type quick-detachables for the custom rifles he designs and builds. Almost flush with the stock there is little chance they will catch on brush, while their low profile does not detract from overall aesthetic lines of the rifle. They also are extremely fast when it comes to installing or removing the sling, and the additional width of the screw studs gives them strong contact with the wood. They cost a bit more than Uncle Mike's, but are an excellent investment for either big-game hunters or custom-rifle collectors.

Installation of the flush-type Pachmayr screws is best accomplished with the Pachmayr installation and jig kit. Retailing for about $24, it should be part of the equipment of the riflesmith. The Pachmayr kit — which includes a holding fixture, specialty cutter, set screws, tap, screwdriver and drill guide — insures professional results in a minimum of time.

Installation is begun with the stock held securely upside-down in a vise equipped with soft jaws. Before any drilling is done, Davenport uses a knife to carefully feather the area to be drilled. This prevents splintering of the wood. He then places the cutter through the drill guide and drills to the depth which has been established by the special stop on the cutter. The hole then is threaded with the ½x13 tap. The Pachmayr screw then is positioned, using the screwdriver that comes with the installation kit. This screw is actually spring loaded. To install or remove the swivel, Davenport merely inserts the swivel base into the screw slot, pushes downward and turns the swivel in either direction to lock it in place.

Installation of the front swivel base screw is accomplished in the same manner, which eliminates the problem of countersunk retaining nuts being placed in the barrel channel. Any amateur gun tinkerer is capable of

Installation or removal of the Pachmayr-made swivels is fast and positive (above and below). Simply place the swivel base pin in the swivel screw, press down and turn in either direction. The screw is spring-loaded as an aid.

Pete Grisel of Bend, Oregon, makes, sells low-profile swivel studs in pre-64 Winchester style. The twin screws offer added strength, for use with Uncle Mike swivels. Author found them simple and relatively quick to install.

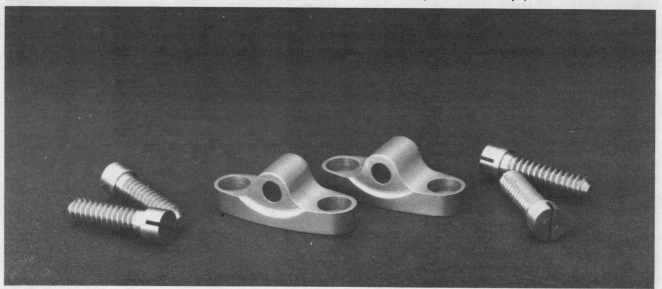

To install the Grisel unit, first establish center-line, then the screw hole is marked with a scribe. (Below) After hole has been drilled, tapped, Davenport secured it to top of stock with screw, then carefully scribed a line around the stud. The area inside the mark is cut away to accomodate the stud. Instructions come with the set.

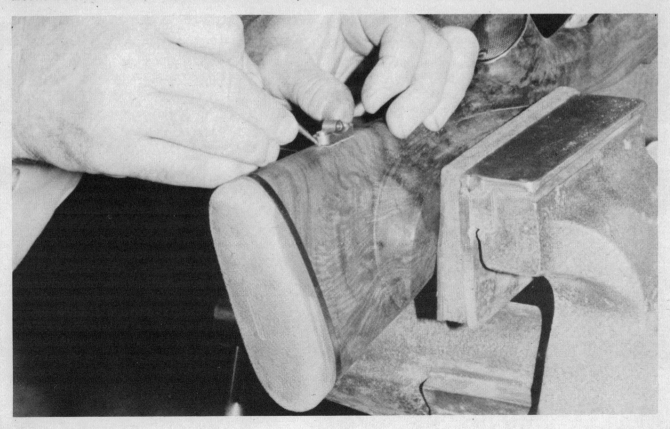

Davenport uses a Grisel screw as a tap screw. This will eliminate the possibility of applying too much pressure on new screws that are to be used with the stud, he says.

center punch to start the holes. The rear hole is now drilled using a #24 drill. He next uses the tap screw to establish the threads. One of the new screws is used to hold the stud to the top of the wood. The stud positioned perfectly, the second hole is drilled. Davenport scribes a careful line around the stud to mark the wood that must be removed.

The wood must be removed carefully inside the scribe line to eliminate any gaps between wood and metal. Davenport discovered that using oil paints available in any art supply house is simpler and less messy than regular inletting black. Falen's Ivory black oil color shows any high spots to be removed and cleans up quickly from hands and tools.

As the Grisel stud is hammered deeper into position in the stock with a rawhide mallet removing it each time becomes more difficult due to the tight fit. Using a scribe placed through the eyebolt solves this problem. Once the

professional results in less than fifteen minutes using the Pachmayr installation kit.

Another strong, low-profile alternative for custom rifles are Grisel sling swivel studs. They are machined to pre-'64 Winchester style, but fit Uncle Mike's swivels. Each stud is held in place by two screws for added strength. The screwheads are purposely left long so they can be crowned or filed flush with the metal.

Davenport keeps a Grisel screw that he has tapered slightly on the grinder as a tap screw for installation of the Grisel swivel studs. After the hole has been drilled for the screws, he uses it to make the threads. This alleviates the possibility of putting too much pressure on the screws that will hold the studs in place.

As with the other methods of swivel-stud installation, a center-line is established and a place three inches from the toe is marked with a scribe. The Grisel stud is positioned with the eyebolt directly over the mark. Davenport then uses a scribe to place it between the two screw holes in the stud to mark for drilling. After marking he uses a

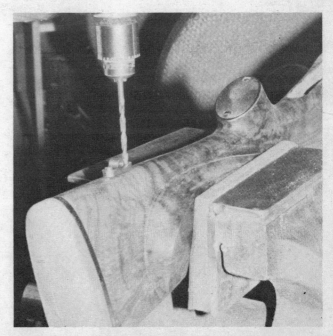

With the Grisel stud screwed securely into the top of the stock in the final position, second screw hole is made.

Inletting black or a substitute can be used to inlet the Grisel swivel stud into the stock without unsightly gaps. Davenport prefers to use oil colors from any art supply house, as it cleans up faster than the traditional black.

The custom Grisel swivel stud is positioned with relief cuts on either side of the eye bolt. The only requirement to complete the riflesmithing job is polishing, bluing.

Left: Grisel swivel stud is tapped gently into stock coated with inletting black or substitute to ensure a perfect fit. High spots are removed with wood tools.

The curved portion of slot in stock housing swivel stud is relieved with curved chisel or gaps between wood, metal will result. (Below) With stud almost flush with stock, use of scribe makes removal easier, pulling straight up.

After the Grisel stud is flush with the stock line and screws have been tightened, heads are filed down flush.

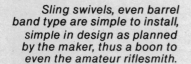

Sling swivels, even barrel band type are simple to install, simple in design as planned by the maker, thus a boon to even the amateur riflesmith.

stud is seated flush with the stock, Davenport uses a grease pencil to mark the recess cuts that must be made on either side of the eyebolt so the swivel will not catch on the stock and scratch the finish. These recess cuts take only a few seconds to make with a small half-round file. The screws then are used to tighten the stud to the stock. They have long screwheads that may be filed flush with the stud. After contouring stud and screws they can now be polished, removed and blued.

Another type of sling swivel base involves the use of barrel band sling swivel studs. I highly recommend them for big-caliber rifles used on dangerous game. A hunter may have to get off a life-saving shot with little time to prepare for it. A rifle in the .375 H&H category has more than

a little recoil. A rifleman trying to fire this type of rifle before he has sufficient time to place his hands properly on the stock can suffer a nasty gash if that portion of his hand between thumb and index finger slides up to the swivel area when the gun goes into recoil. This may seem a remote possibility, but I've been thanked by a customer who had to shoot a grizzly from the hip during an Alaskan hunt and I've seen the scar on the hand of another hunter who faced a similar situation with conventional swivels and base.

Barrel band front swivels are available through Brownell's and Pete Grisel. Diameter of the particular barrel determines the barrel band size that should be ordered. They are silver-soldered or brazed easily into place.

Chapter 24

WOOD CHECKERING

It Can Be Simple Or It Can Be Tough; Degree Of Complication Is Up To Your Expertise

Sterling Davenport preparing to checker a custom stock for a Ruger Model 77 rifle. Note the position of the light above and to the rear of the working area for purposes of highlighting the work to afford better visibility.

Tools of the checkering trade: Checkering tools at left are Full-View type with sixty and ninety degree single line cutters. Top left is sixty degree veiner and plastic straight edge. Top center is adjustable layout guide with three-to-one plastic template just below. On the right is MMC checkering tool with fine carbide cutter above grease pencil, scribe and jointer for straightening lines. Many other variants are used.

OF THE FOUR hundred or more gunsmithing students I met and worked with at gunsmithing school in Colorado many years ago, less than a handful have really worked to perfect the wood checkering phase of gunsmithing. It may be due to the amount of practice and patience required to turn out quality work. Many gunsmiths also realize that checkering is not the most lucrative aspect of the trade to attempt to master. Yet, I can think of no other phase of riflesmithing that will improve and enhance the overall appearance of a custom rifle. Custom checkering is more an art form than a simple mechanical task.

Basic checkering techniques are mastered easily. After all, seventy-five percent of checkering is nothing more than cutting straight lines in a piece of wood in a crisscross pattern within the main boundary lines of the design. Checkering simple patterns or repairing damaged checkering on rifles can be mastered by anyone with a bit of patience and the proper tools. It is this basic form of checkering that is performed in most gunsmithing shops.

Checkering runs the gamut from simple hobby to the level of fine art. Custom checkering is achieved only by practice, patience and an artist's perception. A custom checkering pattern must conform and add to the beauty of the rifle's lines. It is a careful blend of functionality and creative design.

Checkering generally is described as being a series of parallel V grooves cut approximately one-sixteenth-inch into the wood and crossed at a thirty-degree angle by another series of parallel grooves at the same depth. Between this series of crossing lines diamond-shaped high spots will remain. One prerequisite in judging good checkering is that all diamonds be sharp and pointed. The grooves are cut with small saw-like cutters forming either a sixty- or ninety-degree V.

The basic tools required for checkering are inexpensive, unless an electric checkering tool and accessories are considered. Sterling Davenport, an excellent custom checkerer, prefers Full-View tools. They allow the worker to see the cutting edge as it is moved right up to the edge

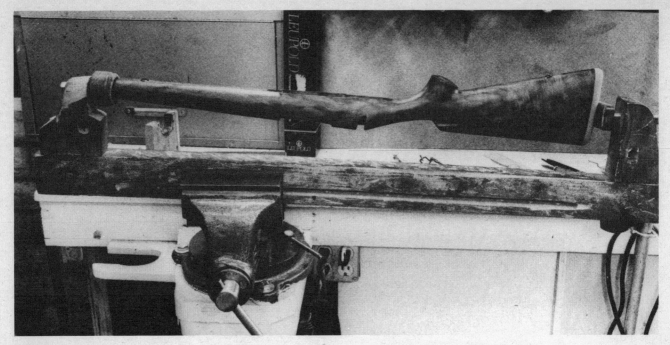

A checkering cradle, such as this, is indispensible in checkering. It frees both of worker's hands, meanwhile holding the workpiece rock-solid at exactly any desired angle as the tool is moved along the line.

of the boundary outline cut. The twin shafts are of quality rigid steel. The cutter has a pivot pin holding the cutter in place and two set screws to adjust the angle of the cutter at precisely the correct angle. For example, the edge of the cutter should be pointing slightly forward and down when cutting to the front edge of an outline, but will be angled in reverse for cutting to an edge closest to the worker. The Full-View checkering tools are available through William Brownell of Vista, California.

A sixty-degree veiner is necessary for cutting boundary outlines. A straight-edge is used for making center lines. Another handy tool is the border-adjustable layout tool to cut borders parallel to the top line of the barrel channel. A jointer, a tool designed by well-known custom checkerer, Monty Kennedy, is necessary for straightening out slightly crooked lines. A grease pencil works well to draw initial pattern lines on the stock. It will not harm the finish and can be erased easily until the desired design is in place. A scribe is useful for cutting the first series of master lines. A four-inch square is needed to measure the distance of each pattern line to align them at equal distances from either side of the barrel channel stock rails.

Anyone interested in learning to checker should begin by purchasing or making a checkering cradle. The cradle holds the stock in a comfortable position and rotates to give the checkerer the best angle for cutting the stock.

Attempting to checker without a cradle generally results in the stock moving just enough to cause a wobbling effect on the cutter; this can cause crooked lines and fuzz the wood grain, producing less-than-perfect pointed diamonds. Although a cradle can be made rather easily, Brownell's sells an excellent model for under $18 which may be easier than hunting around for the various attachments necessary to build one.

The most valuable tool for the professional checkerer is the electric checkering outfit. It allows the checkerer to work much faster. However, it does not guarantee perfect results. One can get in just as much trouble with this as with hand tools if you don't know what you're doing. While I was working with Davenport, he said he'd give up checkering if he didn't have his electric checkerer, but he'd also give up checkering if that was all he had. He feels hand tools always will be necessary for pointing up the diamonds and cutting to full depth.

An electric checkering outfit is an expensive investment. Brownell's new catalog offers them for $541.55. However, anyone doing quantity work will find the tool will pay for itself with the first few jobs on custom rifles. The most popular outfit for electric checkering consists of a Miniature Machine Corp. checkering head and carbide cutter, a Foredom industrial-grade CC motor, flexible shaft, CFL-15 rheostat and an 8D handpiece. There are two types of cutter; the wide version which allows cutting between sixteen and twenty-two lines per inch, and the narrow version which may be adjusted to cut twenty-four to thirty-two lines per inch.

The beginning checkerer should confine his efforts to purchasing cutting tools at eighteen lines per inch. Most factory checkering is between eighteen and twenty lines per inch; quite attractive and gives the shooter the best gripping surface. It also is easier to cut and keep the lines straighter than with fine-line checkering.

There are three ways to learn how to checker. The best is to have an expert standing over your shoulder, watching and coaching as you learn. Another method is to read as much on the subject as possible and then practice on your own. The two best sources I have found on checkering are, *Checkering And Carving Of Gunstocks,* by Monty Kennedy and the chapter on checkering and carving in Ralph Walker's *Hobby Gunsmithing.* The third way to learn to checker is to stand at an expert's shoulder and watch and listen. That is the way I prefer to help beginners pick up valuable tips.

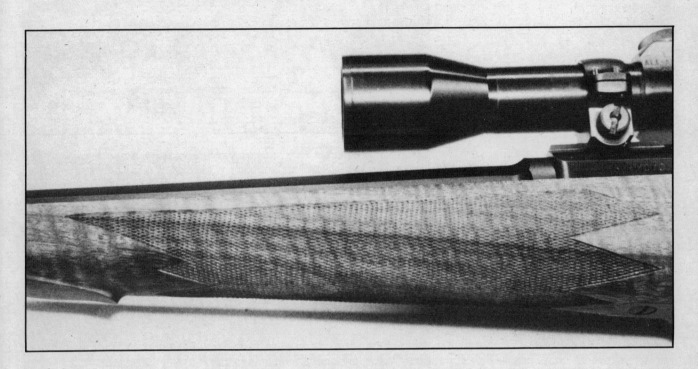

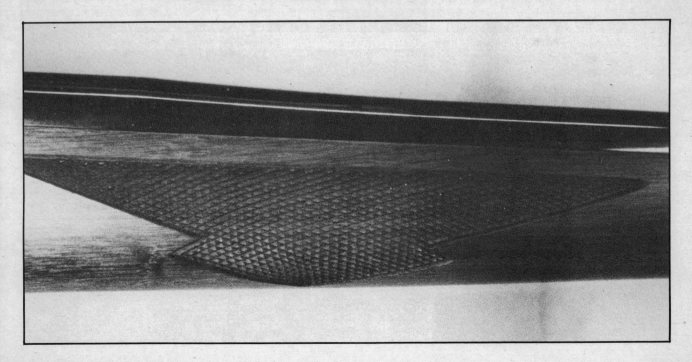

Checkering of forend below is on a factory Model 77 Ruger at eighteen lines per inch; simple, functional and not at all bad looking. The custom-stocked Model 77 Ruger above has been checkered at twenty-six lines per inch in a multi-point pattern by Sterling Davenport. Checkering can enhance rifle appearance.

Davenport commences checkering forend by establishing the boundary lines, using a grease pencil. Area and designs are dictated by size and lines of the firearm. Checkering should add to, not detract from the overall appearance of finished rifle.

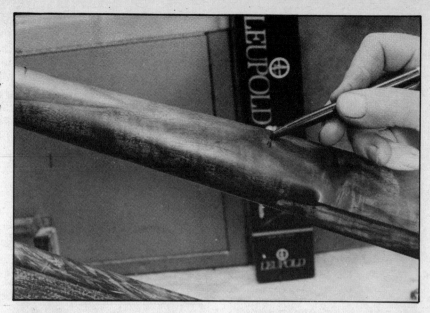

An adjustable layout guide is used to scribe a boundary line parallel to the upper edge of the forend, as well as precisely matching the laid out area of the opposite side.

A plastic straightedge is a must for laying out the centerline with the grease pencil. The line should intersect center of trigger guard recess for proper design balance.

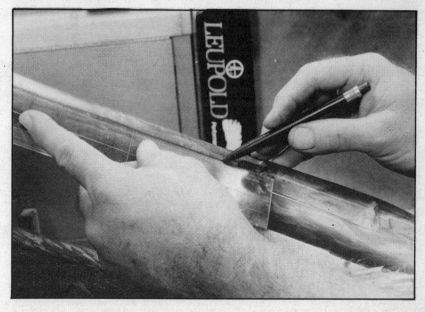

Using centerline as a guide, Davenport employs a three-to-one tool to lay out the multi-point outline with the grease pencil. This tool can be made from a piece of plastic 6"x2", laid out, cut and edges trued using garnet paper.

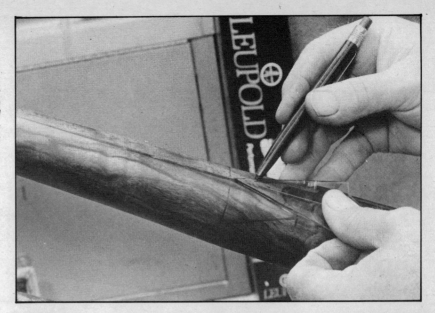

A four-inch combination square is used to measure the distance from each point to top edge of the forend duplicating on opposite side.

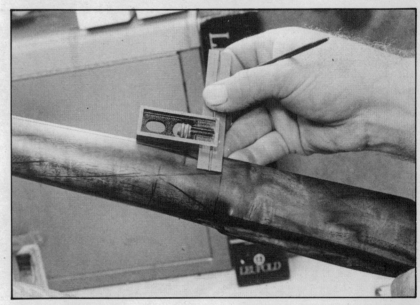

The master checkering lines are now made, using the centerline as a guide, with a scribe to cut through the finish and into the wood. Master lines are extended by means of straightedge. Plastic tape is alternative for scribing straight lines across a curved surface, or Brownell's Checkerchex guide can also be used.

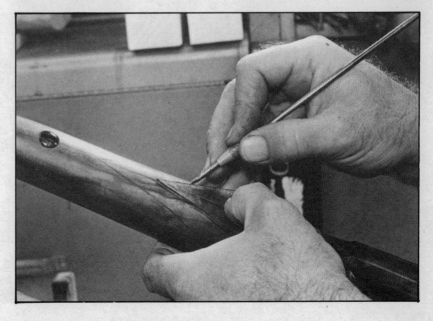

After establishing master line with a scribe and deepening slightly with a single-line cutter, a pair of dividers is used to establish the crossing masterline angle. Dividers also serve to keep each point pattern parallel to the other patterns.

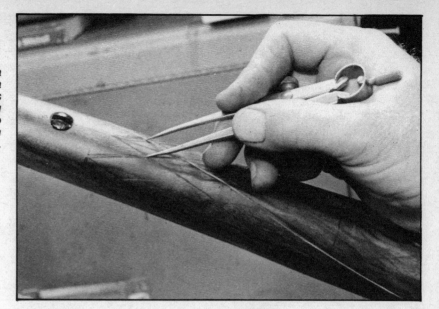

Davenport prefers to use the coarse ninety-degree single-line cutter to cut the masterlines. Unfortunately, the coarse cutter will not cut as sharp a line as the fine cutter, if there are any soft points in the stock wood. Coarse cutters cut faster, but must be replaced by fine ones whenever the former begins to skip, chatter or tear wood.

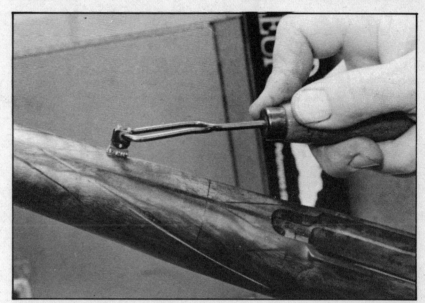

Thread pitch gauge is used to check the narrow carbide cutter. A simple adjustment on side of checkering head sets the cutter for twenty-six lines per inch. Although used for area work, this is not used for working on the boundary lines.

First phase of checkering is to cut all lines in one direction. At this point, they are not cut to full depth. Checkering cradle enables worker to use free hand to keep cutter in a vertical position, assuring straight lines by turning stock during cut.

Lines cut with power checkering tool never run clear to the border of the pattern. Full-View hand tool with cutting edge downward enables worker to cut to the pattern border, eliminating skips and overruns.

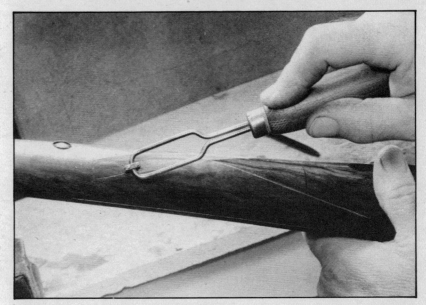

By removing stock from cradle and examining at an angle to the light, it is easy to see if any lines are beginning to curve. This check must be made after cutting four lines over any curved surface. If a curve is developing, use Monte Kennedy's jointer tool to straighten them out.

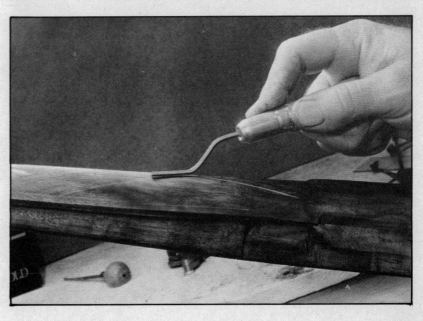

After all lines have been cut with the MMC electric checkering cutter, the master line is recut in the other direction and extended as a boundary line in the multi-point pattern. Note that the lines have still not been cut to the outlines of the pattern. That will be done later, using hand tools.

Here is a valuable pointer for those beginning to checker: Note that Davenport only cuts four crossing lines, then points up the work, using the Full-View hand checkering tool. By cutting only four, he can still use the lines on each side of the crossed pattern as guidelines. If the entire surface of the pattern were cut in the other direction first, the first set of lines would be almost obliterated, making the task of cutting to depth in a straight line much more difficult.

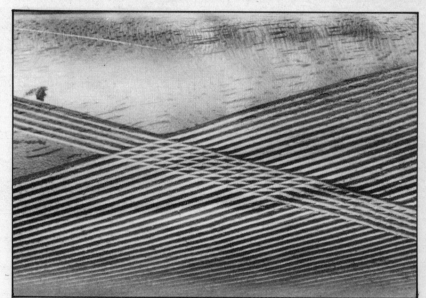

By setting cutter at a slight downward angle to the handle, one can see the cutter edge as it works right up to the boundary line. Thoughtful use of light makes the lines easier to see.

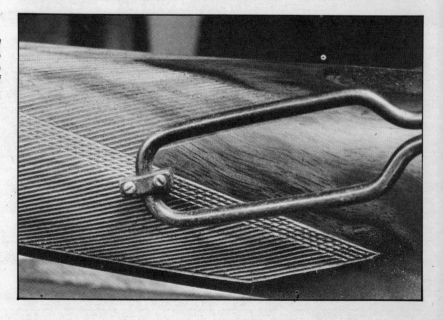

The same basic principles are used to lay out pattern for pistol grip to match the work performed on the forend. Area is much smaller and degree of curvature greater, thus demanding even greater skill.

A sixty-degree veiner is used to scribe the boundaries by tracing the grease pencil markings of layout.

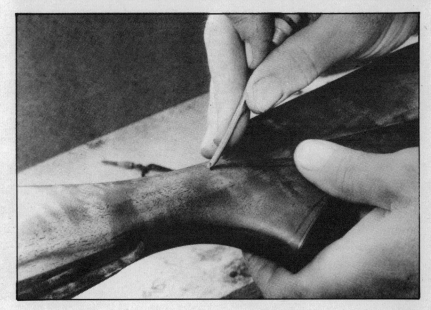

After cutting in the outline of the multi-point checkering, the centerline must be drawn, running from the back of the tang recess to the centerline of stock comb. With that line as a base, the three-to-one tool establishes the crossing lines for the checkering pattern. These lines also extend to become part of the boundary lines for the multi-point pattern. After the initial master lines are drawn, the three-to-one tool may be turned around to continue making new lines for each new point. Note the curved outline running around the back of the tang. It is first drawn in grease, then is scribed by dividers in tang recess. A veiner deepens the layout cut.

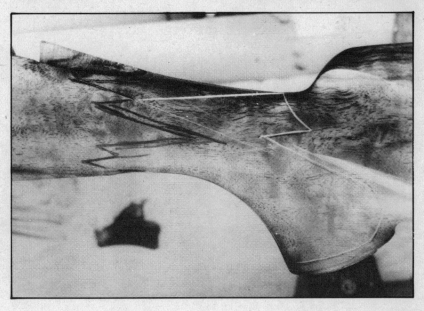

After cutting all the lines in one direction with the MMC tool, the Full-View tool is used to cut each boundary line. If there is a slight overrun in the front point regions, the lines may be extended on either side to match. However, there is no room for error in cutting to the line at the bottom of the grip, close to the grip cap. It pays to move slowly, watching the cutter edge.

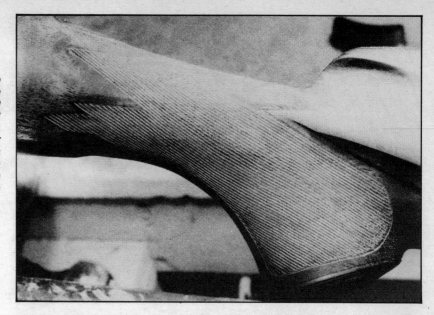

MMC tool is seldom used by custom checkerers to cut to full depth. It is best utilized by pulling it toward the worker. The guide, not visible here, rides in the preceding groove, so as to guide next cut in a straight line.

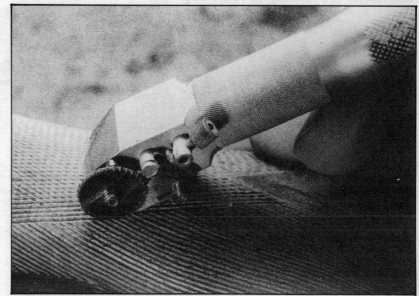

A real test of checkering ability is to be able to cut straight lines over curved surfaces. Continual checking and inspection is part of the key. The jointer is not too effective on concave surfaces such as underside of grip.

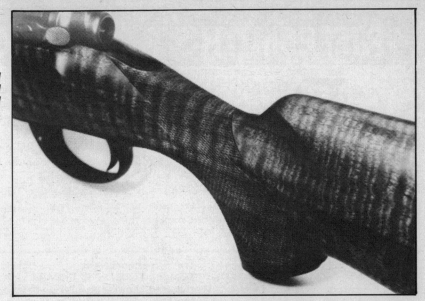

With checkering completed, tung oil is rubbed into it with a cloth or small toothbrush, but not so much as to fill in the cut lines and ruin the final effect.

Views at right and above illustrate the completed checkering of grip area.

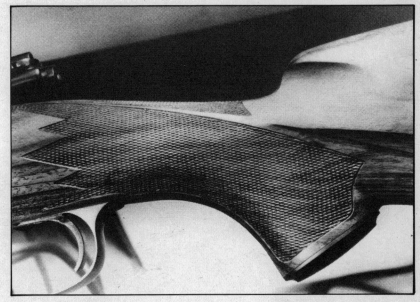

The best way to become proficient at checkering is to practice continually. Cutting tools are inexpensive so change cutting heads whenever they begin to dull. The carbide cutting wheel that comes with the MMC electric checkering tool will last several years. Begin by attempting simple patterns and strive for perfection. The hardwoods checker much better than soft varieties. There is even a difference between French, American, and Bastogne walnut when it comes to cutting. French is considered the best wood to work with by most of the custom checkerers. However, it is also quite expensive so it may be wise to practice with American walnut in the lesser grades until one becomes proficient.

As a person becomes more experienced in the riflesmithing trade he usually begins specializing in one aspect or another because of preference. There are many fine metalsmiths that don't like working with wood and vice versa. Oftentimes a custom riflesmith will send certain parts of his work out to be done by specialists. This practice is especially true when it comes to custom checkering. There is a definite need in this area of the trade today for qualified people. It is also wise for the owner of a fine custom rifle to shop around to find a qualified checkerer to bring out its beauty and design.

One of the best checkerers of custom rifles I know is Sterling Davenport of Tucson, Arizona. The accompanying pictures and information resulted from my watching him lay out and checker a twenty-six-line-per-inch, multipoint pattern on a custom Ruger 77 rifle stocked in French walnut.

RIFLESMITH'S REFERENCE LIBRARY

REFERENCE MATERIALS, constantly updated, are an absolute must for the riflesmith. They are as valuable as his screwdriver or file. Excellent books have been written by the leading firearms authorities on virtually every phase of work the riflesmith will encounter.

Some titles listed here have been out of print for years. If the riflesmith is lucky enough to have come across them at gun shows or through private collectors, he undoubtedly will have to pay premium prices. However, the information contained in them usually outweighs the asking price.

No single book will have all the answers for the riflesmith. The industry is made up of too many facets and complexities. New methods, different types of firearms and tools make it an ever-changing business. However, many of the old ways are still the best. This information is available oftentimes only through reference books like these listed here.

THE MODERN GUNSMITH, VOL. I & II, James Howe; Funk & Wagnalls. The most comprehensive books ever written for the gunsmith; it was last published in 1954. Many methods were a bit out of date with the invention of newer and better tools and products, but the book is loaded with the basic and advanced gunsmithing techniques and formulas necessary for a wide variety of tasks.

GUNSMITHING, Roy F. Dunlap; Stackpole. The edition I have is the eighth, printed in 1979. Like Howe's books, it's loaded with comprehensive gunsmithing methods. However, Dunlap covers more of the how-to aspects of the trade that are encountered on a day-to-day basis. Outstanding and factual.

GUNSMITH KINKS, Bob Brownell; F. Brownell & Sons, 1969. A collabora-tion of tips, formulas and knowledge right from the source. Bob Brownell, one of the most knowledgeable gun people in the industry, imparts his own vast experience with that of hundreds of other gunsmiths to produce a book loaded with information for both the amateur and professional.

FIREARMS ASSEMBLY/DISASSEMBLY, Part IV: Centerfire Rifles, J.B. Wood; DBI Books, Inc. This book has long been needed for both amateur and professional. It covers assembly and disassembly procedures for popular rifles with photos and clearly written text.

DO-IT-YOURSELF GUNSMITHING, Jim Carmichael; Harper & Row Publishers. Almost every phase of basic and advanced gunsmithing is comprehensively written and photographed. A valuable addition to both amateur and professional libraries.

INTRODUCTION TO MODERN GUNSMITHING, Harold F. MacFarland; Stackpole; 1974. MacFarland concentrates on the how-to aspects of gun-smithing. He's opinionated and outspoken, but I tended to agree with the overwhelming majority of his views. He obviously speaks from experience.

HOME GUN CARE AND REPAIR, P.O. Ackley; Stackpole Books. Ackley has probably forgotten more about guns than I'll ever know. This book brings a wealth of general and specific tips to both amateur and professional. The book is a bit brief and lacks needed photos necessary to show how to complete certain jobs, but is an excellent quick reference.

HOBBY GUNSMITHING, Ralph T. Walker; DBI Books, Inc. Although written primarily for the beginning gunsmith, Walker's three decades of working gunsmithing knowledge make this a welcome addition to either amateur or professional libraries. The book is loaded with excellent pictures and is written in an easy-to-understand language. His chapter on checkering is one of the best ever written on the subject.

PROFESSIONAL GUNSMITHING, Walter Howe; Stackpole Books, 1946. This book is intended as a general course in gunsmithing and succeeds quite well. Many excellent riflesmithing tasks are explained clearly. Though not as detailed in specific functions of the riflesmith as others, it is a valuable working text nonetheless.

GUNSTOCK FINISHING AND CARE, A. Donald Newell; Stackpole Books, 1980. This volume proves an entire book can be written on just one phase of riflesmithing. Devoting itself more to professional stockmaking than to general riflesmithing, it explains the properties of stock woods, stains, and finishes in a language the amateur can understand and put into use in his stockmaking efforts. Quite useful for both amateur and professional.

HATCHER'S NOTEBOOK, Julian S. Hatcher; Stackpole Books, 1966. This book aims primarily at scientific and technical data on military weapons and ballistics, but also is loaded with helpful data for the riflesmith, especially the metalworking specialist. More for the professional than amateur.

SEQUENCE OF TAKE-DOWN AND AS-SEMBLY OPERATIONS, WINCHES-TER; Olin Corporation. The Products Service Department of Winchester-Western publishes field service manuals showing complete step-by-step assembly and disassembly of their various models. No riflesmith should be without them.

ENCYCLOPEDIA OF MODERN FIRE-ARMS, PARTS & ASSEMBLY, Vol. I, Bob Brownell; 1975. This is a working riflesmith's bible. It covers everything from assembly/disassembly of a huge variety of different firearms to charts, parts identification and dimensions to allow the riflesmith to make or order re-

placement pieces. Invaluable to amateur or professional.

FIREARMS ASSEMBLY, THE GUIDE-BOOK TO SHOULDER ARMS, National Rifle Association. A standby in the industry for years, it is well illustrated and has easy-to-understand instructions. A handy manual for both amateur and professional.

THE GUN DIGEST BOOK OF EXPLOD-ED FIREARMS DRAWINGS, Third Edition, Harold Murtz; 1982. Contains 477 exploded firearms drawings of past and presently manufactured domestic and foreign firearms. A definite aid to amateur and professional alike.

REMINGTON SPORTING FIREARMS, Field Service Manual, Remington Firearms Company. Easily the finest publication of its kind. Covers everything from assembly/disassembly techniques to cycle of operation, diagnosing problems and repair. The most valuable book you can have on your shelf for working with Remington firearms.

SINGLE SHOT RIFLES AND ACTIONS, Frank de Haas; DBI Books, Inc., 1969. An excellent reference book covering fifty-five different single-shot rifles and actions. Covers development and history of each, wtih accurate photos and drawings of each.

THE RIFLE IN AMERICA, Philip B. Sharpe; Funk & Wagnalls, 1958. Possibly the single finest reference work on American rifles ever written. Loaded with factual data and history of hundreds of different sporting and military rifles. This book has been out of print for several years and commands a high price on the collector market, but worth every penny to any serious gun enthusiast or riflesmith.

MAUSER BOLT RIFLES, Ludwig Olson; Brownell's, 1981. The most authoritative reference work available on the many variations of the legendary Mauser rifle. A must for any collector and extremely valuable to any riflesmith.

THE BOLT ACTION, Stuart Otteson; Winchester Press, 1976. The finest technical and historical work compiled on bolt-action rifle design. Extremely comprehensive and loaded with technical diagrams, measurements, has evaluations of strong and weak points on each. Should be one of the first books purchased by the working riflesmith and quite helpful to any shooter considering purchase of a bolt-action rifle.

THE KRAG RIFLE, William S. Brophy; Beinfield Publishing, 1980. An outstanding authoritative work on the Krag, it is loaded with historical and technical information as well as beautifully illustrated diagrams. This well-written book has been needed for many years by collectors, historians and riflesmiths.

RIFLESMITHING DIRECTORY

CUSTOM GUNSMITHS

Don Allen Inc., R.R. 4, Northfield, MN 55057/507-645-9216
Joe J. Balickie, Rt. 2, Box 56-G, Apex, NC 27502
Al Biesen, 5021 Rosewood, Spokane, WA 99208/509-328-9340
Billingsley & Brownell, Box 25, Wyarna, WY 82845/307-737-2468 (cust. rifles)
Lenard M. Brownell, (See Billingsley & Brownell)
R. MacDonald Champlin, P.O. Box 693, Manchester, NH 03105/603-622-1420 (ML rifles and pistols)
Classic Arms Corp., P.O. Box 8, Palo Alto, CA 94302/415-321-7243
Sterling Davenport, 9611 E. Walnut Tree Dr., Tucson, AZ 85715/602-749-5590
Bill Dowtin, P.O. Box 72, Celina, TX 75009
Bob Emmons, 238 Robson Rd., Grafton, OH 44044/216-458-5890
Jerry A. Fisher, 1244 4th Ave. West, Kalispell, MT 59901/406-755-7093
Jay Frazier, S.R. Box 8644, Bird Creek, AK 99540/903-653-8302
Dale Goens, Box 224, Cedar Crest, NM 87008
Roger M. Green, 315 S. 2nd St., P.O. Box 984, Glenrock, WY 82637/307-436-9804 (rifles)
Griffin & Howe, 589 Broadway, New York, NY 10012
H.L. "Pete" Grisel, 61912 Skyline View Dr., Bend, OR 97701/503-389-2649 (rifles)
Martin Hagn, Herzogstandweg 41, 8113 Kochel a. See, W. Germany (s.s. actions & rifles)
Hal Hartley, 147 Blairs Fork Rd., Lenoir, NC 28645
Richard Hodgson, 5589 Arapahoe, Unit 104, Boulder, CO 80301
Hyper-Single Precision SS Rifles, 520 E. Beaver, Jenks, OK 74037/918-299-2391
Paul Jaeger, Inc., 211 Leedom St., Jenkintown, PA 19046/215-884-6920
Monty Kennedy, P.O. Box 214, Kalispell, MT 59901/406-857-3596
Kennon's Custom Rifles, 5408 Biffle, Stone Mtn., GA 30083/404-469-9339
J. Korzinek, R.D. #2, Box 73, Canton, PA 17724/717-673-8512 (riflesmith)(broch. $1.50)
Harry Lawson Co., 3328 N. Richey Blvd., Tucson, AZ 85716/602-326-1117
Mark Lee, 2333 Emerson Ave., N., Minneapolis, MN 55411/612-938-4540
Al Lind, 7821 76th Ave. S.W., Tacoma, WA 98498/206-584-6363
London Guns, 1528 20th St., Santa Monica, CA 90404/213-828-8486
Bill McGuire, 1600 N. Eastmont Ave., East Wenatchee, WA 98801
Harold E. MacFarland, Rt. 4, Box 1249, Cottonwood, AZ 86326/602-634-5320
Lowell Manley, 3684 Pine St., Deckerville, MI 48427/313-376-3665
Miller Custom Rifles, 655 Dutton Ave., San Leandro, CA 94577/415-568-2447
David Miller Co., 3131 E. Greenlee Rd., Tucson, AZ 85716/602-326-3117 (classic rifles)
Earl Milliron, 1249 N.E. 166th Ave., Portland, OR 97230/503-252-3725
Ted Nicklas, 5504 Hegel Rd., Goodrich, MI 48438/313-797-4493
Maurice Ottmar, Box 657, 113 East Fir, Coulee City, WA 99115/509-632-5717
Pachmayr Gun Works, 1220 S. Grand Ave., Los Angeles, CA 90015
Lynn Shelton Custom Rifles, P.O. Box 681, Elk City, OK 73644
Keith Stegall, Box 696, Gunnison, CO 81230
Walker Arms Co., Rt. 2, Box 73, Selma, AL 36701
Weatherby's, 2781 Firestone Blvd., South Gate, CA 90280/213-569-7186
Cecil Weems, Box 657, Mineral Wells, TX 76067
Frank R. Wells, Tucson, AZ
Fred Wells, Prescott, AZ
Duane Wiebe, P.O. Box 497, Lotus, CA 95651/916-626-6240
Robert M. Winter, Box 484, Menno, SD 57045
Mike Yee, 4700 46th Ave. S.W., Seattle, WA 98116/206-935-3682

CUSTOM METALSMITHS

Ted Blackburn, 85 E. 700 South, Springville, UT 84663/801-489-7341 (precision metalwork; steel trigger guard)
Gregg Boeke, 1812 Coolidge Ct., Northfield, MN 55057/507-645-6346
Tom Burgess, 180 McMannamy Draw, Kalispell, MT 59901/406-755-4110
Dave Cook, c/o Marble Arms Corp., 420 Industrial Park, Gladstone, MI 49837/906-425-2841
John H. Eaton, 8516 James St., Upper Marlboro, MD 20870
Phil Fischer, 2625 N.E. Multnomah, Portland, OR 97232/503-282-7151
Geo. M. Fullmer, 2499 Mavis St., Oakland, CA 94601/415-533-4193 (precise chambering — 300 cals.)
Harkrader's Custom Gun Shop, 825 Radford St., Christiansburg, VA 24073
Huntington's, P.O. Box 991, Oroville, CA 95965
Paul Jaeger, Inc., 211 Leedom St., Jenkintown, PA 19046/215-884-6920
Ken Jantz, Rt. 1, Sulphur, OK 73086/405-622-3790
Terry K. Kopp, Highway 13, Lexington, MO 64067/816-259-2083
R.H. Lampert, Rt. 1, Box 61, Guthrie, MN 56451/218-854-7345
Mark Lee, 2333 Emerson Ave., N., Minneapolis, MN 55411/612-938-4540
Joe Reid, 1902 N. Magnolia, Tucson, AZ 85712/602-795-0526
John Vest, 6715 Shasta Way, Klamath Falls, OR 97601/503-884-5585
Herman Waldron, Box 475, Pomeroy, WA 99347
Edward S. Welty, R.D. 2, Box 25, Cheswick, PA 15024
Dick Willis, 141 Shady Creek Rd., Rochester, NY 14623

GUNSMITH SUPPLIES, TOOLS, SERVICES

Albright Prod. Co., P.O. Box 1144, Portola, CA 96122 (trap buttplates)
Alley Supply Co., Carson Valley Industrial Park, P.O. Box 848, Gardnerville, NV 89410/702-782-3800 (JET line lathes, mills, etc.)
Ametek, Hunter Spring Div., One Spring Ave., Hatfield, PA 19440/215-822-2971 (trigger gauge)
Anderson Mfg. Co., Union Gap Sta., P.O. Box 3120, Yakima, WA 98903/509-453-2349 (tang safe)
B-Square Co., Box 11281, Ft. Worth, TX 76110
Dennis M. Bellm Gunsmithing, Inc., dba P.O. Ackley Rifle Barrels, 2376 S. Redwood Rd., Salt Lake City, UT 84119/801-974-0697 (rifles only)
Al Biesen, W. 2039 Sinto Ave., Spokane, WA 99201 (grip caps, buttplates)
Billingsley & Brownell, Box 25, Wyarno, WY 82845/307-737-2468 (cust. grip caps, bolt handle, etc.)
Bonanza Sports Mfg. Co., 412 Western Ave., Faribault, MN 55021/507-332-7153
Briganti Custom Gun-Smithing, P.O. Box 56, 475-Route 32, Highland Mills, NY 10930/914-928-9816 (cold rust bluing, hand polishing, metal work)
Brookstone Co., 125 Vose Farm Rd., Peterborough, NH 03458
Bob Brownell's, Main & Third, Montezuma, IA 50171/515-623-5401
W.E. Brownell, 1852 Alessandro Trail, Vista, CA 92083 (checkering tools)
M.H. Canjar, 500 E. 45th, Denver, CO 80216/303-623-5777 (triggers, etc.)
Clymer Mfg. Co., Inc., 14241 W. 11 Mile Rd., Oak Park, MI 48237/313-541-5533 (reamers)
Dave Cook, 720 Hancock Ave., Hancock, MI 49930 (metalsmithing only)
Dayton-Traister Co., 9322 900th West, P.O. Box 593, Oak Harbor, WA 98277/206-675-5375 (triggers)
Dem-Bart Checkering Tools, Inc., 6807 Hiway #2, Snohomish, WA 98290/206-568-7536
Dremel Mfg. Co., 4915 21st St., Racine, WI 53406 (grinders)
Forster Products, Inc., 82 E. Lanark Ave., Lanark, IL 61046/815-493-6360
Gunline Tools, Box 478, Placentia, CA 92670/714-528-5252
Half Moon Rifle Shop, 490 Halfmoon Rd., Columbia Falls, MT 59912/406-892-4409 (hex screws)
Paul Jaeger Inc., 211 Leedom St., Jenkintown, PA 19046
Jeffredo Gunsight Co., 1629 Via Monserate, Fallbrook, CA 92028 (trap buttplate)
John G. Lawson, (The Sight Shop) 1802 E. Columbia Ave., Tacoma, WA 98404/206-474-5465
Lea Mfg. Co., 237 E. Aurora St., Waterbury, CT 06720/203-753-5116
John McClure, 4549 Alamo Dr., San Diego, CA 92115 (electric checkering tool)
Michaels of Oregon Co., P.O. Box 13010, Portland, OR 97213/503-255-6890
Frank Mittermeier, 3577 E. Tremont, New York, NY 10465
Panavise Prods., Inc., 2850 E. 29th St., Long Beach, CA 90806/213-595-7621
Pilkington Gun Co., P.O. Box 1296, Muskogee, OK 74401/918-683-9418 (Q.D. scope mt.)
Riley's Supply Co., 116 N. Main St., Avilla, IN 46710/219-897-2351 (Niedner buttplates, grip caps)
SGW, Inc. (formerly Schuetzen Gun Works), 624 Old Pacific Hwy., S.E., Olympia, WA 98503/206-456-3471
L.S. Starrett Co., 121 Crescent St., Athol, MA 01331/617-249-3551
Timney Mfg. Inc., 3106 W. Thomas Rd., Phoenix, AZ 85017/602-269-6937
Williams Gun Sight Co., 7389 Lapeer Rd., Davison, MI 48423

STOCKS (Commercial and Custom)

Don Allen Inc., R.R. 4, Northfield, MN 55057/507-645-9216 (blanks)
Al Biesen, West 2039 Sinto Ave., Spokane, WA 99201
Billingsley & Brownell, Box 25, Wyarno, WY 82845/307-737-2468 (cust.)
E.C. Bishop & Son Inc., 119 Main St., Box 7, Warsaw, MO 65355/816-438-5121
Gregg Boeke, 1812 Coolidge Ct., Northfield, MN 55057/507-645-6346 (custom)
John M. Boltin, 2008 Havens Dr., North Myrtle Beach, SC 29582/803-272-6581
Brown Precision Co., P.O. Box 270W; 7786 Molinos Ave., Los Molinos, CA 96055/916-384-2506
Jack Burres, 10333 San Fernando Road, Pacoima, CA 91331 (English, Claro, Bastogne Paradox walnut blanks only)
Calico Hardwoods, Inc., 1648 Airport Blvd., Windsor, CA 94592/707-546-4045 (blanks)
Winston Churchill, Twenty Mile Stream Rd., Rt. 1, Box 29B, Proctorsville, VT 05153
Reggie Cubriel, 15502 Purple Sage, San Antonio, TX 78255/512-695-8401 (cust. stockm.)
Sterling Davenport, 9611 E. Walnut Tree Dr., Tucson, AZ 85715/602-749-5590 (custom)
Gary Duncan, 1118 Canterbury, Enid. OK 73701 (blanks only)
Reinhart Fajen, Box 338 Warsaw, MO 65355/816-438-5111
Jerry A. Fisher, 1244 4th Ave. W., Kalispell, MT 59901/406-755-7093
Dale Goens, Box 224, Cedar Crest, NM 87008
Gould's Myrtlewood, 1692 N. Dogwood, Coquille, OR 97423 (gun blanks)
Hal Hartley, 147 Blairsfork Rd., Lenoir, NC 28645
Paul Jaeger, Inc., 211 Leedom St., Jenkintown, PA 19046/215-884-6920
Monty Kennedy, P.O. Box 214, Kalispell, MT 59901/406-857-3596
Al Lind, 7821 76th Ave. S.W., Tacoma, WA 98498/206-584-6361 (cust. stockm.)
Gale McMillan, 28638 N. 42 St., Box 7870-Cave Creek Stage, Phoenix, AZ 85020/602-585-4684
Leonard Mews, Spring Rd., Box 242, Hortonville, WI 54944
Pachmayr Gun Works, 1220 S. Grand Ave., Los Angeles, CA 90015 (blanks and custom jobs)
Paulsen Gunstocks, Rt. 71, Box 11, Chinook, MT 59523/406-357-3403 (blanks)
Royal Arms, 1210 Bert Acosta, El Cajon, CA 92020/714-448-5466
Sile Dist., 7 Centre Market Pl., New York, NY 10013/212-925-4111 (shotgun stocks)
Weatherby's, 2781 Firestone, South Gate, CA 90280/213-569-7186
Frank R. Wells, 4025 N. Sabino Canyon Rd., Tucson, AZ 85715/602-887-3559 (custom stocks)
Western Gunstocks Mfg. Co., 550 Valencia School Rd., Aptos, CA 95003

TRIGGERS

M.H. Canjar, 500 E. 45th Ave., Denver, CO 80216/303-623-5777 (triggers)
Custom Products, 686 Baldwin St., Meadville, PA 16335/814-724-7045 (trigger guard)
Dayton-Traister Co., 9322 900th West, P.O. Box 593, Oak Harbor, WA 98277/206-675-5375 (triggers)
Michaels of Oregon Co., P.O. Box 13010, Portland, OR 97213/503-255-6890 (trigger guards)
Miller Single Trigger Mfg. Co., R.D. 1, Box 99, Millersburg, PA 17061/717-692-3704
Timney Mfg. Inc., 3106 W. Thomas Rd., Suite 1104, Phoenix, AZ 85017/602-269-6937 (triggers)